D1254173

HIGHLIGHTS FROM  THE VERITAS FORUM

A PLACE FOR TRUTH

LEADING THINKERS EXPLORE LIFE'S HARDEST QUESTIONS

EDITED BY

DALLAS WILLARD

ASSISTANT EDITORS

DANIEL CHO AND **SARAH PARK**

IVP Books

An imprint of InterVarsity Press
Downers Grove, Illinois

InterVarsity Press
P.O. Box 1400, Downers Grove, IL 60515-1426
World Wide Web: www.ivpress.com
E-mail: email@ivpress.com

InterVarsity Press® *is the book-publishing division of InterVarsity Christian Fellowship/USA*®*, a movement of students and faculty active on campus at hundreds of universities, colleges and schools of nursing in the United States of America, and a member movement of the International Fellowship of Evangelical Students. For information about local and regional activities, write Public Relations Dept., InterVarsity Christian Fellowship/USA, 6400 Schroeder Rd., P.O. Box 7895, Madison, WI 53707-7895, or visit the IVCF website at <www.intervarsity.org>.*

All Scripture quotations, unless otherwise indicated, are taken from the New Revised Standard Version of the Bible, *copyright 1989 by Division of Christian Education of the National Council of the Churches of Christ in the USA. Used by permission. All rights reserved.*

The poetry on page 244 is from Michael O'Siadhail, Poems 1975-1995 *(Bloodaxe Books, 1999). Used by permission.*

Design: Cindy Kiple
Images: The Veritas Forum at USC 2003, Bovard Auditorium. Heather Fuqua© 2003, www.heatherfuqua.com

ISBN 978-0-8308-3845-5

Printed in the United States of America ∞

Library of Congress Cataloging-in-Publication Data

A place for truth: leading thinkers explore life's hardest questions / edited by Dallas Willard; assistant editors, Daniel Cho and Sarah Park.
   p. cm.
 Includes bibliographical references.
 ISBN 978-0-8308-3845-5 (pbk.: alk. paper)
 1. Theology. I. Willard, Dallas, 1935- II. Cho, Daniel. III. Park,
Sarah.
 BT10.P53 2010
 230—dc22

                                          2010014322

P	19	18	17	16	15	14	13	12	11	10	9	8	7		
Y	26	25	24	23	22	21	20	19	18	17	16	15			

CONTENTS

Foreword 7
Harry Lewis, Harvard University

Preface. 11
Daniel Cho, Executive Director, The Veritas Forum

Introduction 15
Dallas Willard

TRUTH

1 Is There Life After Truth? 23
Richard John Neuhaus

2 Time for Truth 39
Os Guinness

3 Reason for God: The Exclusivity of Truth 55
Timothy J. Keller

FAITH AND SCIENCE

4 The Language of God: A Scientist Presents
Evidence for Belief 72
Francis S. Collins

5 The New Atheists and the Meaning of Life 99
Alister McGrath and David J. Helfand

6 A Scientist Who Looked and Was Found 122
Hugh Ross

ATHEISM

7 The Psychology of Atheism 135
Paul C. Vitz

131409

8 Nietzsche Versus Jesus Christ 153
   Dallas Willard

MEANING AND HUMANITY

9 Moral Mammals: Does Atheism or Theism Provide
   the Best Foundation for Human Worth and Morality? 169
   Peter Singer and John Hare

10 Living Machines: Can Robots Become Human? 195
    Rodney Brooks and Rosalind Picard

11 The Sense of an Ending 216
    Jeremy S. Begbie

CHRISTIAN WORLDVIEW

12 Simply Christian 239
    N. T. Wright

SOCIAL JUSTICE

13 Why Human Rights Are Impossible Without Religion . . . 259
    John Warwick Montgomery

14 Radical Marxist, Radical Womanist, Radical Love:
    What Mother Teresa Taught Me About Social Justice 279
    Mary Poplin

15 The Whole Gospel for the Whole Person 300
    Ronald J. Sider

Notes 318

Contributors 319

Photo Credits 322

FOREWORD

Universities today search for the truth, but the terms of success aren't what they once were. Science is the dominant mode of knowledge, and other areas of inquiry have had to adapt to the changed academic ecology.

Scientific knowledge is progressive, mutable and always subject to more precise confirmation. Its successes are practical, resulting in increased power over human life. Atom bombs and the Internet, synthetic insulin and Octomom—none of this would have been possible without the cumulative scientific discoveries of the past century, including many with roots in university research.

And so the scientific enterprise has flourished in universities through the combined effects of freedom of inquiry, huge federal funding and an objective, meritocratic standard of success. Scientific culture has drastically altered university hiring and promotion standards. Peer assessment against objective standards limits both the nepotism and the various ugly forms of discrimination for which universities used to be infamous. These reforms in the academy have made the American university the world's leading engine of knowledge creation and of economic prosperity.

But the same reforms were, with every good intention, adopted across every academic discipline, and their effects on the social sciences and humanities have been less happy. It is now very hard to get tenure as a qualitative social scientist in the old style, a brilliant observer and synthesizer with gifts in human understanding and grand stories, rather than in statistical analysis. Even the successes of economics, the most successfully quantified social science, have been called into question by the startling market collapse of 2008-2009.

Whatever its success in making social science more objective, the scientific paradigm for truth fits humanistic learning most uncomfortably. What used to be the big question of humanistic learning—what does it mean to be human?—now has little place in the academy because there is no way to tell whether the question has been answered correctly or not. No hypotheses can be disproven, no predictions can be tested—so how could we judge, on grounds of veracity, whether one humanist is more successful than another? Instead we judge humanists on what metrics we can: influence and originality and, to be sure, page counts. Productivity has become a proxy for truths discovered. And the mere capacity to change people's minds—which is in science a consequence, not a defining characteristic, of a great discovery—becomes in humanistic scholarship a virtue in itself.

And yet the big old questions haven't gone away. Does human life have meaning? Do suffering and death have a purpose? Are we more than our material selves—is everything about the human condition explicable by biochemistry and physics? What is a good life? Is there any reason to lead a good life rather than a bad one? Should I live for myself or for others? Does love matter?

The essays in this book are based on talks about some of the big questions of life. The discussions took place in universities, not as part of the daily life of the academic family but instead at events sponsored by The Veritas Forum. It is awkward to take up such questions within the academy itself, unless they can be reduced to matters of psychology or cultural study.

And yet students ask these questions when they are very alone under starry skies or in the blaze of city lights, when they confront decisions affecting the lives of their loved ones, and when they are faced with pivotal decisions about their own lives. The discomforts attendant on this search for the truth are afflictions of the young for which college education offers little aid.

I am not among those who regret the departure of God from the academy. I join the atheists in their skepticism about scientific proof of the existence of God or of any meaningful argument for God's existence that is not subject to scientific verification. Yet I regret the extent to which God took with him, when he left the classroom, questions of values and morals and purposes with which young people struggle today as they always have. As much as ever, a good education owes students guidance on examining their own lives.

These essays, mostly by Christian thinkers, are serious dialogue about important questions. Whether you find in them enlightenment and encouragement, or much to challenge, I hope you will agree that The Veritas Forum has done a service to the academy by encouraging the discussions. For those of us who don't agree with the answers suggested here, we are challenged to a simple remedy: do what we can to bring the big questions back into the practice of academic life. The questions aren't going away, and we should not cede to religious thinkers the job of helping youth search for answers.

Harry Lewis
Harvard University
Gordon McKay Professor of Computer Science
Former Dean of Harvard College
Author of *Excellence Without a Soul*

PREFACE

INSPIRED BY THE IDEA THAT Harvard's motto—*Veritas* (truth)—
was more than a meaningless relic of the past, in 1992 a small group of
Christians at Harvard, led by chaplain Kelly Monroe, hosted the university for a weekend of lectures and discussions exploring some of life's
most important questions. Their hope was to restore within the university a space for asking deep questions, seeking real answers and building community around the search for truth.

In the nearly two decades since that first Veritas Forum, more than
one hundred universities in the United States, Canada, the United
Kingdom, France and the Netherlands have hosted their own forums,
and thousands of students and faculty have participated in this search
for truth and meaning in the academy. Individuals have come and gone,
trends and terminology have changed, and academic disciplines have
evolved, but the questioning nature of minds and hearts in the university has endured.

In this volume we have sought to provide a representative sampling
of the best Veritas events over the years, engaging the most lasting
questions and the most compelling responses. Many more are worthy
of print and could be the content of future volumes. In preserving the

oral nature of the presentations and including some of the question and answer sessions, we hope to draw you more intimately into the conversation.

This collection is the fruit of the labor of hundreds of volunteer students, faculty and campus ministers who helped create these Veritas Forum events, as well as of the presenters who so generously shared their words, ideas and lives with us, and have allowed us to extend that gift to a wider audience. Our deep gratitude is also due to Dallas Willard for shaping the content and context for the volume; Sarah Park for her labor in the bulk of the editing; Kelly Monroe Kullberg, founder of The Veritas Forum; the Veritas board of directors; Rebecca McLaughlin and the rest of the Veritas team; countless supporters and partners over the years; and Al Hsu and the team at InterVarsity Press.

As a freshman sitting in that crowd at the first Harvard forum back in 1992, my life was profoundly shaped by the coherence of life, truth and beauty in Jesus Christ that I tasted over that weekend within that community of seekers. May the following pages bring that same life, truth and beauty into your own journey.

Daniel Cho
Executive Director
The Veritas Forum

We create forums for the exploration of true life.

We seek to inspire the shapers of tomorrow's culture to connect their hardest questions with the person and story of Jesus Christ.

For hundreds of video and audio recordings of events like those presented in this volume, visit The Veritas Forum website: www.veritas.org

INTRODUCTION

Dallas Willard

You HAVE IN YOUR HAND a remarkable volume in which a number of outstanding Christian intellectuals, along with a few from other perspectives, deal with questions about *truth itself* and questions about *several particular truths*. Most prominent, in the latter respect, are questions about the existence of God and about how we ought to live, given the existence (or nonexistence) of a God of the Judeo-Christian variety.

Much of the argumentation here concerning the existence of God is actually about whether naturalism, as a form of atheism (or agnosticism), is true, and much of the argumentation about how we ought to live is actually about the nature of the human being—purely physical ("natural") or something radically different from that. Many of the discussions are also devoted to objective as well as personal factors that influence people to accept or reject the basic claims put forward by Christians *as* truths. The Veritas Forum, under whose auspices the talks were originally given, is interested both in the current status of truth on the campus, and in how the basic claims of Christianity are now treated there. Its aim is to restore the university to its age-old character as "a place for truth."

In reading these chapters it will be helpful to keep a few essential points in mind. Most important, perhaps, we should recognize and hold onto the distinction between *truth itself* and particular *truths*, in the plural. There are different battles to be fought over *truth* and over particular truth*s*, and we should not run those battles together. If truth itself is lost, then there is little point in straightforwardly arguing for the truth or falsity of particular claims.

Truth itself is the distinctive property of truths as such, as red is the distinctive property of red things. A belief or idea (a statement or a proposition) is true provided that what it is about *is* as it is represented in the belief, statement or so forth. Truth itself is a very simple property which children encounter (along with its dark counterpart, falsity) and identify well before they have the word *truth*. They encounter truth and falsity as they live out their thoughts and expectations of the world around them. As our experience and understanding grows, we learn more about truth and how and where it shows up. At an early age we learn about the powers and the importance of truth, and we learn how to lie: how to "mess with" truth to gain what we want. But the basic nature of truth itself remains unchanged, in glorious simplicity, however far we grow and however complicated the truths we are dealing with become.

We quickly learn how important it is that our ideas and beliefs be true. Our beliefs and ideas orient us in action toward our world and our future. If they have this property of truth, our actions will be more successful in terms of our objectives and possibly in terms of our well-being. All of this is, once again, something children learn while quite young. Action in terms of beliefs or ideas that are not true lead to unhappy outcomes. Our beliefs are the rails upon which our lives run. We believe something if we are set to act as if it were so. But if our beliefs are false, reality does not adjust to accommodate our errors. A brief but useful characterization of reality is as *what you run into when you are wrong*—that is, when our corresponding beliefs are not true. That can be fatal and often is. Truth is quite merciless, and so is reality.

A major dimension of the importance of truth is how it guides us with respect to what we cannot see, what is not directly given to our experience. That covers a huge amount of life, from our bank account and whether there is gas in our tank up to the nature of the universe and of the human mind or personality. Without truth and the knowledge of truths we would wander blindly through life guided only by what we can get before our face. That would be very dangerous with respect to the ultimate beliefs that guide life as a whole, among which are the claims of religion. Whether there is a great person in charge of the whole universe, including you and me, and whether we are the sort of thing that will never stop existing, are matters about which we do well to gain whatever truth can be gained. Truth in belief and idea is, in a certain respect, similar to the sighting mechanism on a gun or rocket: if correctly used it enables us to hit what we hope to. But in truth's case we need not see what we are aiming at. Truth and the meaning upon which it rests takes care of the aim itself.

So it is fairly easy to see that truth is extremely valuable, but the claims to truth that people make are also *threatening*. That is because they simultaneously are claims to *authority*. Having knowledge of truth puts us in a certain position not otherwise available. Knowledge of truth confers rights and responsibilities. If we indeed "have" the truth, which is what knowing means, then we have the *right* (and perhaps even the responsibility) to act, to direct action, to formulate and supervise policy, and to teach. Sincere belief, sentiment or feeling, mere tradition, or power—none of these confers such rights and responsibilities. Indeed, knowledge gives us the right (and sometimes the responsibility) to *impose our views* on relevant others in appropriate circumstances.

That is explosive stuff now, of course, and we begin to see why, in the contemporary Western world—above all in North America, the land of the free and the home of the brave—the university distances itself from truth and backs away from knowledge into "research." Next, socially certified research methods are allowed to determine which areas of thought and talk can possibly count as acceptable opinion and academic practice, and what might count as knowledge of truth. There are no *knowledge* universities now in the Western world—much less a *truth* one, except in certain countries where theocracy prevails. But everywhere there are "research universities." You cannot get a grant for knowledge or truth, but you can for research. In fact, truth is a joke now on campus, and most of those in responsible positions there rarely even mention it. In John Milton's words (picked up by Thomas Hardy), "Truth like a bastard comes into the world. Never without ill-fame to him who gives her birth." No one is willing to claim it. But now its illegitimacy has dimensions never suspected by Milton.

Nevertheless, truth and knowledge of truth goes its way, striding right through the campus. It remains exactly what it is, and does exactly what it does. It is not running for office or deflected from its role in life by opinions, sentiments or political correctness and incorrectness. It is precisely because of that fact that it is so powerful and important, and that claims to "have the truth" and to *know* are so very frightening in the contemporary academy. It is because these powerful claims have been and are falsely made, and used as a basis for shunting people about—sometimes amounting to oppression or denial of freedom— that the "enlightened" world has ricocheted over into the position of claiming to make no claims to truth or knowledge at all—thus to just doing *research* ("good" research, of course). That shift is based on its implicit claim to have come to know the truth about truth and to have knowledge of knowledge. Alas! It doesn't seem possible. But claimed knowledge of truth—not just research into the matter—itself turns out to be the basis of how the academy acts, directs action, formulates and supervises its policies, and teaches (about teaching, among other things) with reference to truth.

The older tradition of the universities, represented by the word *veritas*, was in no such an intellectual and practical bind as this. It found resources *in* the knowledge of truth, and *moral* truth in particular, to address issues of the misuse of truth and knowledge. Of course, as is now *truthfully* emphasized, that tradition was on many points oppressive. But the academic setting is still oppressive—political correctness is no joke, but a hard-bitten social reality; and there is little hope of it ever being anything else except on the basis of gracious but unqualified allegiance to truth and respect for knowledge of truth. Oppression is after all a moral (immoral) matter and it can be dealt with only on the basis of moral truths pervasively practiced by individuals who know it.

As indicated by a number of the writers represented here, the oppressiveness of the contemporary academy is above all seen in what can and what cannot be freely and sincerely discussed in a generous and inclusive pursuit of truth, in the classroom, in the research setting and in the informal contexts of academic life. It is seen in the limits of collegiality that express themselves ultimately in who gets approved of, celebrated and rewarded in the various ways functional on the campus: from the students who are told that they cannot discuss the teachings of the church and the Bible in connection with their subject matter, to the faculty members who loses status automatically because they take the existence of God and their religion seriously in their teaching or research—or even because of their posture in electoral politics. Any attempt at a generous and rigorous examination of the major questions of life and reality, which the university for most of its history stood for, has to be imported onto the campus from outside, as in the Veritas Forums. It cannot now be done as part of the serious business of earning credits and picking up research methods and letters of recommendations for the next move up. Anyone who does not see oppression here would not recognize it if it ran right over them. Oppression rarely comes without intellectual blindness that sees itself as "obviously" right and true. To reveal it you have to examine what is presumed to be obvious in the context of whatever activity is involved.

The chapters in this book deal both with *truth itself*—its perils and promises, along with some of its essential aspects (e.g., exclusiveness)—and with the significance of and evidence for and against *particular truths* of great concern to traditional education and to life now. The chapters by Richard John Neuhaus, Os Guinness and Tim Keller are especially focused on truth itself, and they are placed at the front of the book because they should be read first. Unless there is a substantial reality and nature to truth itself, little point is left to discussing the evidence and importance of various claims to truth.

At the top of the list among particular truth claims to be discussed is that concerning the existence of a God of the Judeo-Christian variety or something close. The chapters by Francis Collins, Alister McGrath and David Helfand, and Hugh Ross mainly fall here, and some of them also contain a good deal about the authors' personal experiences in dealing with evidence for God's existence. As might be expected, the highly complex order of the natural world plays a large role in these discussions, and significant attention is paid to points made by the "new" atheists, Richard Dawkins and company.

The chapters by Paul Vitz and me deal with various aspects of the effects of atheism on life. Atheism is treated, not just with reference to arguments as to its truth or falsity, but also with reference to its psychological sources and its bearings on a life of freedom and possible human fulfillment. Friedrich Nietzsche comes in for special attention.

The chapters by Peter Singer and John Hare, and Rosalind Picard and Rodney Brooks are records of Christian and non-Christian thinkers in friendly but no-holds-barred debate. They focus in a quite rigorous way on the question of human nature—spiritual or not—and the significance of the pros and cons on that point for possibilities of moral fulfillment and human dignity. They provide a rare illustration of what intellectual engagement could be and should be on the campus.

The chapters by Jeremy Begbie and N. T. Wright provide fascinating insights into the significance of a transcendent reality—God and the spiritual life—for music, art generally and for "echoes" in ordinary human existence of justice, personal relationships, spirituality and beauty. Richly suggestive rather than argumentative, they help us appreciate the nonnaturalism of ordinary life.

The last three chapters deal, in intriguingly different ways, with the need of Christian faith and understanding for issues of social justice. John Montgomery forcefully demonstrates how human rights are not rationally possible without the involvement of an order transcendent to the various factual legal and political systems. Mary Poplin helps us see, through details of her experience with Mother Teresa of Calcutta and of her own professional and personal growth, how she came to understand the essential involvement of education and social work with Jesus and his teachings—in the midst of the willing blindness of her fields to him. Finally, Ron Sider gives real-life pictures of social transformations actually growing out of whole-life discipleship to Christ. His challenge is to what the church—the people publicly identified with Christ—could be and do for good in this desperate world through such discipleship.

As you read these chapters be alert to recognize intelligence at work, in the framework of a worldview and a reality provided only by Jesus Christ and his people on earth—animated by the Spirit of God, which after all is *the Spirit of truth*. His people are not infallible, but they are devoted to truth and knowledge of the truth as the ultimate appeal concerning what to believe and what to do. In these pages they invite the academic and intellectual world to join them in that devotion.

IS THERE LIFE
AFTER TRUTH?

Richard John Neuhaus

The Veritas Forum at Yale University, 1996

IT'S A GREAT PRIVILEGE TO BE HERE, and the earnestness and sense of expectation that I know marks this gathering, *Lux et Veritas* at Yale. *Lux et Veritas*—"Light and Truth." I mean, they really narrowed the subject down, didn't they? You know, it's this passion for specialization in the academy today, you know? Nobody wants to take on a big question. So we just got light and truth.

Now, the title for my talk is "Is There Life After Truth?" I didn't want to keep you in suspense about this title; I wanted to answer the title question right away and say that, yes, there is life after truth, but it's not a life that's really worthy of human beings.

TRUTH AS A CONVERSATION STOPPER?

And yet, the extraordinary thing (every time is an extraordinary time marked by much that is unprecedented, but our time is marked by something that I think we can truly say is quite astonishing) is that, at least at certain levels of intellectual discourse and conversation in American life, and particularly in the academy, it has been concluded that we do not need to deal with the question of truth. That somehow, the question of truth itself is beyond the purview of serious intellectual discourse. That the only truth, if you must use the word, is that there is *no* truth, at least, no truth that has any obliging force for anybody other than yourself.

When our Lord stood before Pilate and said, "For this reason I came into the world, to testify to the truth" (John 18:37), and Pilate's famous, or infamous, answer, depending on your view—I certainly don't want to suggest there's one truth about this that I'd want to impose on you—was, "What is truth?" You can take that as a cynical answer, as many interpreters do—a kind of jaded, nihilistic response on Pilate's part. He was a disillusioned, world-weary man, perhaps, who simply couldn't be bothered by it, especially when truth within the context of the world he was involved in, with all these crazy Jews, was an impossibly perplexing and conflict-ridden thing. "Who has time for truth?" Maybe that's how he said it.

Today, there are many who ask Pilate's question, "What is truth?" and take it to be the mark of sophistication. It is assumed that we can't get into the question of truth and still keep our society and our relationships going, because once you get into the question of truth, you're going to come into conflict. Truth is a conversation stopper, it is suggested.

Today, there are many who ask Pilate's question, "What is truth?" and take it to be the mark of sophistication.

I want to explore with you whether exactly the opposite is not the case—whether, in fact, the only conversation starter, and the only conversation sustainer that is worthy of human beings, is the question of truth.

THE SEARCH FOR TRUTH

Certainly, that is a proposition supported by a very venerable tradition of reflection on these matters. It is supported, I would suggest, by the Christian tradition in all of its variety. To be human is to seek the truth, and the quest for truth is a kind of open-ended adventure. It really is an excitement, and yes, a kind of delight, into an exploration that is never ended in this life. It'll be ended at the time in which, as

Saint Paul says in 1 Corinthians 13, "then I will know fully, even as I have been fully known" and "we see in a mirror, dimly, but then we will see face to face."

Until then, this truth is something that more possesses us than we possess it. It is much more a matter of being possessed by the truth than possessing the truth. It is a matter of walking along a certain way, the way of the One who said, "I am the way, and the truth, and the life" (John 14:6). "Follow me."

The Christian understanding is that truth is found only in following, in a faithful, trusting following. It's a following in which we can't see where the next step is, where we really do say with Cardinal Newman, "O, lead, kindly light." We do not need to see the distant destination, we need to know only the company. We need to know only the One who travels with us, who says, "I am the way, the truth, and the life. And wherever the honest quest for truth is going to take you, it's going to take you to where I am."

This is not a truth we need fear. To know this truth is to be wondrously freed. The same Person said, of course, in John 8, "You will know the truth, and the truth will make you free."

This is very countercultural, isn't it? It's very much against the grain of the way people think about truth today. In our conversation, we bring up the question of truth and say, "Well, this is true," meaning that in some sense it's binding on all of us.

"Hey, whoa, hold on there, that's heavy. You know, don't lay this on me, you know. I wanna be free."

But we get this weird way of turning it all around in someone saying, "'You will know the truth, and you will be free,' and you're not free until you know the truth."

We're not free until we're bound to be free, until there's something that has a claim upon us other than ourself, our aspirations, our psychological and intellectual and sexual tics and yearnings and desires for community. When all of that is somehow brought into a constellation of obedience to something other than ourself, we start to become, to taste, what it means to be free.

It's really against the grain, that *obedience*. Talk about a word that

We're not free until we're bound to be free, until there's something that has a claim upon us other than ourself, our aspirations, our psychological and intellectual and sexual tics and yearnings and desires for community. When all of that is somehow brought into a constellation of obedience to something other than ourself, we start to become, to taste, what it means to be free.

doesn't have a lot of appeal or cachet today. It's a lovely word; it's from the Latin, *oboedire*—"to listen attentively, responsively; to be alert to the other." To be bound to be free: you will know the truth, and the truth will make you free.

In most of our discourse today, and certainly in most academic settings, talk about truth makes people very uneasy, and especially if the truth turns to religion and questions of moral truth. "Moral truth? Surely that's an oxymoron." This is because *morality* in the minds of many people is simply that on which we turn up the motive dial very high. A moral issue is a gut issue. A moral issue is an issue that we *feel* powerfully about. So you have your moral truth, and I my moral truth: whatever works for you.

But that there could be a truth about the way human beings are made to be, built-in ends and destinations and directions, and right orderings of the human life, in such a way that some ways of living and some ways of being are true, and others are false—it's hard to make this case today, especially when people suspect us of coming from a religious commitment. To speak of moral truth is almost to throw open our jacket and expose the T-shirt that says, "Beware—fanatic!"

AN ANTIFOUNDATIONALIST VIEW OF TRUTH

We have to try to understand why. This is a moment in history in which the question not only of moral truth, not only of religious truth, but of truth itself has, in very many circles of powerful culture-forming influence, been very determinedly bracketed off. What has brought us to this pass?

We can call it antifoundationalism, deconstructionism, postmodernism; it goes by many different names and appears in many different variations. But it's certainly in the academy today, and not only in the academy, for the influence of the academy is insinuated throughout society. As Richard Weaver says, "ideas have consequences," and also, very bad ideas have consequences. The idea is insinuated that what we call truth is but social convention, historically contingent, culturally conditioned, or as it's more commonly said, socially constructed.

As Richard Rorty (one could argue, at least in America, that he is the single most influential philosopher, at least in the academy) says, "It's constructed all the way down." So then, maybe there is no foundation, there's no layer. Once you start unpeeling all the things that have shaped your mind and constructed socially what you call truth, and you take off one layer after another—psychological, family influence, all the other stuff—and find there is no foundation anywhere. There is no basis on which you can say that one thing is "more true" than another. All you can say is what you prefer.

And this radical antifoundationalism, not only bracketing of the question of truth, but a very systematic and sophisticated demolition job on the concept of truth, leads to (though not necessarily immediately) Hobbes's war of all against all, and return to barbarity in its most vulgar and extravagant and sensational forms, for some of the nicest people in the world think this way, beginning with Richard Rorty—an eminently nice person.

"What then," you say to Richard Rorty, "is to prevent anything of which human capacities and ambitions and aspirations are capable?" You don't have to go immediately to the Holocaust, but you'd certainly want to ask about that as well. What is to prevent slavery? What is to prevent rape? What is to prevent my simply taking advantage of you in whatever way it would seem to me to be in my interest to do so?

The answer is, "Well, we're not that kind of people. We're not the kind of people who do those kind of things." And the tag that is put on this answer is a style of ironic liberalism, that we ironic liberals believe in certain liberal values about how we ought to be decent to one another, but with a profound sense of irony, knowing that none of them are true. There's no way of demonstrating that they're any better, or that they're superior to anybody else's values. But those are the ones that we, and people like us, "prefer."

And if other people come along and say, "Well, you know, actually, the nice way you guys live is possible because it's true"—if someone comes along and starts talking about truth that way, says Richard Rorty, or if they come along and start talking about truth in a way that contradicts the way we live, well, we'll just have to understand that they're not part of our circle of ironic liberalism. They'll just have to be declared crazy and kept somehow safely confined, where they cannot do public damage, cannot cause mischief by raising the question of truth.

There are many religious folk in the world today, some theologians of considerable intelligence, who welcome this (what's called) postmodernist, deconstructionist, antifoundationalist turn. They say—and there's some truth to this—"You know, this is really good, because now in the academy, all kinds of things can be discussed."

"Once we've decided that the old eighteenth-century secular rationalists—with their narrow, reductionist, stifling, little notions of what constitutes truth on the basis of very scientistic testing of everything by values and by procedures that cannot begin to understand what they, in fact, are dealing with—are no longer in control, and now that we've all decided that there is really no truth—there's simply your truth and my truth and her truth and his truth, and there's simply the truth of this community and of a body defined by some experience of suffering or victimhood or exclusion or marginalization—so that there are just all these different truths, well, that's great for us Christians," some Christian thinkers say. We can understand why some Christian theologians and thinkers are talking that way, welcoming this kind of antifoundationalism, this kind of rejection of the very notion of truth. It gives them an opportunity to insert *their* particular Christian truth.

CHRISTIAN RESPONSIBILITY TOWARD TRUTH

But I think it is a great mistake. We Christians have an inescapable obligation to contend that there is truth, and that all truths finally serve the one truth. There is one truth because there is one God, and one revelation of God in Jesus Christ. And as much as we may find certain tactical advantages in this world of antifoundationalist, postmodernist chaos, we ought to be extremely careful not to sup with the devil, or else we undermine exactly what it is that we, as Christians, have to propose.

It's not only for the sake of the Christian gospel, it's for the sake of our responsibility in our society. It's a socially disastrous, community destroying thing to deny that there is a truth that binds us together—Christian and Jew and Muslim and believer and nonbeliever and atheist and secular and black and white and Asian. To believe that there is a truth, however elusive, however difficult for us to articulate it, however much we may frequently discern it in manners that are sharply in conflict, and to nonetheless insist that there is a truth to discern and articulate is part of our responsibility as human beings, and as Christians. "I am the way, and the truth, and the life—I'm not simply the way, the truth, and the life for people who happen to believe that I am the way, the truth, and the life." It's not just a truth for Christians.

The very heart of the Christian faith is caught up in what sounds like the very esoteric, strange, academic, philosophical discussions that I was talking about, about postmodernism and antifoundationalism and all of that.

You say, "Well, that's just all academic buzz. That's just the way in which the leisure of the classes is consumed. That's just what academics do, because they don't have anything else to do."

No, it's very important to believe that we are part of one world that is brought into being and is directed toward—from eternity to eternity, from alpha to omega—the One who said, "I am the way, and the truth, and the life."

It's publicly important. Aristotle said that our public responsibility as citizens—as people who accept some responsibility for our part in the *polis*, the city of man, the earthly city—is that we are always to be engaging one another and deliberating the question of how we ought to order our life together.

The "ought" there clearly signals that it's a moral question. The fact that we are to be deliberating it as rational, reasonable beings means that there must be something to deliberate; there must be a truth. There must be a right answer or many right answers in various ways, and different ways of putting the question, and many wrong answers. But it is not a futile deliberation.

In a world in which people have stopped talking about truth or have despaired of truth or have agreed with those who say that Pontius Pilate's question was a conversation stopper and not a conversation starter—in such a world there is no way to deliberate the question how we ought to order our life together. There's only power and propaganda and grievance and anger and caucuses and anticaucuses and special interest groups and victims and vengeance. That's the kind of world we increasingly live in, because we've stopped believing, or so many have stopped believing, that there is a truth that we can deliberate together.

At this time in world history, at the end of the twentieth century, the bloodiest and most horrible century in all of human history, we've piled up more corpses and loosed more rivers of blood than any century in human history. Incidentally, it's also the century that produced the great ideologies that denied the Christian and the classic Aristotelian understanding of truth, and denied our obligation as reasonable persons to engage that truth and to engage one another in our quest to engage that truth more fully.

Christians have a great obligation for God's world. This is the world of God's creating and of God's redeeming love. God so loved the world that he gave his only begotten Son. We have a great obligation to defend the *humanum*, to defend the unity of humankind at a time when there are so many powerful, destructive, satanic forces posited against it.

This is a time, as we prepare to cross the threshold into the third millennium, to reassert a genuine, a Christian, biblical, humane humanism that can, with the whole of our tradition, in the spirit of Psalm 8, stand in awe and wonder at what is man: What is this *humanum*? A little less than the angels. Why should God have become *humanum*, to become one of us? To assert truth in public. It's the great task of our generation, to learn how to do it persuasively and winsomely and in a manner that does not violate, but strengthens the bonds of civility.

The American experiment within the *humanum* has been both blessing and curse in so many different ways, but to the extent it has been blessing (and that it has been in at least a penultimate manner), it is because it was premised on certain truths, as in, "We hold these truths to be self-evident." Not just rhetorical ruffle, that. That's a substantive statement. And the whole of the American experiment, the republican, democratic, self-governing people is premised on the fact that there are truths to be held.

Why should God have become humanum, *to become one of us? To assert truth in public. It's the great task of our generation, to learn how to do it persuasively and winsomely and in a manner that does not violate, but strengthens the bonds of civility.*

Today, not only in literary criticism or in the backwaters of academic fashion and cachet, but also in our courts and in the public square, anybody who seriously proposed that there are truths to be held (i.e., "We hold these truths—life, liberty, the pursuit of happiness, endowed by their Creator, nature and nature's God")—would not simply be considered as indulging a propensity for flowery language in public. They'd be laughed or forced out of court.

What's happening in our society today, to a very great extent, when we talk about the culture wars and the conflicts over the definition of what American society is, is that many people speak with great alarm about the extreme religious right. What they're terrified by, for the most part, is due to a moment in American history where things have become so systematic, so cynical and so contemptuous of the common people in this program for the denial of truth in public, that it has triggered a response. The response will often be populist and raucous and rough and vulgar—that's the way democracy works. (The word *demos*, "the ordinary people," are often vulgar and raucous and not the way we do things here.)

But we have to decide whether we believe that in some powerful sense, there is a necessity to this that may look reactive. That whether this may not, in fact, be the portent of a more promising moment in which we might again, in our society (and not least of all in our universities) begin to do what Aristotle says is the human and humanizing political task, mainly, to deliberate how ought we to order our life together.

I tell you what I think about this postmodernist, deconstructionist, antifoundationalist (use what word you will) move; I don't think it's for long. I don't think it's for long because finally, the dogma that "there is no truth other than the dogma that there is no truth" is not very interesting. It's kind of dumb, really.

It's internally incoherent. It cannot provide any interesting answers or proposals or even hypotheses about how we ought to live, what kind of person we ought to be, what's worthy of aspiring to. Indeed, it cannot even supply any stories of real evil and of the demonic and of the terrible and the terrorizing in human life. It's a vacuous moment in-between things.

NEED FOR A BELIEF SYSTEM IN OUR CENTURY

People need some kind of—call it a belief system, call it a *Weltanschauung*, a worldview—way of putting things together amid stories, rituals. Ultimately, Christians know what people are looking for, in all of the floundering about, a belief system, a way of making sense of things. Augustine said it sixteen-hundred-plus years ago, "You have made us for yourself, O Lord, and our hearts are restless until they rest in you."

But for many whose hearts do not rest in God, they'll grab at other belief systems. You recall G. K. Chesterton's wonderful line: "The problem with people who don't believe in God is not that they will end up believing in nothing. The problem is they'll end up believing in anything."

Of course, Chesterton was right. God knows that our century has borne witness to this. As distinct from today's fashion of—let's just use the word *postmodernism* for the moment—think of what earlier in the twentieth century were the great belief systems, the great kind of functional religions, explanatory systems for making sense of reality. Think of Marx, Freud, Darwin.

As a youngster and coming to an intellectual age, I have to confess that Marx's notion of class struggle and the economic being the real epicenter of reality and of world historical-defining change always seemed to me rather preposterous. It was, to me, as preposterous as Freud's notion of sexual infant experience being determinant to the development of the person and community.

But at least it was something to believe. They claimed to have the truth. These theories were in the current jargon of the day, the hegemonic theories of Western intellectual life at the most elite, the most educated, sectors of cultural influence.

Today Marx is dead, for all practical purposes—though there are still a few in academic departments who have not received the news. Freud is dead, at least as a major belief system. There are a few psychoanalysts who are motivated by self-interest, rightly understood as Tocqueville would say, "who resist the announcement of the death of Freud." But there you are.

And Darwin? Well, it's two down and one to go. Darwin still continues because for many he's the last redoubt of the indubitable—which is to say that if you really want to hold on to an absolutely rock bottom, empirically verifiable, indisputable fact of sheer matter, then you'll want to say, as incoherent as it may be to many other people, that matter causes itself. But if you want to get more sophisticated, you don't say that matter causes itself, because that assumes some kind of contingent cause-effect relationship. You simply say, "Matter is." You become, in as radical a way as you possibly can, a materialist, all the way down. Well, then you still have company in Darwin.

Richard Rorty in *The New Republic* had an essay on some of the critiques that have been raised about Darwinism recently, and he concludes his essay in defense of Darwin with the words, "Whatever may be the truth of these critiques, we must *keep faith with Darwin.*"

I thought, *Gee, this is touching. This is poignant.* I mean, my heart goes out to a devotee of a belief system so besieged, so embattled, yet he holds on, keeping faith with Darwin. In his better moments he knows that we can't keep faith with Darwin or anyone else. Darwin is no foundation. There is no foundation, and no one's pointing to one. There is no faith at all.

There is what has been aptly described in our culture as a mode of debonair nihilism. It's a nihilism that doesn't understand how deadly nihilism is. It's a nihilism that dances and makes jokes at the edge of the abyss—and it's not gallows humor, not black humor, as it used to be called, because they don't know it is the abyss. Lionel Trilling, the great literary critic at Columbia University, describes his students to whom, through the great literary works of history, he would introduce the prospect of nothing, the abyss, the heart of darkness. And he describes his students, the brightest and the best of America, who looked over and said, "Oh, that's the abyss is it? Interesting."

There is what has been aptly described in our culture as a mode of debonair nihilism. It's a nihilism that doesn't understand how deadly nihilism is.

So much for the abyss. So much for the loss of truth, which is the loss of the capacity to lose ourselves to that at which we wonder, at which we live in awe, and which inevitably is conjoined to the loss of the capacity to recognize evil. It's now debonair nihilism.

What is our historical moment like? It's like what Nietzsche rightly described as the Last Man. The Last Man, you will recall, is the last man to receive the news that God is dead, or he had perhaps heard it but didn't know that it meant the end of everything. He still went on talking, chattering about justice and about fairness and about love and about community, and even words like right and wrong. He went on and on talking this way, programmed to talk that way as he was, without realizing that now that God is dead, all that language is empty. It is just noise.

FEARS ABOUT TRUTH CLAIMS IN THE PUBLIC SQUARE

Well, an extraordinary time. One thing that we have witnessed, and it's still happening in different ways, is the collapse of the aggressive confidence of the secular enlightenment of the eighteenth century, understood as a kind of rationalism. Very few people today believe that. Very few people today really believe that you can get down by a course of radical skepticism, by a systematic hermeneutic of suspicion, to some kind of truth that is indubitable.

It was René Descartes, a fine Christian, who introduced that train of thinking. He basically said, "I will not accept anything as true that I can reasonably doubt." And others took it farther—David Hume. And so did many others, in many different ways—try to get down to that lost redoubt of the indubitable, of the undoubtable.

Why did they do that? For a good and important reason, one we should understand: because they lived in a world in which dogmatic truths and conflict were destroying the world. They lived in a time that had been scarred and bruised and bloodied by the wars of religion. In 1996, we are still living the consequences of the wars of religion in the sixteenth and seventeenth centuries.

It's very important for you to understand this: Why is it that so many secular academics and leaders here at Yale University, or any other university in the country, believe that religion does not really have an appropriate role in public, in the public life of the university? Why do they even fear religion as something divisive and as destructive of the kind of community and excellences that a university ought to pursue? Because deep within the history of the Western world is the experience of religion being precisely that, as were the wars of religion.

The philosophers and the thinkers, many of them admirable Christians, Protestant and Catholic, very committed, nonetheless believed that it was their task to develop a kind of public discourse that could prescind, or bracket, the question of truth. This

Why is it that so many secular academics and leaders here at Yale University, or any other university in the country, believe that religion does not really have an appropriate role in public, in the public life of the university? . . . Because deep within the history of the Western world is the experience of religion being [something divisive and destructive], as were the wars of religion.

became, over time, not simply a well-intended effort in order to avoid certain kinds of religiously based conflict in the public square, but an effort to advance an aggressively militant secularism, to create what someone has called, "the naked public square." It was a public life, a public university, and all public space sanitized of any religion or religiously grounded truth claims, moral or otherwise. And that's the world in which we live.

And yet that world is coming to an end, at least at this moment, by ushering in the multicultural, antifoundationalist, postmodernistic fads that we have already talked about. But we have to believe that in the years ahead, and especially if Christians and Jews and other reasonable people do their job and press for the unity of truth—for the reality of truths which must, of necessity, be one—ultimately, this present moment of chaos, of debonair nihilism, of ironic liberalism, will not be for long.

Kay Coles James, LaminSanneh, Richard John Neuhaus, N. T. Wright and Nicholas Wolterstorff on a panel at Yale.

But we have to demonstrate also that we, as Christians, have understood some of the lessons of the past. We have understood how Christians claiming to possess the truth can indeed be destructive of public discourse. Christians who are overwhelmingly confident that they actually possess the truth in the sense of being in control of the truth can become the enemies of civil discourse. It is not yet clear, by any means, in the Christian community across the board, that Christians have come to understand why it is a matter of religious obligation for us to be not simply tolerant of those with whom we disagree but to eagerly engage them, for that's the course of love.

People who worry about the role of religion in public life say, "Look, at all those religious fanatics out there—they're going to have at one another. There's going to be blood all over the place." We cannot simply brush off that fear, as though it has no historical justification. We have to make clear that we, today, understand that we do not kill one another over our disagreements about the will of God, because we know it is the will of God that we not kill one another over our disagreements about the will of God. We must demonstrate that our tolerance, our respect for civility, our respect for discourse around Aristotle's question, "How ought we to order our life together" is itself grounded not in a half-held, half-hearted religious conviction, but in religious, specifically Christian, biblical imperatives.

Until that is clear to our secularist friends, their suspicion and their fear of the tonalities of religious truth claims in public will not be allayed—not at all.

CHALLENGE OF THE CHRISTIAN INTELLECTUAL

These are the great questions of our time, *Lux et Veritas.* It's a grand adventure to be a Christian intellectual. I was surprised to see, I think it was in *Christianity Today*, about a Veritas Forum at Harvard, and some undergraduate at Harvard was quoted as saying, "This was the biggest surprise, that you could say you're a Christian intellectual and not be crazy."

I thought, *Gee, what a strange thing to have to say.* Why, to be a Christian is to be in a grand, noble, intellectual tradition, so much grander, so much more various, so much richer in its diversities than anything that the brightest and best of our academic leaderships today could possibly produce. I mean, who, just in terms of intellectual excitement, in terms of provocation, in terms of depth of thought, would you rather read on the nature of the subject itself, in search of truths? Would you rather read Michel Foucault or Augustine? Would you rather read John Rawls's *A Theory of Justice* or Augustine's *City of God?*

Not because they're Christian, but because they're *more interesting*— ever so much more interesting. They're ever so much more daring to ask the big questions about the *why* of everything and the *what for* of everything. It's an intellectual tradition of breathtaking audacity. The company that we are in, sisters and brothers, the company of classic Greece, which has been incorporated into the Christian tradition, of Plato and Aristotle, all of Paul, of Origen, of Augustine, Thomas Aquinas, Catherine of Sienna, and Teresa of Ávila, among the moderns

—C. S. Lewis, Dorothy Sayers, Hans Urs von Balthasar—the list goes on and on.

It is the largest, the richest, the grandest evidence of God in Christ reconciling the world to himself, which means also reconciling the human intellect to himself, tending us toward our proper end, ordering us toward the truth, ultimately toward the One who is the way, the truth, and the life. It is open-ended, and it'll go on all our lives, and all the lives of our children and our children's children, until our Lord Jesus returns in glory, and we know, even as we are known, and see no longer through a glass darkly but then face to face.

So, it can be construed that Pilate asked the right question, "What is truth?" Yeah, that's the right question. And it's not a conversation stopper; it's a conversation starter. Now, let the conversation begin.

2

TIME FOR TRUTH

Os Guinness
The Veritas Forum at Stanford University, 2005

THE YEAR THAT THE SOVIET UNION fell—1989—was described as "the Year of the Century." Those of us who can remember have our favorite memories of that extraordinary time: the joyous dismantling of the Berlin Wall, flowers jauntily poking out of Soviet gun barrels, the toppling of the statuary of the men-gods—Marx and Lenin and Stalin.

My favorite image of that year was when, night after night in November 1989, more than a third of a million people packed into Wenceslas Square, Prague, to listen to a short, boyish, mustachioed, then-dissident, now president, Václav Havel. Again and again, he painted the contrast between the Velvet Revolutionaries and the Soviets. The very quick-witted Czech crowd picked up a chant: "We are not like them. We are not like them." Some of the contrast was the violence, that the Velvet Revolution would not reply to violence with violence. But another contrast in the course of that week was that the Soviets were people of lies and propaganda, and they, the revolutionaries, were people of truth. The Charter '77 Movement had as its motto: "Truth prevails for those who live in truth."

Just a few years earlier Alexander Solzhenitsyn had electrified the world with his line, the old Russian proverb, "One word of truth out-weighs the entire world." Now as we look back on that, we realize how they were aware there were only two ways they could bring down the Soviets: either they had to trump Soviet power with equal or more power—they were a handful of dissidents—unthinkable, or they had to counter Soviet power with another type of power altogether. So that's what they did, with the power of truth. "Truth prevails for those who live in truth." And the unthinkable happened: they won.

As we look around Europe and the United States today, particularly in many of our elite, intellectual establishments, we have to say that though people throughout the West applauded this tremendous cour-age and this principled stand, in many parts of America there isn't a similar solid view of truth on which anyone could make such a stand today. You can see assaults and confusion surrounding the notion of truth, so that truth is seen as dead.

Anyone who believes in an objective truth, or an absolute truth, is Neanderthal and reactionary. Truth, at very best, is relative: all depends on the interpretation, all depends on the perspective. At worst, it's so-cially constructed; it's a testament to the community that said it and made it stick, and the power they had in expressing it. And you can see the many people today who stand for a solid, traditional view of truth are considered reactionary if not far worse: arrogant, exclusive and thoroughly wrong-headed.

Far from being Neanderthal and reactionary, truth is a very precious, simple, fundamental, human gift, without which we cannot negotiate reality and handle life. The truth is absolutely essential for a good human life. Equally important, truth is absolutely essential for freedom.

I want to argue that this crisis of truth is enormously important for both individuals and for the American Republic. Far from being Neanderthal and reactionary, truth is a very pre-cious, simple, fundamental, human gift, without which we cannot negoti-ate reality and handle life. The truth is absolutely essential for a good human life. Equally important, truth is abso-lutely essential for freedom. And in the American republic, where the challenge is not just becoming free but sustaining freedom, any people who would be free and remain free have to grapple seriously with the real challenge of truth.

I will do it, in the space we have for an enormously complicated and controversial subject, by outlining a series of pairs that introduce us to some of the themes that need to be thought through:

- First, two companion crises to the crisis of truth.

- Second, two arguments for those who do believe in truth but have grown rather careless about it.

- Third, two arguments for those who are radically skeptical about truth and have no interest in it.

- Fourth, two challenges the truth brings to us all, even if we're deeply committed to a solid view of truth.

1. Two Crises to the Crisis of Truth

I begin with two companion crises to the crisis of truth. What we see as we look at the American Republic is that the present crisis of truth has gone hand-in-hand with a crisis of character and a crisis of ethics. Together, these three are a very serious erosion of what was once considered essential to this nation.

The crisis of character. First, the crisis of character. In 1979 in a little Guatemalan town called Chajul, the whole town was herded into the public square one day to witness the execution of twenty-three Marxist guerillas who had been captured by the Guatemalan army. As the story goes, the guerillas were stood up, and a soldier explained to the crowd how each of the hideous wounds had been given. Another soldier took a pair of scissor and cut all their clothes off and left them naked, and then other soldiers came and bludgeoned them with bayonets to the ground, poured kerosene over them and burned them alive. They writhed hideously until they died.

All over Europe, in the thirteen years following that event, the sister of a sixteen-year-old who was one of the guerillas told this story in conferences and to all sorts of packed audiences; with the spotlight on her alone, it was credibly dramatic. Many people would be in tears. The red carpet was rolled out, the pope and royal heads of state invited her to speak. Then, to climax it all, she was given the Nobel Peace Prize over Václav Havel and various people who were also candidates that same year. It was 1992, five hundred years on from Christopher Columbus, how extraordinarily appropriate that a young, native Mayan Indian woman should be given the Nobel Peace Prize, standing up for the truth of their people.

But then one of her supporters, an anthropology professor, investigated her story, and in his words, after looking at the facts he decided she should have been given the Nobel Prize for fiction, not peace, because much of the story was concocted. Part of it was true—her parents had been killed by the police, her brother had been killed by the army, but not in that way. No one had actually been burned alive in the town square in Chajul. But when the professor said this, a firestorm of outrage came on *him*. He was imposing his Western journalist views of veracity on this Native American woman who lived in a different world. After all, she was expressing the larger truth of her people. She had the victim's right to lie—you name it, and it went on.

A left-wing example, undoubtedly. But we can find examples across the board today—left, right and center—of what's now loosely called "creative invention" or "creative reinvention." And we can see how, when it comes to character, in the last one hundred years there's been a profound sea of change in American culture. Truth is dead, character is dead, and we can create whatever image we want for ourselves.

Now this is clearly different. Go back to the Greeks, Plato or Aristotle, or to the Bible. Character was the inner stuff that made a man or a woman what he or she was. The inner form was below all the external things like words, behavior, let alone personality and image. It was, in the biblical understanding, who a person was when no one sees except God. You can see that the traditional view of character was very much captured by Jesus' word *hypocrite*, which before him was actually the Greek word for "actor," someone playing a role which he or she isn't. Jesus morally charges that as hypocrisy, because it is not in line with what God sees of their character inside.

Now of course, there have been other voices. Say Machiavelli: Character is nice, he says, but the bottom line is the survival of the Prince. Whatever it takes. If you can be filled with good character, fine, but if you have to go another way, by all means be thoroughly evil if that means the survival of your rule. You can see that those lone voices, like Machiavelli's, are now the general rule. What is behind this?

Well, on the one hand we've moved from the country to the city, from a few deep relationships to an enormous number of relationships, and from words to images. So increasingly, there is a sense that the first impression is the only impression, face value is what counts,

Os Guinness meets with student planners over lunch at Stanford

until we arrive down to the 1950s and 1960s, to the whole art of impression management, where all that matters is the appearance. "The perception *is* the reality," as the politicians say in Washington, D.C. All is impression management, and each of us is now the impresario of our own images. The notion of "designer personality" is very powerfully abroad in this country, so character is dead. All that matters for many people today is image and appearance and packaging.

Mark Twain said, "In America, the secret of success is sincerity. If you can fake that, you've got it made."

Or as Groucho Marx said, "Hey, these are my principles, my moral principles. And if you don't like them, I've got others."

In other words, there is no solid core today. There is only this world of appearances. And we can see in politics and in advertising and many, many areas how profoundly that has come in, largely I think not a result of ideas but of living in modern society with its mobility and media and so on.

The crisis of ethics. How about the other crisis? The crisis of ethics. Do you know the story of Kay Haugaard and her teaching of Shirley Jackson's story "The Lottery"? You may have done "The Lottery" in high school: Midwestern community, tremendous suspense building up, something crucial to the community is going to be enacted. Who knows what it is? And suddenly, with a stunning denouement: human sacrifice. When it was published in *The New Yorker* in 1948, there was a storm of outrage. "Unthinkable!" "Morally outrageous!" And sacks full of mail were received by *The New Yorker* in protest to its publication.

Kay Haugaard, a teacher in Pasadena, taught this over many years. When she began, it was the 1960s. And the first reactions were equally outrage. Unthinkable. Impossible here in America. Human sacrifice? And then came Vietnam, and people came back with the stories of death and violence and maiming and the perversions they'd seen with prostitutes or whatever. And the whole discussion changed. She described the various trends going through America, until one summer's evening in the mid-1990s, with more than twenty in the class, this story, which had always evoked a strong passionate outrage, got *none*.

"What a neat ending!" one person said, seeing it only in literary terms. "Well, we believe in religious liberty and cultural differences, and hey, if this is their religious liberty, who am I to judge?" By the end of the evening, not a single adult in the class objected. For the first time she injected her own views, trying to stir some discussion. Not a single one would make any stand against any moral judgment. She writes, "in the warm Californian night, she left the classroom shivering—chilled to the bone."

> *I've been on campuses where, to put it simply, today it is worse to judge evil than it is to do evil.*

I've been on campuses where, to put it simply, today it is worse to judge evil than it is to do evil. The confusion, the uncertainty, the stress on tolerance, on nonjudgmentalism, is such that with many groups it is now worse to judge evil than it is actually to do evil, so profound is the ethical confusion. Now in this case, it does go back largely to ideas.

There are many roots, of course, but one of the supreme ones is Friedrich Nietzsche. Nietzsche, who was the self-proclaimed immoralist, the "anti-Christ" who called himself "the old artilleryman who delighted in doing philosophy with a hammer," assaulted truth and ethics from two sides. The first is the more obvious, what he called, "perspectivism." As Nietzsche says, "There are many eyes, so there are many truths, so there is no truth." Everything is a matter of perspective, where you're coming from, how you see it. And race, class, gender and so on are fundamental.

But that's not actually the deepest assault of Nietzsche's on truth and ethics. It's what he calls "the genealogy of morals." In other words you take virtues, say pity or compassion, and behind these magnificent-seeming virtues are actually sniveling vices, dressing themselves up, using the virtues to express their power agendas, so that the herd has control over the heroes, and the slave morality finally conquers the master morality.

So strip away the genealogy, get down behind the family tree, don't look at anything as it seems to be. Nothing is what it seems. And behind these great virtues are really vices. And behind everything, the will to power. Strip it all away. Dismantle it. Deconstruct it. And then you get down to the will to power. Very deadly assault on truth.

His book means that truth, in its objective sense, is dead, knowledge is only power. And certainly right and wrong are dead. And we're beyond good and evil in that sense. As I said, this is not universal in America—thank God. But you can see it in many places, including the academic world.

2. Two Arguments About Truth

Let me move on to two arguments, to people who actually believe in truth, mostly, but are very careless about it, which is, on the one hand, many Christian believers, and on the other hand, many citizens.

Arguments for the truth to believers. Let me address two arguments to believers, first. There's a lower and a higher argument for truth. The lower argument, for people who are believers, is that they should be committed to truth because unless there is truth in faith, faith is always vulnerable to the charge of either bad faith or poor and inadequate faith.

Bad faith, particularly in the way the French existentialists put it, is exhibited by people who believe in God only because they're afraid of the alternative, the terror of meaninglessness, or whatever. So because they fear the alternative, they believe in God. There are many answers to that profound objection to faith, but the deepest of them is simply: No believer should believe because he or she is afraid of the alternative. That may make us think and care and search. But fundamentally there's only one, final, adequate reason to believe, because we are convinced that it is true.

How about poor faith? I've met many people in this country who have extraordinarily inadequate views of faith. They believe because "it's true for them," which is *relativism*. Or they believe because "they felt it and experienced it very deeply," which is *subjectivism*. Or they believe because "it works for them," which is basically *pragmatism*. But for followers of Jesus, relativism, pragmatism and subjectivism are three fundamentally inadequate views. The Christian faith is not true because it works, it works because it's true. And very often people have inadequate faith because of bad teaching. Sometimes they use that lack of reason as a drawbridge to raise the portcullis against skepticism and objections—in other words, as a way of escape, which is fundamentally dishonest.

No believer should believe because he or she is afraid of the alternative. That may make us think and care and search. But fundamentally there's only one, final, adequate reason to believe, because we are convinced that it is true.

There's no answer either to bad faith or to poor versions of the faith without the notion of truth. But that's the lower reason for believers.

The higher reason is that for both Jews and for Christians (and they would be exactly one here) the ultimate reason to believe in truth is not fancy philosophy but solid theology. In other words, in the biblical family of faiths, unlike the secularist family or the Eastern family, truth is central to faith, because God himself is the true One—he who is a personal, infinite God is the true One. He speaks and acts truly, and his words and deeds can be checked out in history. So the notion of trustworthiness and truthfulness are very closely linked. Ultimately truth, for both Jews and follows of Jesus, is finally a matter of who God is.

Arguments for truth to non-believers. But what about those who are not believers, just citizens who traditionally should believe in truth but don't? I think there are two arguments here: negative and positive. The negative argument's the simpler and more dramatic one, but the positive one is equally important.

The negative argument is this: without truth there is only manipulation. In other words, many of our postmodern people suggest there's a brave new world. Dismantle all these fancy claims to truth and we get down to the fundamental agendas of power. So just strip it all away and we're in a great state. If our power game is stronger than everyone else's, we're in great shape. But what happens if we're weaker than others? If there's no truth and truth is dead, and knowledge is only power, then might makes right. The victory goes to the strong, and the weak go to the wall. That of course was what Aleksandr Solzhenitsyn and Václav Havel were standing against. They did not have the power, but they had truth. Because of truth, they could not and would not be manipulated.

But that's true not only in the grand cosmic sense, like bringing down the Soviet Union, it is also true in all sorts of other ways, for example, when people have a family member who is a tyrant emotionally, or a boss is extremely controlling, or a professor is thoroughly unfair in his manipulations. Whatever the situation is in human life, the only way to stand is on the basis of truth. Without truth, there is only manipulation.

An extraordinarily poignant example is Pablo Picasso, a genius of an artist, maybe, but a monster of a man in his relationships. His great friend Alberto Giacometti called him a monster. He devoured his friends, especially women and mistresses. He called himself "the Minotaur," the classical monster who devoured maidens. He said, "When I die," and he said this long before the filming of the *Titanic*, "it will be like a great ship going down and many will go down with me." And when he did, three of those close to him committed suicide, unable to live without this devouring, consuming personality at the center of their lives in such a powerful way. Only one was really able to stand with security: Francoise Gilot, one of his mistresses, who was forty years younger than Picasso. She said,

The simple fact is that while any thought can be thought and any argument can be argued, there are some thoughts that can be argued but not lived.

"I would have to go into Pablo every day like Joan of Arc, wearing the armor of truth." Without truth, there is only manipulation. It's a simple but very powerful argument, because none of us like to be manipulated. Let's be clear: without truth, there is only power, and all of us will be at the mercy of those stronger than us, because the name of the game is manipulation.

That's the negative argument. The more positive argument sounds a little more abstract but is equally important: without truth there is no freedom. When I was at Oxford, one of the grand old men of the university was Isaiah Berlin, the great Jewish philosopher. And repeatedly I saw him teasing American graduate students. He would say, "You know, in America you come across to England with only half of your freedom," and they would look at him. He would expound freedom with two dimensions, and said that most Americans only had one dimension (but he said the same to the British too).

In other words, most people, for example, the archetypal teenager, would say that freedom is "freedom *from*." The teenager is free from parents, from professors, from the police, from any parental supervision, and thinks that's free: *freedom from*. And of course that is a very vital part of freedom, whenever there are tyrants and repressive authorities, becoming free *from* is a big deal.

But Berlin would point out that negative freedom is only half of freedom. Freedom is not just freedom *from*, it's freedom *for*. As Lord Acton, the great Catholic historian, put it, "It's not just the permission to do what we like, it is the power to do what we ought." Real freedom depends on knowing who we are, because we're most free when we are ourselves. G. K. Chesterton says we can free a tiger from its cage, but we can never free it from its stripes. Stripes are part and parcel of the tiger. We can free the camel from the zoo, but for heaven's sake don't free it from its hump. The hump is part and parcel of being a camel.

In other words, we have to discover the truth, the character, the nature of what something is in order for it to be itself and be free. We need to know the truth of what it is. And without truth, there is literally no freedom.

I suggest that many of our fellow citizens do, sort of half-consciously, believe in truth. But in a day when it's unpopular, and now it's associated with religious totalitarianism and Osama bin Laden and so on, many people are ashamed to say that they believe in truth, and we need to build back in some of these fundamental arguments for the importance of truth.

3. TWO ANSWERS TO SKEPTICS OF TRUTH

Let's move on to two arguments for those who are much more radically skeptical about truth, who are opposed to truth, who are openly dismissive of truth in a very skeptical way. Here two arguments are very powerful. The first is negative, the second positive. We could put it in many ways, but I'll put it in the terms of my own mentor, the eminent social scientist Peter Berger.

Lack of consistency in relativity. The negative approach to the radical skeptic is, as Peter Berger says, to "relativize the relativizers." People glory in relativism, but if you look at their relativism, there's usually a hidden double standard. They'll be skeptical about the past, but not the present. Or they'll be skeptical about everyone else, but not themselves. In other words, they don't apply the relativism to their own position. There's a clarity in consistency, and as people try to be true to what they say they believe, they find they can't be. The simple fact is that while any thought can be thought and any argument can be argued, there are some thoughts that can be argued but not lived. And the best way to expose this is not to put in all sorts of contrary claims, but to say, "All right, very well," and push them to be true to what they think.

When I was a student, my own field was the social sciences, but as an undergraduate one of the things I was very interested in was philosophy. And back in the early 1960s, the influence of the Vienna Circle and logical positivism was still enormously powerful in the British universities, particularly the thought of A. J. Ayer, who extolled the verification principle: we have to judge types of claims. Analytical claims, for instance, "All bachelors are male," were accepted automatically because the end of the conclusion was written into the assumption. But other claims had to be verified through the five senses, or they were dismissed as nonsense.

So all religious claims, all metaphysics, were dismissed as nonsense. As A. J. Ayer said, famously, the word G-O-D is a great deal less meaningful than the word D-O-G. The dog is in the world of the five senses and can be empirically verifiable. God isn't. So God is nonsense. But those who know philosophy know well what happened. His verification principle itself could not be verified through the five senses. In other words, the principle itself was nonsense!

Years later, when I was at Oxford and A. J. had retired, I found myself on the train with him for an hour one day. We were chatting over his life, and he said to me, "That whole verification principle of skepticism was a blind alley." Then he said, "Any debunker ought to be forced in public to wield his own debunking sword over his own cherished beliefs."

That's exactly right. He wielded a sword and wiped out all sorts of things. And then someone returned the favor, and his principle collapsed overnight. Relativize the relativizers, and don't let them get away with the cheating they so often do.

Signals of transcendence. The second answer to the radical skeptics is more positive. Peter Berger calls it, "pointing out the signals of transcendence." They're skeptics. They're debunkers. They believe nothing. And yet, as Berger points out, embedded in their experience are things that point beyond their experience, yet are not allowed for in their experience. In other words, some things contradict their experience, and some yearnings point to something that goes way beyond their experience. Signals of transcendence.

I'll give you an example: one of the great twentieth-century English-speaking poets was W. H. Auden. He came to the United States in the late 1930s to escape the war in Europe and was happy to settle in Manhattan. Two months after the war broke out, he was in a cinema in Manhattan, on the Upper East Side, which he did not know was in the largely German-speaking Yorkville area. He would go to the cinema every week to follow the documentaries, because there was no television in those days. One particular day in November 1939, two months after the war broke out, the documentary was on the siege of Poland. Nazi storm troopers were going in, bayoneting women and children. And the German-speaking audience (to be fair to them, they did not yet know about the death camps and so on) cried out, "Kill them! Kill them!" egging on the storm troopers.

Auden sat there in the darkness of the cinema, and he said in five minutes his whole worldview was turned upside down. Two things just struck home immediately. The one was, there is evil in human nature. All his life, he said, he had believed in the goodness of human beings, and that with better psychology and a little more education and improved political this, that and the other, we'd have the glories of good human beings coming out. He said he just knew instinctively, seeing on the screen and seeing the audience reaction, there is evil in our human nature, "including me," he said.

He said, "the second thing I saw instinctively, if I was to say that was evil, I had to have a standard by which to do so. I didn't have one." He said, "I knew intuitively Hitler was absolutely evil." He said, "I'd spent all my adult life as an intellectual, destroying the absolutes, and now suddenly I needed one to be able to say that this was wrong."

Have you ever heard an atheist say, "God damn it!" and really mean it? In other words, ninety-nine times out of one hundred that's just idle and maybe even blasphemous. But even an atheist who confronts real evil will often intuitively, almost despite him- or herself say, "God damn it," and they're not wrong. Some things are so profoundly wrong that we need a standard, and an absolute standard by which to judge them. That's what Peter Berger calls "a signal of transcendence," a contradiction of what Auden believed before, and a yearning of what he didn't yet believe. Auden says, "I left the cinema a seeker after an unconditional absolute," and he came to faith. Pointing out signals of transcendence.

As you can see, many people are brave skeptics, radical skeptics, enormously proud of their debunking skills. Don't bother to give them counterarguments. Just relativize the relativizers or love them enough to be in their lives when the signals of transcendence go off and bleep and point beyond their lives. And you will see some of these radical skeptics turning 'round and realizing how profoundly wrong they are and how precious truth is.

4. TWO CHALLENGES OF TRUTH

One last point: truth and its double challenge to all of us. I'm not talking about just skeptics here; I mean all of us, including those of us who are people of faith who are openly and strongly committed to truth. Truth is very tough. At the heart of the biblical position, both for Jews and Christians, is the fact we are truth-seekers, and unlike the East and secularism, the biblical position has a framework for why human truth-directedness is important. So we have notions like trust and honesty in business, or integrity and truthfulness in journalism, or character and truthfulness in political communication, or truth in science. All these things have a fundamental place in the biblical position, which, because of the view of God, as I said earlier, has a powerful view of why human beings are truth-directed. But, the Bible points out, we're not just truth seekers, we are truth-twisters. The biblical ideal is not just that we speak for truth or that we fight for truth, but that there is no final answer here unless we become people of truth, and live and act in truth.

Here we come across the real moral challenge of truth, because as we look down the centuries of how thinkers have thought and related to truth, there are two ways we can go. And we are always all tempted by the two. One way is to try and shape the truth to our desires. The other way is to seek to shape our desires to the truth.

Shaping the truth to our desires. Let's look at the first: people who try to shape the truth to their desires. Many people think that the intellectual is passionately and totally committed to truth, and many have been. The great hero in the social sciences Max Weber said, "Truth or nothing." And Kierkegaard, Camus and many others had that passionate commitment to truth. They would follow truth wherever it leads. Truth or nothing. But is that the general intellectual picture? Not on your life. The more sophisticated the education, the more sophisticated the potential for rationalization. The sharper the mind, the slipperier the heart. The record of intellectuals, particularly in the modern world, is a very cautionary tale. Paul Johnson, among others, says, at the end of it, "beware intellectuals."

The most brazen example I know is Aldous Huxley, the author of *Brave New World*, who died not far from here. If you read Huxley's story in his book *Ends and Means*, he says when he left Oxford, he and his friends decided the world had no meaning. He says, "We

There are two ways we can go. And we're always all tempted by the two. One way is to try and shape the truth to our desires. The other way is to seek to shape our desires to the truth.

were open about it. We decided it had no meaning"—not *discovered* it had no meaning, we *decided* it had no meaning—"because if it had no meaning, we were free to make whatever meaning we wanted, sexually, politically and other ways." Huxley says, quite openly in the book, that for him meaninglessness was an "instrument of liberation." Not that he sought the truth, but he decided it had no meaning, in order to live his own way. Not surprisingly, as many have discovered, if you do that, in the short run—magnificent! Do your own thing—make up your own reality. But because truth is this handle on reality by which we negotiate life, in the long run, for Huxley and many others—the result is confusion and lostness.

One of the key words for people who do this was made very popular by President Clinton: *compartmentalize*. Remember when Clinton explained that he learned it from his mother. If life had any part that was unpleasant, you cordoned it off as a separate compartment and lived as if it wasn't there. He used it positively. Most people would say that was behind his schizophrenic, "split-screen presidency," as ABC News put it. Or put more simply: If you don't have integration with truth in the whole of your life, compartmentalization is another word for lack of integrity—shaping the truth to our desires.

Shaping our desires to truth. The alternative: seeking to shape our desires to the truth. Unquestionably in the short run, this is far less comfortable. I don't like the truth sometimes. It perhaps shows what I've just said is a lie, or that I morally violated a principle. Truth is uncompromising, as is reality. But in the long run it's liberating, because when our life is aligned with reality, we are able to live humanly and freely.

And here the word that contrasts with *compartmentalism*, a word very strong in both the Jewish and the Christian faiths, *confession*. Michel Foucault is well known as a great postmodern thinker who hated the Christian faith. But Foucault acknowledged he admired one thing about the Jewish and Christian faiths: confession. Not coerced confession but voluntary confession is actually an act of extraordinary moral rarity. Why? When humans confess, "I was wrong; I did wrong," they are going on the record publicly against themselves, which in the short run is very painful, but in the long run is very healing and liberating.

So truth is not an easy thing today. You can see that for the framers of the Constitution, truth was one of those fundamentals, without which this nation would not and could not remain free. It's extraordinary how in the last thirty years many of the foundations that the framers would have considered essential have been blithely torn up or thrown away by so many. Both on the individual level and on the level of the Republic, there is no freedom unless there is truth. Follow the argument through, no matter how complicated we might get through all the controversies, at the end of it what shows up with a stunning simplicity and clarity is that the words of Jesus of Nazareth were not a cliché but extraordinarily profound: "You will know the truth, and the truth will set you free."

No motto adorns more American university walls than that verse from the eighth chapter of the Gospel of John. America's tragedy today is that while the motto adorns the walls, it doesn't animates the minds. Truth, humanness, freedom. We're at a place where, put simply, the choices are ours. Your generation. Will you rethink and courageously go back, or will you flow with the current skepticism of much of loose postmodernism? The choices are yours, but what I want to tell you tonight is, so also will be the consequences. Without truth, there is no freedom.

3

REASON FOR GOD

THE EXCLUSIVITY OF TRUTH

Timothy J. Keller
The Veritas Forum at the University of Chicago, 2008

I WOULD LIKE TO TALK TO YOU about one of the biggest reasons why people today are skeptical about belief in God, which is the exclusivity of the truth claims that go along with that kind of belief. If you say, "I know God and what God really likes," you're saying, "I know the truth. I know what spiritual reality is like. I have the truth, and if you don't believe in the God that I believe in, you don't have the truth." Many people today find that unpalatable. It's divisive, narrow and destructive in a pluralistic society. So one of the reasons people have trouble believing in orthodox religions, and Christianity in particular, is because of the exclusivity of the truth.

I'd like to drill down to that: the apparent exclusivity of truth claims regarding belief in God, in Christianity in particular. Actually, I think the exclusive truth claims of religion are to some degree one of the main reasons for conflict, strife and division in the world. Religion does contribute to the lack of peace in the world today. Does that surprise you? I, a Christian minister, am coming right out and saying, yeah, it's true. Does this mean I agree that exclusive truth claims are narrow and need to be stopped? No.

I will discuss the five ordinary ways people deal with the exclusive truth claims in religion, and show that they don't work. Then I will give you a suggestion for how we can deal with the divisiveness of religion.

But, first, let me tell you how most people today tend to deal with the exclusive truth claims in religion. They are

1. hoping it away
2. outlawing it away
3. explaining it away
4. arguing and condemning it away
5. privatizing it away

I want to show you that all five don't work.

Hoping It Away

First, hope it away. When I was in college, everybody believed, including me, that the more technologically advanced the society got, religion would become irrelevant, and that eventually it would die out. Most people said the more educated and economically developed a country became, and the more sophisticated people became, the more religion would thin out. People might still go to church, but they would take it all metaphorically. For instance, they would take the resurrection as a symbol of good triumphing over evil. Most people looked at Europe and said, "See how secular Europe is getting, how unreligious religious people are? That's where all of humanity's going." Except it's not working that way at all. Robust orthodox religion is growing everywhere.

Mark Lilla, who teaches history at Columbia University, has recently written a book called *The Stillborn God*. You know who the stillborn God is? It's the God of liberal mainline Christianity. It was supposed to be the religion of the future, where we would take all of the doctrine metaphorically and would be very tolerant of everyone. Basically Christianity means living a good life and making the world a better place, and we no longer believe in miracles and having to be born again, and all that stuff. He points out in the book that this kind of Christianity has failed. Instead, what we have now, in Western society, is growing secularism and growing orthodoxy. Growing, robust, crunchy, supernatural, miracle-believing religion. We're polarized.

Orthodox people are not going away. And truth claimers are not going away. And we can't just hope that they will. They won't. In fact, interestingly enough, it's even true in the academic world, though we might not notice it. For example, Stanley Fish, the very famous professor in critical theory, had an article in the *Chronicle of Higher Education* a couple of years ago that said: "The university is about to be influenced by a whole new generation of top academics who will be seeking guidance and inspiration from orthodox religion. Are we ready for it?" This is amazing. Fish said:

> We'd better be, because that is where the action is going. When Jacques Derrida died, I was called by a reporter who wanted to know what would succeed, what was coming next after higher theory, and the triumvirate of race, gender, and class is the center of intellectual energy in the academy of the next generation? I answered like a shot, religion.[1]

It may not seem that way right now. But I think Fish knows something's going on. So if you're a secular person, you need to be thinking, *Well, how are we going to get along then in a pluralistic society with all these people who feel like they've got the truth.* Instead of just hoping they go away, or grumbling at them, or telling them that they should know their place, you've actually got to learn to deal with them.

What about the secularization theory, this idea that eventually religion will die out? In the early *Star Trek* episodes with Spock and Kirk, there's no religion around because the science fiction writers of the time figured that a couple hundred years from now, nobody's going to have any religion at all. But the second round of *Star Trek*, the Jean-Luc

The secularization thesis, that religion is all going to go away is so discredited now that last year the New York Times Magazine *had an article on how evolutionary scientists are trying to figure out why the great majority of the human race still believes in God.*

Picard *Star Trek*, there's religion all over the place because the writers knew better.

The secularization thesis that religion is all going to go away is so discredited now that last year the *New York Times Magazine* had an article on how evolutionary scientists are trying to figure out *why* the great majority of the human race still believes in God. They recognize the fact that to the great majority of the human race (but not the average student on elite university campuses) the idea of God makes perfect sense, and they're starting to realize that's just the way it is. What are they going to do about it? They can't hope it away. That's no way to deal with exclusive truth-claiming religion, hoping somehow it's going to die out, or that it will stay up there in the hills with the snake handlers, where we don't have to work it out. It's not going to happen.

Outlawing It Away

Second, people have tried to do to truth-claiming religion what was done in the Soviet Union and in China, that is, suppress or control it. That doesn't work, and I'm not going to talk too much about this because I don't think anybody here is actually considering that. However, as many of you probably know, when the communists kicked all the Western missionaries out of China in 1945 or 1946, they thought, *That's the end of that awful Western religion. Now that the missionaries are gone, what little there is will die out.* But Christianity there is growing enormously.

There are probably more Christians in China than there are in America, and China is probably going to go from about 1 percent Christian to about 30 or 40 percent Christian in the next hundred years. That's going to change the course of history. And the reason it's happening is that by kicking the missionaries out and suppressing Christianity, the Chinese communist leaders made it indigenous. It really became a Chinese Christianity, still devoted to the Apostles' Creed and still orthodox, but it became far more powerful and is growing like crazy. So religion can't be outlawed. Persecuting religion never helps. It only makes it better, makes it stronger. It purifies it in many ways.

EXPLAINING IT AWAY

Third, explain it away. People today are trying to deal with exclusive truth claims of religion by attempting to weaken it; they're trying to diminish it. The evolutionary scientists mentioned in the *New York Times Magazine* article are asking, Why is religious belief so prevalent? It's not going away. They've even done studies showing that children are almost prepared for belief in God. When children are told about belief in God, they almost always immediately find it makes as much sense, if not more sense, than anything else they hear. There are a lot of other kinds of beliefs that children seem to resist, but not this. So the scientists ask what is the source of this seemingly innate human belief.

And of course an evolutionary scientist says, "Ah, the answer is that it's hard-wired into us by the process of natural selection." That is, belief in God is something that helped our ancestors survive. Therefore, in a sense, evolution selected that trait, so that's why we all have it. But there's a problem with this. One of the things I found fascinating in these new atheist books written by Richard Dawkins, Christopher Hitchens and Daniel Dennett—and they all take this approach—is they say that if you believe in God, it's not because there is a God out there, but because you're hard-wired to believe in God. You kind of can't help it. It helped your ancestors survive.

What amazes me is that almost all the book reviews, especially in the high-end journals like the *London Review of Books*, the *New York Times Review of Books* and the *New York Review of Books*, have been pretty negative. Though the reviewers themselves aren't Christians (like Thomas Nagel at New York University, a great philosophy professor who's an agnostic, and Leon Wieseltier, who reviewed Dennett in the *New Republic*), here's what they say, and they're absolutely right: The problem with saying that belief in God or morality is hard-wired into us—that our belief-forming faculties or moral impulses are the product of evolution and therefore can't tell us the truth about things but only help us survive—is that you've proved too much. If we can't trust what our belief-forming faculties tell us about God and morality, because it's just to help us survive, why should we trust our belief-forming faculties when they tell us evolution is true? How dare you use the scalpel on every other thing, everybody else's belief, but not your own?

Alvin Plantinga of Notre Dame has argued this at a very high level in a number of his books. He's a philosopher, and he says: If we believe that everything in us is only the product of evolution, and that all our belief-forming faculties are there only because they help us survive, not because they tell us the truth, then we cannot trust our cognitive faculties to tell us what's really out there. In fact, if anything, a mildly paranoid take on reality will certainly help us survive more than an accurate take on reality. And therefore, if we can't trust what our faculties tell us about God or morality, how dare you say, "But you *can* trust what your faculties tell you about the theory of evolution?" Therefore, if we have a theory like evolutionary theory, we can't trust our mind.

If we can't trust what our faculties tell us about God or morality, how dare you say, "But you can *trust what your faculties tell you about the theory of evolution"? Therefore, if we have a theory like evolutionary theory, we can't trust our mind.*

At the end of the *Abolition of Man*, regarding people who explain away religion and morality as "Well, it's just evolutionary" or "It's just this, just that," C. S. Lewis writes:

> You cannot go on "explaining away" forever: you will find that you have explained explanation itself away. You cannot go on "seeing through" things forever. The whole point of seeing through something is to see something through it. It is good that the window should be transparent, because the street or garden beyond it is opaque. How if you saw through the garden too? It is no use trying to "see through" first principles. If you see through everything, then everything is transparent. But a wholly transparent world is an invisible world. To "see through" all things is the same as not to see.

So if as Nietzsche says, "All truth claims are really just power grabs," then so is his, so why listen to him at all? And if, as Freud says, "All views of God are really just psychological projections to deal with our guilt and insecurity," then so is what he says about God. So why listen to him? And if, as the evolutionary scientist says, what our brain tells us about morality and God is not real, it's just a chemical reaction designed to pass on our genetic code, then so is what their brains tell them about the world and evolution itself, so why listen to them? In the end, to see through everything is the same as not to see anything. And if we try to explain away belief in God like that, by appealing to evolution, then we've explained away everything. So we can't explain it away.

ARGUING IT AWAY

The next strategy is to argue or condemn belief in God to make it go away. This is the main way most people try to stifle others who say they have the truth. It's divisive, they argue. How dare you say your religion is the right religion? How dare you say that? It's narrow, it's divisive, it's exclusive.

One of the most famous of all the exclusive religious truth claims is that Jesus is the only way to God. Jesus says in John 14, "I am the way, and the truth, and the life. No one comes to the Father except through me." That's the classic exclusive truth remark. Jesus is the true way to God.

How do we respond to this? Well, there are three things we can say. The first is to say, "All religions are equally right, and how dare you say that Jesus is the only way?" But may I respectfully say, that's impossible. Let me explain why. Every religious founder of every other major religion says, "I'm a prophet who has come to show you the way to find God." But of all the major religions of the world, only Christianity has a founder who has the audacity to say "I *am* God, and I have come to find *you*." Do you realize how different that is?

Do you know how often Jesus says that? In Luke 10 Jesus says to his disciples, "I watched Satan fall from heaven like a flash of lightning." I imagine his disciples sitting there thinking, *When did you see that? Where were you standing? And who the heck are you?* In Matthew 23 Jesus says to his critics, "I've been sending you wise men and prophets, and you've killed them all." By this, Jesus causally says, "I'm the power behind the universe who's been sending prophets, wise men and sages into the world, and you've been killing them." Jesus says in John 8, "Before Abraham existed, I am." And if you say, "Well, I don't know about that, and I don't like all that doctrine about Jesus being the same as God, all I know is I love his teaching. In fact, I accept all the teachings of Christianity." If you say this, with all due respect, it shows you have not read his teachings, because they are absolutely, inextricably bound up with his claims about who he is. It's everywhere!

Every religious founder of every other major religion says, "I'm a prophet who has come to show you the way to find God." But of all the major religions of the world, only Christianity has a founder who has the audacity to say "I am God, and I have come to find you." Do you realize how different that is?

Once I was on a panel with an imam and a rabbi. We were talking to a bunch of people at the New School of Social Research in downtown New York. And one thing that really upset them: I said, if Jesus is not just a prophet showing us how to find God, but is actually God come to find us, then Christianity would have to be a superior religion. It would have to be a better way of finding God, if it's actually God coming to find us. On the other hand, if what Jesus said is not true, then it would be an inferior religion, it would be a blasphemous religion, and Jesus would be either deranged or a fraud. Christianity is either far better or far worse than religion, but it's not the same.

Guess what? The Muslim cleric and the rabbi absolutely agreed. They had no problem agreeing with it, but the students were very unhappy. No, no, no. You're all equal, they said. And we responded, How dare you violate us? You're not listening to us. It's who we are. You can't say all religions are equally right.

There's another way to deal with exclusive truth claims, which is to say they're all equally wrong. In fact, that's what Dawkins, Hitchens and company do. They say that all religions are wrong because they all say that they have the truth, but the fact is, nobody knows the truth. All the religions have a little bit of wisdom in them, but nobody knows the whole truth. And the way that is put forth is usually with the illustration of the blind man and the elephant. Here's how the illustration goes. Five or six blind men are walking along and they encounter an elephant. Everyone grabs a different part of the elephant, and the guy with the trunk says, "Oh, well elephants are kinda like snakes. You know, they're kind of long and flexible." Another guy says, "I don't think so. Elephants are more stumps of trees," because he's got the leg. And so they're all arguing about what the elephant is. And many people think, *Ah, there's a perfect picture of all the religions of the world.* All the religions think they see the whole elephant, the whole truth. But nobody really knows anything but a little tiny bit of the truth. They're all blind—and so are all religions. So how dare any religion say it knows the truth?

But there's a huge problem. The philosopher Michael Polanyi came up with this response, and Lesslie Newbigin, a British scholar and Christian minister, put it into this narrative. Newbigin said that the point of the story is often overlooked. The story is told from the point of view of someone who is not blind. How could you know all the blind men only have part of the elephant unless *you* can see the whole elephant? If you were equally blind with the blind men, then there's no way you could know that nobody could know. So the only way you could say nobody can know the truth is if you assume you've got more knowledge than anybody else. The only possible way that you could know that no religion can see the whole truth is if you yourself have the very kind of superior comprehensive knowledge of spiritual reality that you just said none of the other religions have.

> There is an appearance of humility in the protestation, that the truth is much greater than any one of us can grasp, but if this is used to invalidate all claims to discern the truth, it is in fact an arrogant claim to a kind of knowledge which is superior to [all others].[2]

If you say, "I don't know which religion is true," that is a statement of humility. But if you say, "No one can know the truth," you're being dogmatic in presuming you have the ultimate view of reality greater than any other religion, and that's the very claim you're criticizing. You're hoisted on your petard, as they say in philosophy class.

I've had a number of conversations that go like this. I'm talking to somebody who does not believe about Christianity or Christ. At some

point he or she says to me suddenly, "Wait a minute, what are you trying to do to me?"

I respond, "I'm trying to evangelize you."

"You mean you're trying to convert me?"

"Yeah."

"You're trying to get me to adopt *your* view of spiritual reality and
convert *me?*"

"Yeah."

"How narrow! How awful. Nobody should say that their view of
spirituality is better than anybody else and try to convert them to it. Oh
no, no, no. Everybody should just leave everybody else alone."

"Wait a minute, wait a minute," I say. "You want me to adopt your
take on spiritual reality, you want me to adopt your view of all the
various religions. What are you doing to *me?* What you're saying is,
you have a take on spiritual reality and you think I would be better off
and the world would be better off if we adopted yours. I have my take
on spiritual reality and I think mine's better than yours, and I'm trying to convert you to mine. You're trying to convert me to yours. If
you say 'Don't evangelize anybody,' *that* is to evangelize me, into your
Western, white, enlightenment, individualistic, privatized understanding of religion."

Do you understand? Who's more narrow? It's not narrow to make an
exclusive truth claim because *everybody* makes an exclusive truth claim.
What does it mean to say nobody can know the truth, that there are no
such thing as universal truth claims. Oh, you mean, *universally?* But
everybody makes an exclusive truth claims. Everybody has a take on
reality. Everybody thinks the world would be better if those people over
there adopted mine. Everybody.

Well then, what is narrowness? Narrowness is not the *content* of a
truth claim. Narrowness is our attitude toward the people who don't
share our view. If we look down our nose in disdain and think, *They're
primitive, unenlightened*, and if we make jokes about them all the time,
we're narrow. I don't care what your view is of reality, of religion or
how skeptical you think you are—*you're* a fundamentalist. To simply
argue and say we can't make exclusive truth claims because that's nar-

row—because nobody knows the truth, because all religions are equal—doesn't work at all. If you think about it, to say nobody should make exclusive truth claims is actually inconsistent, and in many cases hypocritical.

> *Narrowness is not the content of a truth claim. Narrowness is our attitude toward the people who don't share our view.*

PRIVATIZING IT AWAY

Let me go one step further. The last thing that people say in order to try to neutralize exclusive truth-claiming religion is, "Okay, you can have your view, but you have to keep it private. In particular, you've got to keep it out of politics." When we come into public discourse and we start to argue for public policy, the broad understanding is that we must never use religious reason, only secular reason.

Richard Rorty, a really good (pragmatist) philosopher who has recently died, would say religion in the public realm is a conversation stopper. As soon as people start to argue that this is how society ought to go, and they give a religious reason for what they're suggesting, it stops the conversation because other people who don't share their religion don't have access to that reason. So, he says, let's keep our religious views totally private, and let's just pragmatically come together and work on practical solutions on the big problems we've got, like education, poverty, social cohesion and these sort of things. Let's work together and leave our religious ideas behind. This is privatizing.

This won't work, and here's the reason why. As soon as we start to say society ought to be like this or like that, we're arguing from a worldview. This is sometimes called a narrative identity, an understanding of what life is about. So, for example, some people say there is no God and morality is basically relative; therefore, they say, every human being has a right to determine what is right or wrong for him- or herself, and we should live any life that fulfills us as long as it doesn't get in the way of somebody else doing the same. Can we prove any of that? Can we prove there is no God? Can we prove morality is relative? Can we prove this individualistic understanding of what life is all about?

There are two ways we could call something a fact. It's a fact if it's self-evident. We can't prove that we are here, philosophers will tell us that. Anyone who's watched *The Matrix* knows we can't prove we're really here. We can't really prove much of anything, and yet it's self-evident to everybody that we're here—anybody can walk in the room and look around and say, yeah, you're here. Second, if we can prove it empirically, then that's a fact.

But what if we say human beings are really important, and no one should trample on the rights of any human being. Or everyone has the right to determine what is right or wrong for him- or herself. Guess what? Those are religious statements, and not everybody has access to them. Remember, Richard Rorty says the problem with arguing from a religion is that many other people don't have access to it. The fact of the matter is *anything* we say comes from a worldview that lots of other people don't have access to.

Here's a quick example: divorce laws. Should getting a divorce be really easy or hard? In traditional cultures that have a different narrative identity, the individual is not as important as the family. For them, what's important is to fulfill the expectations of the family and the tribe. Western individualism and the Enlightenment says the individual and individual happiness, fulfillment and consciousness is more important than the clan and the community, tradition and values. Right? Do you know what this means? Those who come from a traditional culture—for example, Confucianism, Hinduism, Protestantism, Catholicism or Judaism—and have that understanding of the meaning of life, are going to want getting a divorce to be difficult. But those who come from a Western Enlightenment understanding of individualism are going to want getting a divorce to be easy, because they think the purpose of marriage is the fulfillment of the two individuals. Other people think the purpose of marriage includes the flourishing of children and the broader community.

And where does Richard Rorty's idea go? Richard Rorty says let's all put our religion behind us and work together on practical solutions to our problems. But any practical solution to a problem that we think is a good, practical solution depends on a particular view of human flourishing and the meaning of life that is rooted in nonprovable faith assumptions. That's why we're all religious, whether we admit it or not.

Carolyn Fluehr-Lobban used to teach cultural anthropology, and she believed that all morality is basically socially constructed. Thus she believed we should never impose our morality on another culture. She was working in Africa and she saw the terrible oppression of women. In the *Chronicle of Higher Education* she wrote a fascinating article about the agony she felt when she tried to tell the leaders of the African societies that what they were doing to the women was wrong. They responded, "Don't impose your values on us." They said, "You're imposing your religious beliefs on us."

She retorted that she was not religious. But she began to realize that of course she is: she is a secular humanist and believed in human rights. Human rights are not self-evident to everybody. Human rights are not things we can prove. It takes religious commitment. It's a faith assumption, and therefore we cannot say to religious people, "Don't talk about your doctrine in the public realm, whereas we can talk about our less institutionalized doctrine in the public realm." That's not right.

That's the reason why increasingly there are people saying there's a difference between privileged secularism and procedural or passive secularism. *Privileged* secularism says, in the public realm when we argue for laws, we can use the secular worldview—the enlightenment individualistic worldview—to build our laws, but not any other. We can't argue out of any other worldview, which would be a form of state-sponsored religion. But *procedural* or *passive* secularism

> *Human rights are not things we can prove. It takes religious commitment. It's a faith assumption, and therefore we cannot say to religious people—people who go to church and synagogue—"Don't talk about your doctrine in the public realm, whereas we can talk about our less institutionalized doctrine in the public realm." That's not right.*

says that the state stays neutral, the state is not going to support any religion or church with its tax money and so forth. And yet anyone in the public realm who's fighting for certain approaches to social arrangements and is working for certain public policies has the freedom to argue out of any religious stance he or she wants to. But unless that person has fairly broad arguments, he or she is not going to be able to appeal to a broad body of people and will not get the votes. So, let the best appealers win, whether they're being overt or covert, implicit or explicit in their religious appeals. See? Privatization doesn't work either. So now what are we going to do?

A NEW SUGGESTION

Here's what I'd like to suggest (I already gave you half of the suggestion): We need to distinguish the privileged propagandist kind of secularism, in which we're really imposing a secularist worldview on everybody, from procedural secularism. There are too many Muslims, Christians, Protestants, Catholics, Jews and people with robust orthodox belief in God to say, "Stay out of the public realm; we're going to handle it." It's not equitable. Instead, there has to be a way of keeping the state neutral, but at the same time allowing people to put their policies into place regardless of their roots.

For a minute I'd like to talk directly to Christians. I want Christians to recognize one big reason why we have problems in the United States now, and over the years, is because of religious belief. I want us to take responsibility for part of the problem that is our fault. Only when we realize we've been part of the problem will we perhaps become the heart of the solution, which is a society in which we're able to talk civilly about these matters.

Here's what I mean. There are two ways to think about self-image. There is a performance narrative that says "I am a good person, I'm a significant person because I've achieved this, I've done that, I've performed." Basically, there are a hundred million forms of this: "I'm a pretty good person because I'm a liberal activist," for example. And if that's the basis of our self-image, it's hard not to look down our nose at bigots and feel superior to them.

If, on the other hand, we are a traditional religious person—"I read the Bible and pray, and I'm trying to follow Jesus"—and that's why we feel good about ourselves, it's almost impossible not to look down our nose and feel superior to people that don't have the right doctrine and aren't living the right way. In fact, even if we're not religious, even if we just have a lot of pride in the fact that we're decent hard-working chaps, and *that's* the basis for our self-image, it's hard not to feel superior to the people we think of as slackers.

But there is another way to build up identity. It's not the performance narrative but the grace narrative. The grace narrative is this: Jesus Christ came to earth to accomplish our salvation, but he didn't do it through strength. He didn't get on a horse, brandish a sword and shout, "Charge!" He went to the cross and died. He became a servant. He sacrificed. He became weak and paid for our sins on the cross. This means salvation that is accomplished in weakness can only be received in weakness. We only get Christ's salva-

Tim Keller presents the reason for God to students at the University of Chicago.

tion and mercy when we admit our failure. Because we can never even live up to our own standards, the only possible way to know God is to say, "I'm a failure, and I need mercy and grace." Then, in him, we're loved—not because of our performance, but because of his.

That means we can't despise anybody. If we really understand the grace narrative, we can't. If we feel superior to anyone, it shows we've slipped back into the moral performance narrative. I have a Hindu neighbor who for nineteen years has lived right across the hall from me in New York City. That man could easily be a better father than me. That man could easily be a better man in every way. He could be more calm, could have better character, could be more patient, could be more noble and more courageous than me. And why not? The truth, for a Christian, is being saved by grace; that's the truth. And I'm not basing my relationship with God, or even my own self-image, on me being better than him! That's not what saved me.

If we had even a little piece of the Christian church living out of the grace narrative, there would not be all these complaints about self-righteousness, divisiveness, condemning attitudes and judgmentalism. It would be impossible. Christians have to realize we've been a big part of the problem. We're part of the divisiveness, because religion sets up a slippery slope in our hearts where we begin to feel superior to people. Then we caricature them in our heart, and eventually we start to oppress them. Christianity explains that those attitudes and actions come from works righteousness. They come from self-salvation projects. They come from the moral performance narrative. And Christianity has a way of expunging it. Here's how.

> *Christians have to realize we've been a big part of the problem, that we're part of the divisiveness, because religion sets up a slippery slope in our hearts where we begin to feel superior to people. Then we caricature them in our heart, and eventually we start to oppress them.*

Here's one of the great historical conundrums and riddles: Why did Christianity eventually overrun the Roman Empire, and when it wasn't even trying to gain political power? The Greco-Roman world believed everyone had their own god. That's very open isn't it? No one has the truth, everybody has their own God. But the Christians came along and said, "We have the true God." So the Greco-Roman world had what looked like the more tolerant worldview, and the Christians looked like they had the more narrow worldview. But the way the Christians and Greco-Romans *lived* was actually the exact opposite.

In the Greco-Roman world the poor were despised; in the Christian world the poor were loved. In the Greco-Roman world women were looked down on; in the Christian world women were empowered. The Greco-Roman world kept the races and the classes apart. The Christian world brought them together promiscuously, offending the Greco-Roman world. When the plagues came in the second century and people were dying in the cities, and the streets were littered with people abandoned by their loved ones, the Christians stayed. And in many cases the Christians died taking care of their pagan neighbors. In other words, Christians had the absolute most narrow worldview because they thought they had the truth.

The Greco-Roman world said, "We don't know who has the truth. Everybody's got their own." So why did Christians live the most peace-loving, the most generous, the most sacrificial, the most inclusive possible lifestyle out of the most exclusive possible truth claim? Here's the answer. Actually, my wife Kathy gave this to me some years ago, right after 9/11. All the papers were saying this is the problem with religious fundamentalism. If you're a fundamentalist, if you really believe you have the truth, this is what happens. Kathy said, as I tried to show you here, everybody's a fundamentalist, in a way. Everybody believes fundamentals; everybody's got exclusive truth. I remember Kathy said, "Fundamentalism doesn't necessarily lead you to terrorism. It depends on what your *fundamental* is. Have you ever seen an Amish terrorist?"

And if the *Amish* are not fundamentalists, there ain't no such thing. So why will there never be Amish terrorists? I'll tell you why. If your "fundamental" is a Man dying on the cross for his enemies, if the very heart of your self-image and your religion is a Man sacrificing and praying for his enemies as he died for them, loving them—if that sinks into your heart of hearts—it's going to produce the kind of life that the early Christians produced. The most inclusive possible life out of the most exclusive possible claim. This is the truth. But what is the truth? The truth is a God who became weak, who loved and died for the people who opposed him, forgiving them.

Take that into the center of your heart and you will be at the heart of the solution that we need in this world. And that is the "divisiveness" of exclusive truth claims by the Christian.

4

THE LANGUAGE OF GOD

A SCIENTIST PRESENTS EVIDENCE FOR BELIEF

Francis S. Collins
The Veritas Forum at California Institute of Technology, 2009*

WE ARE HERE TO TALK ABOUT big questions, maybe the biggest question of all: does God exist? I won't give you a proof, but I hope to give you some things to think about, things that have led me from being an atheist to becoming a believer and a follower of Jesus. I will also explain why I see no conflict between that perspective and that of being a scientist who is rigorous in my views of data, but who also sees that the study of nature is not all there is.

So come, let us reason together here and see what we might learn. As Socrates said, "Let us follow the truth whithersoever it leads." And of course, *veritas* means "truth," which is what this Forum stands for.

THE HUMAN GENOME PROJECT
I would like to start by telling you a little bit about the science that I've had the privilege of being involved in, which is the study of our human DNA instruction book, the human genome. When the popu-

---

*This Veritas Forum took place in February 2009, six months before Collins was appointed director of the National Institute of Health.

lar press reports on this, they often use iconic images such as a *Time* magazine cover featuring the double helix with Adam and Eve. As to whether these images are connected, I will certainly argue that the faith and the science perspectives are appropriate to consider together. (I have a sneaking suspicion that magazine editors have another motivation, because they always feature double helixes with naked people. You can draw your own conclusion about what editors have decided sells magazines.)

We are going to talk about this amazing double helix molecule, spilling out of the nucleus of the cell, carrying the information that needs to be passed from parent to child, generation after generation, by the series of these chemical bases, here abbreviated A, C, G and T. The order of those letters provides the instructions to take each organism from its original, rather simple, beginnings as a single cell to a fancy organism like a human being.

The genome of an organism is its entire set of DNA instructions. The human genome adds up to 3.1 billion of those letters. If we decided we were going to read the human genome tonight, we would probably regret it after we got started because we would be reading seven days a week, twenty-four hours a day, for thirty-one years.

We have that information now, which is pretty amazing. And you already had it, even before we sequenced it, inside each cell of your body. Every time the cell divides, you've got to copy the whole thing. Occasionally mistakes get made, and if they get made during your life in a particularly vulnerable place, they might start you on a path toward cancer. If a mistake is made in passing the DNA from parent to child, then that child might end up with some kind of a birth defect.

But once in a very long time that change might actually be beneficial. That, of course, is how evolution works. It is gradual change applied to this DNA sequence over long periods of time by the means of what Darwin identified as natural selection, resulting in gradual evolution and the appearance of new species.

So, DNA is at the center in terms of trying to understand how the whole system works. The Human Genome Project was proposed rather controversially in the late 1980s, and most of the scientific community was deeply skeptical about whether or not this was a good idea. It might cost too much money. It might not be feasible. It might just attract mediocre scientists because it seemed kind of boring. Well, none of those things turned out to be true. It certainly wasn't boring.

I'm happy to report that it went better than expected. As the person who had the privilege of serving as the project manager of this enterprise, we were able to announce not just a draft, which we had in June 2000, but a finished human genome in April 2003, fifty years after Watson and Crick described the double helix. We completed all of the goals of the Genome Project more than two years ahead of schedule, and more than $400 million under budget. That doesn't happen very often.

I could give you hours of descriptions of what's happened since April 2003 in terms of taking this foundational information and building upon it, particularly for medical benefit. As a physician, the promise for better health was one of the most exciting aspects of why we did this in the first place. I will spare you the details, but I think the dream of application for medical benefit is beginning to come true.

With these tools from the Genome Project, we have been increasingly able, especially in the last couple of years, to identify specific genetic risk factors for cancer, heart disease, diabetes, asthma, schizophrenia and a long list of conditions that previously were very difficult to sort out. And in circumstances where someone is at high risk, knowing this allows that person to reduce that risk by changing a diet, lifestyle or medical surveillance. This opportunity to practice better prevention on an individualized basis is getting pretty exciting. This is called "personalized medicine." It applies not only to this kind of prevention, but if we do get sick, it may provide us with a better chance to get the right drug at the right dose instead of something that doesn't work or perhaps even gives us a toxic side effect. That's what pharmacogenomics is about.

Perhaps the biggest payoff in the long term will be to take those discoveries of the real fundamentals of what causes these diseases and turn those into insights that will lead us to novel therapeutics, be they gene therapies or drug therapies, targeted to the fundamental problem instead of some secondary effect. We are beginning to see that future now, especially in the field of cancer. We will see much more of it over the coming decade. I would predict that in another fifteen years, medicine will be radically different because of all of these developments stimulated by the Genome Project. The scientific community is plunging in with great energy and creativity to make the most of these discoveries.

That's what I've had the chance to do over the last twenty-five years, through the Genome Project and before that, chasing down genes for disease. It's been a wonderful experience as a professional working with lots of other skilled people, making great friends and having the chance to learn new things about biology and medicine that were not known before.

MERGING SCIENCE AND FAITH WORLDVIEWS

But now let me ask you the question that many people pose, and which I pose to you tonight: There are two fundamental worldviews, the scientific and the spiritual. Do we have to choose? Do we have to throw in our lot with one and neglect the other? Or is there a possibility of merging the two?

Many people today argue that these worldviews are at war and there is no way to reconcile them. That has not been my experience, and that's what I particularly would like to share this evening. Then I hope we will have some time for questions from those of you who would like to pursue this in one way or another.

At this point, I want to share a little bit more of a description about my spiritual perspective. I described my scientific pathway. But how is it that I can stand up

There are two worldviews, the scientific and the spiritual. Do we have to choose?

here before you at a distinguished university to talk about being a believer in God?

I was raised in a family that was wonderfully unconventional. My father had been a folk song collector in the 1930s in North Carolina. After the war, he and my mother did the sixties thing, except it was still the 1940s. I don't think it involved drugs, but they did buy a dirt farm and tried to live off the land, which didn't go very well. They discovered that was not a credible way to have enough income to serve a growing family. I was born on that farm. By that time, my father had gone back to teaching at the local college, and my mother had started writing plays. They founded a theater in a grove of oak trees near our farmhouse, which I'm happy to say is about to have its fifty-fourth consecutive summer season.

I was raised in this wonderful mix of ideas, music, theater and the arts. My mother taught me at home until the sixth grade, which was also very unconventional in the 1950s, and she taught me to love the experience of learning new things. But one thing I didn't learn much about was faith. My parents didn't really denigrate religion, but they didn't find it very relevant.

When I got to college, even though I might have had some spiritual glimmers along the way, those quickly disappeared in those dormitory conversations where there's always an atheist who's determined to put forward the argument about why faith is flawed. My faith wasn't even there at all, so it was pretty easy for the resident atheist to dismiss my leanings.

I was probably an agnostic at that point, although I didn't know the word. Then I went to graduate school and studied physical chemistry, and was immersed in a theoretical approach to trying to understand the behavior of atoms and molecules. My faith then rested on second-order differential equations (which are indeed pretty cool). But just the same, I adopted an increasingly reductionist and materialist mode. I had even less tolerance then for hearing information of a spiritual sort, considering that to be irrelevant information left over from an earlier time that should appropriately be cast off.

Then I had a change of heart about what I wanted to do professionally. I loved what I was doing in chemistry, but I discovered biology, which I had pretty much neglected. Recombinant DNA was being invented. There was some chance that we might actually begin to understand how life works at a fundamental level. Realizing that this was becoming a real calling for me, and also being unsure whether I wanted to be a researcher or a practitioner, I went to medical school. That had not previously been part of my life plan. It's still rather amazing that medical school let me in with that story, but they did.

I arrived in medical school as an atheist, but it didn't last. In the third year of medical school I found myself taking care of patients, wonderful people with terrible illnesses. They were people who saw death approaching. To my surprise, many of them seemed to be at peace about it because of their faith. That was puzzling.

As I tried to imagine myself in that situation, I knew I would not be at peace. I would be terrified. That was a bit disturbing, and I tried to put it out of my mind. Then, one afternoon when we had run out of medical options for a wonderful elderly woman with advanced heart disease, she told me in a very simple, sincere way about her faith. It gave her courage, hope and peace about what was coming. As she finished that description, she looked at me quizzically. I sat there silently, feeling a little embarrassed, and she said, "Doctor, I've told you about my faith, and we've talked about my family, and I thought maybe you might say something."

And then she asked me the simplest question, "Doctor, what do you believe?"

Nobody had ever asked me that question before, not like that, not in such a simple, sincere way. I realized I didn't know the answer. I felt uneasy. I could feel my face flushing. I wanted to get out of there. The ice was cracking under my feet. All of a sudden, by this simple question, everything was a muddle.

That troubled me. I thought about it a little bit and realized what the problem was. I was a scientist, or at least I thought I was, and scientists are supposed to make decisions after they look at the evidence. I had made a decision that there is no God, and I'd never really thought about looking at the evidence. I had to admit I didn't really know whether I had chosen the answer on the basis of reason, or whether because it was the answer I wanted.

I wasn't sure there was any evidence, but I figured I'd better find out because I didn't want to be in that spot again. I figured I should learn about world religions—what do they believe? I tried to read through some of those sacred texts, and I got totally confused and frustrated.

There was no Wikipedia to help me either. Now there's even a book called *World Religions for Dummies*, but there wasn't then.

At a loss, I knocked on the door of a minister who lived down the road from me in Chapel Hill, North Carolina, and said, "I don't know what these religious people are talking about, but I figure it's time for me to learn. So you must be a believer, at least I hope you are, since you're a minister. Let me ask you some questions." I asked him a bunch of probably blasphemous questions, and he was gracious about that.

I had made a decision that there is no God, and I'd never really thought about looking at the evidence.

After a while he said, "You know, you're on a journey here, trying to figure out what's true. You're not the first one. In fact, I've got a book written by somebody who went on that same journey, from an academic perspective. In fact, he was a pretty distinguished Oxford scholar. He found there were people around him who were believers, and he was puzzled about that. So he set about to try to figure out why people believe. He figured that he could shoot them down. Well, why don't you read the book and see what happened."

He pulled this little book, *Mere Christianity*, off the shelf, and I took it home and began to read. In the first two or three pages I realized that my arguments against faith were really those of a schoolboy. They had no real substance. The thoughtful reflections of this Oxford scholar, whose name of course is C. S. Lewis, made me realize there was a great depth of thinking and reason that could be applied to the question of God. That was a surprise! I had imagined faith and reason were at opposite poles, and here was this deep intellectual who was convincing me quickly page by page that actually reason and faith go hand in hand, though faith has the added component of revelation.

I had to learn more about this. Over the course of the next year (kicking and screaming most of the way because I did not want this to turn out the way that it seemed to be turning out), I began to realize that the evidence for the existence of God, while not proof, was actually pretty compelling. It made me realize that atheism would no longer be an acceptable choice for me, as it was the least rational of the options.

NATURE PROVIDES INTERESTING POINTERS TO GOD

I won't go through the whole chronology as it actually happened. Let me just summarize for you the kinds of arguments that ultimately brought me around to the position of recognizing that belief in God was an entirely intellectually consistent event, and also something that I was increasingly discovering I had a spiritual hunger for. Interestingly, some of the pointers to God had been in front of me all along, coming from the study of nature. I hadn't really thought about them, but here they were:

1. There is something instead of nothing. This seems like an obvious statement, but maybe it's not so obvious: There is something instead of nothing. There's no reason that should be.

2. The unreasonable effectiveness of mathematics. This phrase from Eugene Wigner, the Nobel laureate in physics, caught my eye because as a graduate student working with quantum mechanics, I had studied Schrödinger's Equation. One of the things that had appealed to me so much about mathematics, physics and chemistry was how it is that this particular kind of depiction of matter and energy works; it really works *well.* A theory that is cor-

Francis Collins answers questions before a packed crowd at Caltech.

rect often turns out to be simple and beautiful. But why should this be? Why should mathematics be so unreasonably effective in describing nature?

3. The big bang. The fact that the universe had a beginning (as virtually all scientists are now coming to the conclusion) about 13.7 billion years ago, in an unimaginable singularity, where the universe, smaller than a golf ball, suddenly appeared and then began flying apart, and has been flying apart ever since. With observations like the background microwave radiation, the echo of that big bang, we can calculate the timing of that singularity by noticing just how far those galaxies are receding from us.

Of course, that presents a difficulty, because our science cannot look back beyond that point, and it seems that something came out of nothing. Well, nature isn't supposed to allow that something came out of nothing. So if nature is not able to create itself, how did the universe get here? We can't just postulate that it was created by some natural force, because then, what created that natural force? We haven't solved the problem. So, it seemed to me the only plausible explanation is that there must be some supernatural force that did the creating. Of course, that force would not need to be limited by space or even by time.

So this seems to lead to the hypothesis of a Creator. Let's call that creator "God," who must be supernatural, not bound by space or time, and is a pretty darned good mathematician. It's starting to make some sense.

4. The precise tuning of physical constants in the universe. Well, God must also be an incredible physicist, because another thing I began to learn is that there is this phenomenal fine-tuning of the universe that makes complexity, and therefore life, possible. Those who study physics and chemistry know that there's a whole series of laws that govern the behavior of matter and energy. They are simple, beautiful equations, but they have constants in them, like the gravitational constant or the speed of light. At the present time we cannot derive the value of those constants, nor do we think we will in the future. They are what they are. They're givens. We have to do the experiment and measure them.

Suppose these constants were a little different. Would that matter? Would anything change in our universe if the gravitational constant was a little stronger or a little weaker? That calculation got done in the 1970s by John Barrow and Frank Tipler, and the answer was astounding. If we take any of the fifteen physical constants and tweak them just a tiny little bit, the whole thing doesn't work anymore.

Take gravity, for instance. If gravity was just one part in about ten billion weaker than it actually is, then after the big bang, there would be insufficient gravitational pull to result in the coalescence of stars and galaxies and planets and you and me. We'd end up with an infinitely expanding, sterile universe. If gravity was just a tiny bit stronger, things would coalesce all right, but a little too soon. The big bang would be followed, after a while, by a big crunch, and we would not have the chance to appear, because the timing wouldn't be right.

We can't look at that data and not marvel at it. It is astounding to see the knife-edge of improbability on which our existence exists. What's that about? Well, I can think of three possibilities:

- First, maybe theory will some day tell us that these constants *have* to have the value they have, that there is some a priori reason for that. Most physicists I talk to don't think that's too likely. There might be relationships between the constants that have to be maintained, but not the whole thing.

- A second possibility is that perhaps we are one of an almost infinite series of other universes that have different values of those constants. And, of course, we have to be in the one where everything turned out right, or we wouldn't be having this conversation. This is the multiverse hypothesis. It is defensible as long as we're willing to accept the fact that we will probably never be able to observe those infinite series of other parallel universes. That requires quite a leap of faith.

- The third possibility is that this is intentional, that these constants have the value they do because the Creator God, who is an awesome mathematician and physicist, also knew that there was an important set of dials to set if the universe that was coming into being was going to be interesting.

Which of these three possibilities seems most plausible? Ockham's razor says that the simplest explanation is most likely correct. I come down on number three, but in part because I've already arrived there in terms of arguments 1, 2 and 3 about the idea of a Creator.

This is interesting, but how far have we gotten? We've gotten to Einstein's God now, because Einstein was a deist, and certainly marveled at the way mathematics worked. Einstein was not aware, as far as we know, of the fine-tuning arguments at quite this level, but he probably would have embraced them in the same way.

5. Moral law. So how do we get from deism to theism? We now go back to Lewis. In the first chapter of *Mere Christianity*, titled "Right and Wrong as a Clue to the Meaning of the Universe," Lewis talks about the moral law. I didn't take philosophy in college, but as I began to recognize what the argument was, it rang true. It rang true in a really startling way. It was one of those moments where you realize, I've known about this all my life, but I've never really thought about it.

What's the argument? That we humans are unique in the animal kingdom by apparently having a law of right behavior that we are under, although we seem free to break it. There's something called right and something called wrong, and we're supposed to do the right thing and not the wrong thing. Of course we break that law. But when we do, we make an excuse, which means we believe the law must be true, and we're trying to be let off the hook.

Some will quickly object, "Now, wait a minute! I can think of human cultures that promoted terrible things. How can you say they were under the moral law?" Well, when we study those cultures, we find that the things we consider terrible were to them "right" because of various cultural expectations. It seems the moral law is universal, but it is influenced in terms of particular actions in how a culture sizes up what counts as "right" or "wrong."

The moral law sometimes calls us to do rather dramatic things. An example is altruism, where people do something sacrificial for somebody else, without expectation of reward. What about that? People may argue, and they have, that this can be explained by evolution. For instance, if a man is altruistic to his own family, we can see how that might make sense from an evolutionary perspective, because they share his DNA. If he's helping their DNA survive, it's his too, so that makes sense from a Darwinian argument about reproductive fitness.

If we are being nice to others in expectation that they'll be nice to us later—a reciprocal form of altruism—we can see how that might also make sense in terms of benefiting our reproductive success. We can even make arguments, as Martin Nowak of Harvard has, that if we do computer modeling of things like the Prisoner's Dilemma, we can come up with motivations for entire groups to behave altruistically toward each other.

But a consequence of that, and all the other models that have been put together, is that we still have to be hostile to people who are not in our group. Otherwise, the whole evolutionary argument falls apart. Well, does that fit? Is that what we see in our own experience? Where are those circumstances where we think the moral law has been most dramatically at work? I would submit they are *not* when we're being nice to our family, to people who are going to be nice to us, or even just when we're being nice to other people in our own group.

Where are those circumstances where we think the moral law has been most dramatically at work? I would submit they are not when we're being nice to our family, to people who are going to be nice to us, or even just when we're being nice to other people in our own group.

The things that strike us, that cause us to marvel and to say, "That's what human nobility is all about," are instances when radical altruism extends beyond categories of self-interest. When we see Mother Teresa in the streets of Calcutta picking up the dying. When we see Oskar Schindler risking his life to save Jews he doesn't know from the Holocaust. When we see the actions of the good Samaritan.

Or when we see Wesley Autrey. Autrey, an African American construction worker, was standing on the subway platform in New York City, when next to him a young graduate student went into an epileptic seizure and, to the horror of everybody standing there, fell onto the tracks in front of an oncoming train. With only a split second to make a decision, Wesley jumped onto the tracks, pulled the young man still having the seizure into the small space between the tracks, and covered him with his own body as the train rolled over both of them. Miraculously, there was just enough clearance for them both to survive.

This was clearly radical altruism. These two had never met, had no likelihood of seeing each other in any other circumstance, and belonged to different groups as we seem to define them in our society, one African American, the other white. And yet New Yorkers went crazy with admiration, understandably. What an amazing act. What an amazing, risky thing to do.

Evolution would say, "Wesley, what were you thinking? Talk about ruining your reproductive fitness opportunities!" This is a scandal, isn't it? Think about that. Again, I'm not offering you a proof, but I do think when people try to argue that morality can be fully explained on evolutionary grounds, that's a bit too easy. That's a bit too much of a just-so story. Perhaps indeed there is another answer.

Lewis asked, if you were looking for evidence of a God who was not just a mathematician and a physicist but who cared about human beings and who stood for what is good and holy, and wanted his people to also stand for those things, wouldn't it be interesting to find written in your own heart this moral law which is calling you to do just that? That made a lot of sense to me.

I do think when people try to argue that morality can be fully explained on evolutionary grounds, that's a little bit too easy.

After going through these arguments over the course of a couple of years (and it was a long fight), I began to realize that I was beginning to experience awe of something greater than myself. I had to agree with Immanuel Kant: "Two things fill me with constantly increasing admiration and awe, the longer and more earnestly I reflect on them: the starry heavens without and the Moral Law within."

That's just where I was. But I had to figure out what God is really like. It was time to go back to the world's religions and try to figure out what they tell us about that. As I read through them, now somewhat better prepared, I could see there were great similarities between the great monotheistic religions, and they actually resonated quite well with each other about many of the most important principles. I was a bit surprised, because I had assumed that they were radically different. But there were differences as well.

About this time, I had also arrived at a point that was not comforting. If the moral law pointed to God, and if God was good and holy, I was increasingly sure that I was not. And as much as I tried to forgive myself for actions that were not consistent with that moral law, they kept popping up. So just as I was beginning to perceive the person of God in a blurry sort of way, that image was receding because of my own failures. I began to despair of whether this would ever be a relationship that I could claim or hope to have, because of my own shortcomings.

Into that cloud of increasing uneasiness came the realization that there is a Person in one of these faiths who has the solution to that. That's the person of Jesus Christ, who not only claimed to know God but to *be* God. In this amazing and sacrificial act, he died on the cross and then rose from the dead to provide this bridge between my imperfections and God's holiness. I had heard phrases before about Christ dying for our sins, and I thought that was so much gibberish. Suddenly it wasn't gibberish at all. It made more sense than anything I'd ever dreamed of.

So two years after I began this journey, on a hiking trip in Oregon's Cascade Mountains, with my mind cleared of those distractions that so often get in the way of realizing what is really true and important, I felt I had reached the point where I no longer had reasons to resist. And I didn't want to resist. I had a hunger to give into this. That day I became a Christian. That was thirty-one years ago. I was scared; I was afraid I was going to turn into somebody very somber, lose my sense of humor, and be called to Africa or something. But instead I experienced this great sense of peace and joy about having finally crossed that bridge. Contrary to my earlier expectations faith was not something I had to plunge into blindly, but faith and reason went hand in hand.

I guess I should have known, because as I began to learn a bit more about the Bible, I encountered Matthew 22:37. There Jesus is being questioned about which is the greatest commandment in the law. The Pharisees are trying to trap Jesus into saying something they could point out as being inconsistent with the Old Testament, and Jesus replies, "Love the Lord your God with all your heart, and with all your soul, and with all your mind." Wow, there it was: "all your mind." We're *supposed* to use our minds when it comes to faith. Mark Noll has written a book called *The Scandal of the Evangelical Mind* to suggest that perhaps we haven't done such a good job of that part of the commandment lately. "Love the Lord . . . with all your mind!"

CONVERSATIONS ABOUT FAITH AND SCIENCE

This was an exciting time, but I was already a scientist studying genetics. As I began to tell people of this good news, they said, "Doesn't your head explode? You're in trouble and you're headed for a collision. These worldviews are not going to get along." "Isn't evolution incompatible with faith? What are you going to do about that?"

I had a lot of those conversations. In fact, I've continued to have those over the course of quite a few years. Including with Stephen Colbert! If you want to see a humorous version of the proposition that science and faith are incompatible, see www.colbertnation.com/the -colbert-report-videos/79238/december-07-2006/francis-collins.

What really is the problem here? If evolution is such a stumbling block in this science-faith conversation, we better ask the question whether that tension is well-founded or not. Certainly there are religious people saying, "Evolution is on its last legs." Evolution is known by scientists to have many flaws, but nobody wants to admit it. What are the actual facts of the matter?

Genes and pseudogenes. I can tell you that from my perspective, as somebody who studies DNA, that DNA has become probably the strongest window into this question that we could imagine. Darwin could not possibly have imagined a better means of testing his theory, except maybe for a time machine, because along comes DNA with its digital code, and it provides us insights that are really quite phenomenal.

In fact, the bottom line is that DNA tells us incontrovertibly that Darwin's theory was right on target. We have not worked out some of the mathematical details, but I think it's fair to say that here in 2009 nearly all serious biologists see evolution as so fundamental that you can't really think about life sciences without it.

What's some of the evidence to support what I just said? Well, looking at the fossil record is one thing. I'm not going to talk about that, I'm going to talk about DNA because I think it gives us more detailed information. But the fossil record is entirely consistent with what I'm going to say.

We have now compared the genomes of multiple organisms. We have sequenced not only the human genome but the mouse, the chimpanzee, the dog, the honeybee, the sea urchin, the macaque and, good heavens, the platypus. And those are just the ones that made the cover of *Nature* or *Science*. There are now about thirty more.

When we put the DNA sequences into a computer, the computer doesn't know what any of these organisms look like, nor does it know about the fossil record. But the computer comes up with a diagram, which is an evolutionary tree, entirely consistent with descent from a common ancestor. It includes humans as part of this enterprise and agrees in detail with trees that people have previously put together, whether based on anatomy or the fossil record.

We could argue, and people certainly have, that this doesn't prove that common ancestry is required. If all those organisms instead were created by God as individual acts of special creation, it's entirely plausible that God might use some of the same motifs in generating those organisms' genomes. The ones that looked most alike would have genomes that were most alike for functional reasons. I could not refute that alternative argument on the basis of overall genome similarity.

But let's look a little deeper. Let's look into the details of one little snippet of DNA. Consider three genes that happen to be in the same order in humans, cows, mice and quite a lot of other mammals as well: EPHX2, GULO and CLU are in that same order for these three species. This arrangement in itself is at least suggestive of a common ancestor; otherwise why would these genes be clumped together this way? They are totally different in their functions. There doesn't seem to be any logical reason why they need to be near each other, but they are.

But I chose this particular set of genes for a reason, because they tell a very interesting story. For the cow and the mouse, all three of those genes are functional. For the human, the one in the middle, GULO, is really messed up. In fact, it is what we call a pseudogene. About half of its coding region has been deleted; it's just not there. It cannot make a protein. It can't do much of anything, except travel along from generation to generation as a little DNA fossil of what used to be there.

Does this have a consequence? This is a downgrade, not an upgrade. This one tells a particularly interesting story. GULO stands for gulonolactone oxidase. What is that? It's the enzyme that catalyzes the final step in the synthesis of ascorbic acid, also known as Vitamin C. Because of this deletion of GULO, sailors of old got scurvy, but the mice on the ship didn't. For humans this is one of those things that we apparently get along fine without, except in unusual circumstances. Apparently a long time ago a mutation arose. There was no evolutionary drive to get rid of it. We humans are altogether completely deficient in being able to make Vitamin C, whereas most other animals are not. Interestingly, chimps have the same problem we do.

Now try to contemplate how that could have come about in the absence of a common ancestor. If we're going to argue that each species comes about by an individual act of special creation, then we would have to say that God intentionally placed a defective gene in the very spot where common ancestry would have predicted it to be, presumably to test our faith. He would have to do that for humans and also for chimps. But this sounds like a God that I don't recognize. It sounds like a God who's involved in deception, not in truth.

THE GOD DELUSION?

I could give you many more examples like this, but when you look at the details, it seems inescapable that evolution is fundamentally correct, and we humans are part of it. Well, if that's true, does that leave any room for God? There are certainly those who say no, and are using evolution as a club over the head of believers.

Richard Dawkins, perhaps, is the most visible of club-wielders. His book *The God Delusion* has sold millions of copies—one of those rare books that does not need a subtitle to tell you what it's about. Dawkins, who is an incredibly gifted writer and articulator of evolutionary theory for the general public, has more recently become a very antagonistic critic of religion, not only claiming that religion is unnecessary and ill-informed, but that it is evil and basically responsible for most of the bad things in the world.

Dawkins uses science as the core of his argument, trying to demonstrate that in the absence of scientific proof of God's existence, the default answer should be that there is no God. But of course, there is a problem here. One of the problems, as G. K. Chesterton points out, is that atheism requires the assertion of a universal negative, which is a daring dogma indeed. The other problem is a category error. If God has any significance in most religions, God has to be at least in part outside of nature, not bound by nature. Pantheism might be an exception, but most other religions would certainly agree that God is not limited by nature itself. Science is. Science really is only legitimately able to comment on things that are part of nature. And science is really good at

If God has any significance in most religions, God has to be at least in part outside of nature, not bound by nature. . . . God is not limited by nature itself. Science is. Science really is only legitimately able to comment on things that are part of nature.

that, but if you're going to try to take the tools of science and disprove God, you're in the wrong territory. Science has to remain silent on the question of anything that falls outside of the natural world.

Dawkins and I had a debate about this in *Time* magazine, which is still posted on the Web if you want to look at it. Basically, we went back and forth about a number of the issues, but I challenged him about how it was possible from a scientific perspective to categorically rule out the presence of God. At the end of the interview, he did admit that he couldn't, on a purely rational basis, exclude the possibility of a supernatural being. But, he says, such a being would be grander and more complicated and awesome than anything humans could contemplate. I wanted to jump up and shout, "Hallelujah, we have a convert!" (But I didn't.)

This reveals something important. Often, when people are trying to disprove or to throw stones at belief, they caricature belief in a way that makes it seem very narrow and small-minded, the sort of thing that a mature believer wouldn't recognize. Of course, that's an old debating trick: mischaracterize your opponent's position and then dismantle it,

and your opponent is left wondering, *What happened there?* That has
very much been the strategy with the atheist books by Christopher
Hitchens, Sam Harris, Daniel Dennett and Richard Dawkins.

RECONCILING EVOLUTION AND FAITH: BIOLOGOS

So what then? How can evolution and faith be reconciled? Have I led
us into an unsolvable dilemma here by talking about my own faith
conversion and then telling you that I think evolution is true? Well,
actually, no. Forty percent of scientists are believers in a personal
God. Most of them, from my experience, have arrived at the same
way of putting this together, a way that is actually pretty simple and
almost obvious. But it's amazing how little it gets talked about. It
goes like this:

Almighty God, who is not limited in space or time, created our universe 13.7 billion years ago, its parameters precisely set to allow the
development of complexity over long periods of time. God's plan included the mechanism of evolution to create the marvelous diversity of
living things on our planet. Most especially, that plan included us, human beings. After evolution, in the fullness of time, had prepared a
sufficiently advanced neurological "house" [the brain], God then gifted
humanity with free will and with a soul.

Thus, humans received this special status, which in biblical terms is
"made in God's image," but that is about mind, and not about body. We
humans, having been given those gifts, used our free will to disobey
God, leading to our realization of being in violation of the moral law.
And thus, we were estranged from God. For Christians, Jesus is the
solution to that estrangement.

That's it. A very simple view that does no violence to either faith or science. It identifies God as the Creator, natural laws as the means of creation,
and puts us in a position to be able to further explore the consequences.

This is often called "theistic evolution." It's not a term that necessarily has a lot going for it. *Evolution* is the noun, *theistic* is the adjective,
which sounds like we're tipping the balance in the favor of the scientific
view. A lot of people aren't quite sure what *theistic* means anyway, so
maybe we need a better term. I have proposed one: BioLogos. It comes

from life, *bios*, arising by God speaking us into being, the *logos*. "In the beginning was the Word" (John 1:1); life came through the Word, bios through logos, or simply BioLogos.

In that regard, as the title of my book indicates, maybe we could think about this universal code of life, the DNA molecule, as the language of God.

Some objections to BioLogos. *1. Didn't evolution take an awfully long time?* Some people are troubled about the *long* time that evolution seems to require to do this. Why would God be so slow in getting to the point? But that's our perspective; we are limited by the linear arrow of time, where yesterday had to come before today, which has to come before tomorrow. But remember that thing about God having to be outside of time in order to make sense as a Creator? That solves this problem too, because if God is outside of time, then a process that seems really long to us may be incredibly short to God.

2. Isn't evolution a purely random process? Doesn't that take God out of it? Again, it might seem random to us, but if God is outside of time, randomness doesn't make sense anymore. God could have complete knowledge of the outcome in a process that seems random to us. I suppose in that way we could say God is inhabiting the process all the way along. So I don't think this is a fundamental problem, despite the way it is often portrayed as such.

3. Can evolution really account for highly complex biomachines like the bacterial flagellum? This is the intelligent design (ID) question: can evolution really account for all of those fancy structures that we find in living things? A favorite poster child of ID is the bacterial flagellum. The bacterial flagellum is a little outboard motor that allows bacteria to zip around in a liquid solution. That flagellum has about thirty-two proteins that must come together in just the right way for the whole thing to work. And if we inactivate just one of those thirty-two proteins, it doesn't work. So, in a simplistic way, we wonder how this motor could come to pass on the basis of evolutionary steps, because how could thirty-one of those proteins appear by chance with no positive benefit, and then only when the thirty-second one joined them would the organism have a reproductive advantage. That doesn't seem to be mathematically feasible.

But as we study the bacterial flagellum and other examples like this, it becomes increasingly clear that this motor did not arise out of nowhere. Parts of the bacterial flagellar motor have been recruited bit by bit from other structures and used in a way that gradually built up its capacity to serve the function that we now so admire. And with this additional knowledge, the development of the flagellum doesn't sound so different than the standard process of gradual change over time, with natural selection acting upon it.

So intelligent design turns out to be—and I'm sorry to say this for those who have found this a very appealing perspective—putting God into an apparent gap in scientific knowledge, which is now getting rapidly filled. The God of the gaps approach has not served faith well in the past, and I don't think it serves it well in this instance either. Unfortunately, many in the evangelical Christian church have attached themselves to ID theory as a way of resisting a materialistic and atheistic assault coming from the evolutionists. But attaching the church to an alternative theory that turns out to be flawed is not a successful strategy.

If we think about it, ID is not only turning out to be bad science; it's also bad theology. It implies that God didn't quite get it right at the beginning and had to keep stepping in and fixing things. Wouldn't it actually be a more awesome God who started the process off right at the beginning and didn't have to step in that way? I think so.

4. Doesn't this view conflict with the Bible? The question that I think is of most concern to believers is how to rectify evolution with Genesis 1–2.

All of this comes down to the questions, what do science and Scripture really say, and are they really in conflict? That requires us to get deeply into questions of scriptural interpretation: What is the meaning of a verse? What was the intention of the author, and who was it written to? What is the original language? What do those words mean in that language? Does this section read like the history of an eyewitness? Does this read like something that is more mythical, lyrical and poetic? I'm not an expert in biblical hermeneutics, but there are a lot of people who have spent their lives on that.

Ultimately, when it comes down to the perceived conflict between Genesis and science, it primarily results from an interpretation that insists on a literal reading of the Bible. That literal reading is a relatively recent arrival on the scene. Down through the centuries many deep thinkers in theology did not conclude that a literal reading is required.

Furthermore, if you read Genesis 1–2 carefully you will notice there are two stories of creation, and they don't quite agree in terms of the order of appearance of plants and humans. So they can't both be literally correct. Maybe that's a suggestion to us as we read these two creation accounts that this is not intended to be a scientific treatise.

Given all of this, I think it is entirely possible to take the words in Genesis and fit them together with what science is teaching us about origins. I was particularly gratified as I was wrestling with this to run across the writings of St. Augustine. Augustine was obsessed about this question of Genesis, and wrote no less than four books about it. Ultimately he concluded that there was no real way to know precisely what is intended by those verses. He warned in a very prescient way, sixteen hundred years ago, that people should be very careful, therefore, not to attach themselves to a particular interpretation that might turn out, when new discoveries are made, to be indefensible. Here's his exhortation:

> *Ultimately, when it comes down to the conflict between Genesis and science, it seems that it primarily results from an interpretation that insists on a literal reading of the Bible. That literal reading is a relatively recent arrival on the scene. Down through the centuries many deep thinkers in theology did not have the sense that a literal reading is required.*

> In matters that are so obscure and far beyond our vision, we find in Holy Scripture passages which can be interpreted in very different ways without prejudice to the faith we have received. In such cases, we should not rush in headlong and so firmly take our stand on one side that if further progress in the search for truth justly undermines this

position, we too fall with it. (*The Literal Meaning of Genesis* 1.18, trans. J. H. Taylor)

I wish Augustine's exhortation were referred to more often, so I've written about this in more detail in *The Language of God*. Two other books refer to these issues in very thoughtful ways: *Coming to Peace with Science* by my friend Darrel Falk and *Saving Darwin* by Karl Giberson.

Though I'm encouraged that we're having this conversation, I'm troubled by the fact that the stage often seems to be occupied by those at the extremes of the spectrum: on the one hand, atheists, who argue that science disproves God, and on the other, fundamentalists, who say that science can't be trusted because it disagrees with their interpretation of particular Scripture verses. But I think there is hope here for having this conversation go somewhere.

I have had the privilege of starting the BioLogos Foundation. The foundation's website (biologos.org) provides suggested answers to the thirty-three most frequently asked questions from more than three thousand e-mails I've received about science and faith. I hope it turns out to be a useful resource for people who want to dig deeper.

We started with the most important question: Is there a God? My answer is yes. I can't prove it, but I think the evidence is fairly compelling. If this question interests you, and you haven't spent a lot of time on it, I would encourage you to do so. It's not one of those questions you should put off till the last minute. After all, you might get a pop quiz along the way.

I am delighted that the Veritas Forum provides this kind of opportunity for discussion and that Caltech has welcomed this conversation.

Q&A

Questioner 1. Thank you for a very nonantagonistic discussion. I really appreciated it.

Collins. Thank you.

Questioner 1. I was wondering, since you did mention pantheism, and I've personally had an affinity with that worldview, if you could speak about why you don't feel that is consistent with your view of God.

Collins. Pantheism, of course, sees God in all nature, and that is an appealing concept, I think, to many people. And it's certainly, from my perspective, compatible with the idea of God, but it's not sufficient for me. It doesn't solve the problem of the Creator that seems to be cried out for by the big bang. It doesn't explain some of the other issues about fine-tuning, about the mathematical nature of the universe. Nor does it provide me with a concept of the holiness of God as reaching out to me and me reaching back that has come to be such a central part of my own faith.

Of course, as you heard, another big part of my faith is the person of Jesus, a person who I considered to be a myth, but when I began to study the history, found that he is incredibly well-documented. We know more about the life of Jesus than we do about Julius Caesar. And we have very good evidence, in fact, for Jesus' death and resurrection. Of course, that is a very different kind of perspective than pantheism can offer.

But, again, I think the notion of considering nature as an extension of God, which of course obligates us to be responsible to nature in ways that I think we're increasingly coming to realize, is an entirely comfortable concept. It's just not enough from where I stand.

Questioner 2. Just this afternoon I heard a radio program about a book called *Born to Be Good: The Science of a Meaningful Life* by Dacher Keltner. He talks about the evolution of gratitude, compassion, altruism and all that, and he cites a study from Israel that has supposedly identified a gene coding for altruistic and moral behaviors. Can you just comment on that?

Collins. I don't know that particular gene. You know, it is possible by personality tests to categorize people in terms of their level of generosity and altruism, and if you look at identical twins, they tend to be more alike than people who aren't related. So that might tell us that there are some hereditary influences on being generous and altruistic, but they're going to be pretty minor compared to other influences, and particularly free-will decisions. And if, in fact, there are some neurological pathways that play a role in altruism, that in no way seems to reduce the likelihood that this is a divinely inspired action on the part of humans. After all, it has to have some mechanism of being implemented.

Similarly, we see these exciting stories of imaging done on people who are in deep meditation, experiencing deep prayer life, and the images show a certain part of the brain lights up that normally wouldn't be. Some people look at that and say, "Aha, you see, that says that spirituality is not a real event." Other people say, "Well, that proves it is a real event." If there's going to be a spiritual experience or a special human attribute in terms of altruism, it has to have some way of being carried out. It seems like it would have to involve some genes and neurons.

Questioner 3. The first question is about agnosticism. You mentioned that you might have considered yourself agnostic at some point. I consider myself agnostic, and I don't disagree with anything you said tonight, and I kind of felt like it was a good argument for agnosticism, with the added fact that I feel that a belief in a God is psychologically a crutch, to put it bluntly.

The second question is, if physics can tell us everything about making a world deterministic, where does that leave room for free will? Because I think it only leaves room for free will in the long-term scale; in other words, God planned it all out and set it in motion, and I don't feel like that has any meaning for what people usually want to call free will.

Collins. Okay. Those are a couple of doozies. I'll take the second one first, and then come back to the first. Back in Newton's day, when we only had classical mechanics, it seemed as if there was going to be no solution to the free-will problem, that everything in the universe was really all predetermined by the motions of particles under the influence of classical mechanic laws.

But then quantum mechanics came along—and whether or not it's fair to bring quantum mechanics into a philosophical discussion, it certainly is something that you have to deal with. In that perspective the uncertainty kicks in, and there is nothing that is defined so precisely, just in terms of pure physics, once that uncertainty principle becomes part of reality. So that's maybe a little bit of a dodge, but I think it's a legitimate one.

When it comes to your question about agnosticism, I agree, agnosticism can be a totally principled position. In my own experience there are principled agnostics, but I will say most of the people I encounter who say they're agonistics are like I was, which was to say, "I don't want to think about this." So that's perhaps not such a good position to be in, because it's a really important set of questions there.

Now, if one is an agnostic and he or she looks closely at all the evidence for and against, and concludes, I can't really find any evidence conclusively for either perspective, then that's where you are. And I suspect a lot of people in this room may very well find themselves in that position. But don't be surprised if over the course of time that might change.

For me, the agnostic position ended up feeling like a bit of a cop-out, like it had not really resolved the question after all. And that made me want to go further. And again, while I can't prove my position as a theist, and particularly as a Christian, the evidence to me, including the evidence for Jesus Christ and his life—which is really very strong—was difficult to dismiss. Coming back to C. S. Lewis, the argument many agnostics might put forward that Christ was a great teacher (because it is hard to read the words of Christ and not conclude that) but we shouldn't consider Christ as divine, is hard to sustain, because the words say that Christ was divine. And you can't take someone who claimed to be God, dismiss that claim and save the "great teacher" part without doing something a little strange. Somebody who claims to be God is either evil or crazy or exactly who he said he was. And if it's the last of those, it's pretty hard to walk back into agnosticism. And that's where I found my difficulties. Ultimately, it led me to the decision that I made.

But every one of you is on your own journey here. And I worry as I've talked about my own faith that I might be coming across as pushing the

I agree, agnosticism can be a totally principled position. In my own experience there are principled agnostics, but I will say most of the people I encounter who say they're agnostics are like I was, which was to say, "I don't want to think about this."

idea that you have to think exactly the way I do or you're not a spiritual person. Please don't take that as the message for this evening. Christians all too often come across as narrow in this way, and I don't want to be of that sort.

I do hope all of you who have sat through this long discussion will go away with a sense that this journey is a fascinating one to be on, and that there are answers out there—though not easy ones. There are other people around you who would love to talk about this, including the students who organized this gathering. Therefore I hope this will not be just one more evening that comes and goes, but something that has more lasting significance for at least some of you. It will for me. You've asked great questions. It's been wonderful being here at Caltech.

5

THE NEW ATHEISTS AND
THE MEANING OF LIFE

Alister McGrath and David J. Helfand
The Veritas Forum at Columbia University, 2006

ALISTER McGRATH

Is GOD A DELUSION? That certainly is the view you find in Richard Dawkins's recent book *The God Delusion*. I want to talk a little bit about that book, and set out the agenda we will talk about, and then see where our thinking goes.

When I was younger, if I had known I would be speaking here at Columbia University tonight on this topic, I would have been extremely surprised. I grew up in Northern Ireland. And those of you who know Ireland well will know that it is not an island of great excitement. As I remember it, one of the greater things I looked forward to was the annual donkey derby. So, the idea of actually coming to Columbia to give a lecture like this is very exciting.

But the other reason I think it would have surprised me is this: when I was growing up in Northern Ireland, I was an atheist. Atheists, as you know, come in different shapes and sizes. There is the very gracious kind of atheist, who doesn't believe in God but is so pleased you do. Then there's the other kind of atheist, and I have to say with a certain degree of embarrassment that I belonged to this second category of atheist, who basically held that religious people were simply utter fools who would one day discover the true light. In the meantime, one had to tolerate them. But a godless dawn was on its way.

I was one of those who, back in the late 1960s, was absolutely convinced that religion was on its way out, that the brighter godless dawn was just around the corner. I took the view that sociology was on my side, that there was this very strong expectation that religion was just fading away into the past and would simply cease to be a major social and cultural and intellectual force in the very near future.

Of course, I was encouraged in that view by the situation in Northern Ireland. As you know, it was a very difficult situation with Catholics and Protestants being pitted against each other. That, I think, led me to the conclusion that religion simply led to polarization and violence.

The story is told of the Englishman who went to visit Northern Ireland and he was in Belfast on a Saturday night, rather late. He was confronted by a group of youths with baseball bats and they asked him menacingly, "Are you a Protestant or are you a Catholic?"

I was one of those who, back in the late 1960s, was absolutely convinced that religion was on its way out, that the brighter godless dawn was just around the corner.

The Englishman thought, because he realized the answer he gave might have no small importance for what happened next. Then he had a stroke of inspiration: "I'm an atheist!"

There was a pause. They asked, "Are you a Protestant atheist, or . . . ?"

As I was growing up studying the sciences, it did seem to me there was this inexorable link between the sciences and atheism, and that religion was on its way out. But when I went up to Oxford to really begin to study the sciences seriously, I found myself going through a radical rethink. Basically, I came to the conclusion that the intellectual case for atheism wasn't that good, and certainly did not rest adequately on the scientific foundation. And so, I made an intellectual pilgrimage from atheism to Christian belief.

But interestingly, here is a point I'd like you to think about. Those of you who have read Richard Dawkins's book *The God Delusion* will know that for Dawkins the only valid intellectual pilgrimage is from religion to atheism. That is a constant theme throughout his books—that God is a delusion, that real science disproves Christianity and that religion simply lingers on because in some way, we are biologically or psychologically preprogrammed to believe in God.

And so, what I'd like to do is try to open up some of the arguments in that book for discussion tonight. The first point very simply is this: Why does Richard Dawkins have to write four hundred pages telling us that God is an illusion when religious belief is meant to have disappeared generations ago?

Certainly, back in the 1960s there was a very strong expectation that religion was on its way out. "We will not be having this conversation in forty years time," and yet, we are tonight. And the fact that so many of you are here is indication that (a) this is interesting, (b) this is important, and (c) this is a live issue, not a debate that our grandparents might have had but has ceased to be relevant to us.

SCIENTISTS BUT NOT ATHEISTS

So, it's a very significant question. Let's begin to look at what Richard Dawkins says. First, he argues that science is an intellectual superhighway to atheism—that real scientists are atheists.

In the same year, three other very interesting books appeared. Owen Gingerich at Harvard University published his very interesting book *God's Universe*. And many of you will have read Francis Collins's book *The Language of God*. Collins is director of the Human Genome Project. Also some of you will have read Paul Davies's very intriguing book *The Goldilocks Enigma*, all about this phenomenal fine-tuning.

Gingerich and Collins give what I think are traditional Christian responses arguing that their astronomy and their biology are perfectly compatible with Christian faith, and that it actually brings enhanced intellectual appreciation to the disciplines. Paul Davies argues that while the God of Christianity is at some distance from this, there is something out there that has to be described in terms of some kind of intelligent Author—in other words, God, by some name or other.

Besides these three books I've mentioned, I could add many others to the list. But the simple fact is there are an awful lot of scientists who do believe in God, who do not see this as being intellectual suicide and, indeed, believe their faith brings added resilience and dynamism to their scientific studies.

How does this fit with Richard Dawkins's rather simplistic world-view: science leads to atheism? I think that the real issue is much more complex and much more interesting. I think as I read things very carefully, it seems to me that we can read nature in a Christian way. We can read nature in an atheist way. In fact, we can read nature in an agnostic way, as well. Nature is patient of all these interpreta-tions, but in and of itself, it mandates and demands none of these.

Alister McGrath, Ron Choong and David Hel-fand on stage at Columbia.

Now, take someone like Stephen Jay Gould, a very interesting per-son who died in 2002 from lung cancer. Gould was an atheist. But he was very clear that it wasn't his science that brought him to that posi-tion. He argues in his very interesting book *Rocks of Ages* that science simply cannot, by the legitimate application of its method, comment on the God question. In other words, it simply lies beyond the scientific method. That raises for me a fascinating question about whether there are limits to what the sciences can tell us. Again, I can explore that later.

FAITH VERSUS SCIENCE

But let's move on and look at Dawkins's other arguments. A very important argument throughout *The God Delusion* is that religious people engage in the process of nonthinking called faith. In other words, faith, to quote from his *Selfish Gene*, is a process of simple disengagement, refusal to look at the evidence, running away from reality. It is simply about believing impossible things, whereas science proves things with absolute certainty. In other words, there's a very strong polarization. Science means 100 percent certainty; religion, 0 percent. Only fools, charlatans and dishonest people would therefore believe in religion.

There are some very interesting points made there. I think it's extremely important to say that evidence-based thinking matters enormously for anyone who takes the sciences seriously. Certainly, although I disagree with Dawkins on many things, he is right to stress that. Without evidence, we are nowhere. The importance of evidence is, for me, supreme. But evidence is open to multiple interpretations. That is what radical theory change in science is all about.

My real problem is that Dawkins does not seem to take into account the intellectual malleability of nature. In other words, we can all look at this and yet see it in different ways. Terry Eagleton, in a very powerful review of Dawkins's book in the *London Review of Books*, simply makes the point that we all know that people hold views they know cannot be 100 percent defended and justified, but nevertheless believe that they are right in doing so.

I think that is an extremely important point, here. I want to argue that atheism is certainly a defensible interpretation of things—as is Christianity—but there is no knockdown argument on either side. This remains a live issue about the best interpretation of nature. Gilbert Harmon's famous foundational paper "Inference to the Best Explanation" establishes that there is a real debate about what the best way of evaluating things is, and what criteria should be used.

I want to argue that atheism is certainly a defensible interpretation of things—as is Christianity—but there is no knock-down argument on either side. This remains a live issue about the best interpretation of nature.

RELIGION CAUSES VIOLENCE

But I move on to the third point. It seems to me this is Dawkins's strongest point: religion leads to violence. Certainly, from my own Northern Ireland situation, I can easily relate to this. As I was growing up, it seemed to me to be self-evident that religion led to violence. I thought that if we got rid of religion, there would be none of this violence that we saw, for example, in my homeland of Northern Ireland.

That was what I thought back in the 1960s. Nowadays, I'm not quite so sure. Let me try to explain why. Let me begin by saying there is no doubt that religion can cause violence. But I don't believe that religion is either a necessary or a sufficient cause of violence. Robert Pape's very interesting study of suicide bombings makes very telling points in relation to this.[1]

I also want to make the point that in the twentieth century, we have seen atheism move from being on the periphery of things to actually taking power in the Soviet Union and elsewhere. And certainly for me, as I read the history of the twentieth century, atheism also has been guilty of violence and oppression.

It seems to me, actually, it's not really either religion or antireligion that is the issue. It may well be there's something about human nature: it inspires us to do great things but also draws us down to do some dreadful things. In other words, inspiration can cause us to do good but also to do bad things as well.

Again, I go back to Terry Eagleton's review in the *London Review of Books*. Professor Dawkins, he says, spends four hundred pages "scientifically" and "impartially" evaluating religion, but not in one of those pages can we find a single good thing to say about it. It does have its good points, but it also has its bad points, but therefore surely, the agenda ought to be working for reformation, not abolition.

Which brings me to the final point I want to make in this opening section: Suppose Dawkins were to get his way; suppose religion were to be abolished, would that end violence in our societies? Sociologists will make the point that it won't because in many ways societies are extremely good about constructing causes for disagreement. These social constructions could be religious. They could be gender-based. They could be class-based. They could be race-based. They could be tribal-based. They could be financially based. They could be whatever you want, but the issue is that humanity posses a remarkable capacity of generating division and then offering explanations and motivations which move these from mere differentiation to lethal conflicts between people groups.

So, I wonder if religion were to be abolished whether the violence we see would actually disappear at all. Certainly, specifically religious violence would, but others would come in very quickly to fill that vacuum. Dawkins shows us very powerfully that religion can cause things to go wrong, but he tends to present the pathological as if it were the normal. It seems to me that needs to be challenged.

I end with one very simple example. When I was studying chemistry at Oxford, one of my set texts was called *Reagents for Organic Synthesis* by Louis Fieser and Mary Fieser. It was a long book, and I have to say it was a rather dull book. I later learned more about Louis Fieser, professor of chemistry at Harvard, a remarkable man who invented synthetic roots to various steroids, to the blood's anticoagulating factor. He's done a lot to help hemophiliacs. But back in 1942, he invented something else: Americans were discovering the Japanese were rather deeply entrenched in certain well-defended positions in the Pacific. A weapon was needed to be able to deal with this. Fieser came to the rescue and invented napalm. Now, I could take a very simplistic view and say, Hey, that shows science is evil. Let's stop it.

But I wouldn't say that, and none of you would either. It just brings home to us that that's what human nature is like. Sometimes, we do great things, sometimes bad things. Those bad things need to be critiqued, and we need to get rid of them. But there are still some good things there. I want to say that religion is like that. Let's work to reform it, but actually trying to get rid of it will simply bring in its wake much worse things than Richard Dawkins, I think, allows.

DAVID HELFAND

You can probably tell I'm not Richard Dawkins, although I do confess that I covet his title, which is Professor in the Public Understanding of Science, which I thought is a very nice title to have. I will not, therefore, on a point-by-point basis attempt to defend his book *The God Delusion* or his opinions, although I must say that I share the underlying basis of many of his opinions.

Throughout history, and I have no doubt prior to recorded history, humans have found meaning in mystery. A comet in the sky (a "guest star," as the Chinese so charmingly called it) would appear, and the fates of armies and empires were sealed. The sun, the seasons, tsunamis and storms all found explanation in supernatural phenomena until, of course, we understood them.

ANTHROPOMORPHIC, ANTHROPOCENTRIC, ANTHROPOMETRIC UNIVERSES

Ted Harrison, the cosmologist who wrote a wonderful book called *Cosmology: The Science of the Universe*, divides human thinking about these notions of our existence in the universe, and our reality, into three major regimes of time: the anthropomorphic universe, the anthropocentric universe, and the anthropometric universe.

The anthropomorphic universe is an age of magic in which there is no division between the self, the mind, and the external environment. Some of this notion, which we imagine dominated prehistory, remains in our language. We talk about "angry" storms and "gentle" breezes, investing natural phenomena with human emotions. That is largely thought to be the realm of prehistory, although I must confess that I find it rather prevalent in certain places today, in Southern California, for example.

The anthropocentric universe, which came next, was the age of myth. We created pantheons of powerful gods that controlled the forces of nature, and yet, of course, they were driven by human emotions and obsessed by human concerns. This, in a very deep sense, was an earth-centered universe. We sit here and look out on the universe, and the rest of the universe is controlled by these powerful gods.

The anthropometric universe is the age of science, not (as Protagoras would have it) that man is the measure of all things, but that we can use our rational cognitive capabilities to take their measure, to assess rationally our place in the universe and attempt to explore what the universe is from within this interesting product of biological evolution that is our minds.

NONOVERLAPPING MAGISTERIA

Now, I'm not an expert on this subject, as Professor McGrath is. So, I had to do a little reading to get prepared for this. Besides his book, and Richard Dawkins's book, one of the books I read was by Kenneth Miller. Kenneth Miller is a professor of biology at Brown University, a very distinguished professor there and winner of many teaching awards, and I would like to meet him someday. He has been known to the public mostly for his spirited, articulate defenses of evolutionary biology against the attacks, first, of young earth creationists and, then more recently, of intelligent design; he was the principal witness at the Dover, Pennsylvania, case in 2005.

He's written this wonderful book called *Finding Darwin's God*, in which the first two hundred pages is a detailed dissection and destruction of the arguments for intelligent design, young earth creationism and various other fantasies that some of the (out of the mainstream, I would hope to say) religious people in the United States have come up with recently and attempt to inflict on the government.

But in the last two chapters he goes on to take what I must confess I regard as a sophomoric misunderstanding of quantum mechanics, and uses it prove the existence of God to justify his deep Catholic faith. I must say I find this truly mysterious. He makes statements like the following: "Any God worthy of the name has to be capable of miracles, but what can science say about miracles? Nothing. By definition, the miraculous is beyond explanation, beyond understanding, beyond science."

Well, if this is so, I have to ask, why is it that the Vatican convenes learned panels of experts to adjudicate the reality of each miracle attributed to a potential saint, a candidate for beatification or canonization? I don't understand why they would do this if science had nothing to do with it.

Stephen Jay Gould had an acronym—NOMA: nonoverlapping magisteria—for the notion that was mentioned by Professor McGrath of there being two separate entities; religion is religion and science is science. I've always had trouble with this. First, I think on Gould's part it was quite disingenuous because he was, as Professor McGrath said, an atheist. I find it even more disingenuous and disturbing that the National Academy of Sciences of the United States of America also adopts the NOMA view despite the fact that polls of its members, the most distinguished scientists in the country, have shown that over 90 percent of them are atheists. Nonetheless, they adopt this view that science is science and religion is religion.

The problem I have with this is that it's a one-way nonoverlap. Let's take the Shroud of Turin project for an example. The Shroud of Turin project began in the late 1970s when a group of scientists and engineers, a large fraction of whom came from the Los Alamos Nuclear Weapons Laboratory (which I find a frightening thought) lugged millions of pounds of equipment over to Turin and were granted unlimited access to the shroud in order to perform scientific experiments on it to prove that it was the burial shroud of Christ. And indeed, the first experiments, all released through press releases and not scientific journals, were very encouraging. There was iron in the blood on the places where the nails had gone through the hands. The image on the cloth was not possible to produce prior to the age of photography and on and on.

Finally, ten years later, when the church relented and allowed two square centimeters of the cloth to be shipped off to two independent laboratories for double-blind tests of the age dating of this shroud, the age in both cases came back at about 650 plus or minus 20 years, or roughly, 1351, when historians had also already shown that the Avignon Pope had excommunicated a French bishop for displaying a fraudulent burial cloth of Christ, "very cleverly painted." My question is, suppose the Carbon-14 data on the shroud had come back differently. Suppose it had come back with a date of A.D. 26. Would then Professor McGrath or anyone else have said, "Oh, but science has nothing to do with religion, so we won't take that data into account?"

I seriously doubt it. I suspect every Christian in the world would have said, Here is a scientific validation for the belief in the Holy Scripture.

What about DNA evidence? We all read in the newspapers the remarkable fact that Neanderthal DNA from a 40,000-year-old bone was going to be sequenced—the entire genome of the Neanderthal. Suppose we found in a reliquary in some European cathedral a shard of bone, and we did DNA analysis on it, did a Polymerase Chair Reaction, and found out that lo and behold, it had one X chromosome and no Y chromosomes, and it was supposed to be a piece of Christ's body. Well, that would be sort of peculiar. I would regard that as truly miraculous, but I suspect this would be regarded as supporting faith.

I don't like the whole idea of the nonoverlapping magisteria because the nonoverlap only goes one way. When it doesn't work out, we say, Well, we have faith and there's religion. When it does work out, we say, Oh, science supports our faith in religion.

And so, I don't like the whole idea of the nonoverlapping magisteria because the nonoverlap only goes one way. When it doesn't work out, we say, Well, we have faith and there's religion. When it does work out, we say, Oh, science supports our faith in religion.

I have a number of things I want to say in response to what Professor McGrath said, but rather than stand up here and say them, I think it might be more productive if we tried to have a conversation. And so, I'm going to sit back down again and our moderator will lead that.

DIALOGUE

Moderator. Professor McGrath, would you respond to Professor Helfand's argument?

McGrath. I'll just make some very preliminary remarks. And then I'm sure we can have a much more detailed discussion. Yes, Kenneth Miller is a fascinating author, but I wouldn't want to be judged by him, if I can just put it like that.

Regarding Gould: it's very interesting. I probably didn't express myself very well—I don't agree with his nonoverlapping magisteria at all. I think it's wrong. The point I was simply making, if he was setting out the thesis of the epistemological limits of science, I think that's a very defensible thesis. For example, take Peter Medawar's very famous book *The Limits of Science.* One of the points he makes is that there are fundamental big questions. For example, why are we here? What's the point of life? Those are real questions, and nevertheless, science isn't able to give answers. The point he's trying to make is that scientists may well need to recognize there are limits to what science can actually answer. So, I think the basic issue here is whether we can calibrate the sciences as to where they're able to answer these big metaphysical questions and where they're not.

I think, for example, I prefer the approach we find in Collins's book *The Language of God,* which I would say is a partially overlapping magisteria. In other words, these things do interpenetrate. They do have overlapping areas, and my own view, for what it's worth, is that these actually reinforce each other.

So I think that's certainly something I'd be very interested to talk about. I'm just very anxious to see where this conversation goes. So, I'll be quiet now.

Helfand. Yes, I had to smile when I saw the posters advertising this, which had the famous quote, "The unexamined life is not worth living," and my wife will be smiling at this now because my dictum tends to be "The examined life is not worth living."

[Laughter]

McGrath. That's good.

Helfand. And therefore, my only difference with you is that I don't think "why are we here" is an interesting question. I agree science can't answer it, but I don't find it interesting, and it's not because science can't answer it. I just simply don't find it interesting.

I find it quite marvelous that our one kilogram of a trace constituent of the matter of the universe can apprehend its age and size and composition, and can understand its origin in the evolution of primitive bacteria out of the amino acids found in interstellar clouds. I find all that fascinating, but I don't see a need for why.

McGrath. I think it is an interesting question, and I think it's a very fundamental question for many. And I think, as I read Richard Dawkins, what I see is a kind of "let's keep this out of the question" almost as a matter of principle, that to even begin to speak of purpose is seen as something kind of illegitimate.

It seems to me, that while it may be a very difficult question to ask (and I take your point about it not being very interesting), I find it *very* interesting. It does seem to me to be a question which many people want to ask. Therefore we might say, "Well, maybe the scientists can't answer these, so maybe there's no answer available at all." Or we might have to say, "Maybe this has to be answered on the basis of something else." In which case, we're trying to say, "Well, the sciences are very good insofar as they go. Maybe we need to look somewhere else if this question can be answered at all."

Helfand. Well, I think it's actually possible, while I personally don't find it interesting, that this question can be answered by science. In a very fascinating, deeply flawed but deeply interesting book called *The Robot's Rebellion*, Keith Stanovich, a cognitive psychologist at the University of Toronto, discusses how the development of the human brain has a number of mechanisms or kinds of processes it uses. Most of the processing in the brain is done autonomously. Most of it is developed over several hundred thousand years of evolution in order to be able to reproduce, to be able to avoid getting eaten, and to be able to find food. And so, we do lots of things like:

[Helfand throws a ball at McGrath.]

Oh, you flinched, you didn't react. You flinched because circuits in your brain over which you have no control quickly responded to the fact that a ball was coming at you. Now, those circuits are very useful for surviving. Most of those circuits are very useful for surviving, and all were developed on the plains of the Serengeti. Those circuits are not so useful in the modern technological society. (The scariest thing about living in this country is that we have a president who goes with his gut feeling. Those gut feelings developed in a rather different environment and therefore are highly inappropriate most of the time in today's modern world. Not just his, but anybody's gut feelings.)

Stanovich points out, however, that we have an overlay on this; a set of processes that are not running in parallel all the time but are serial in nature, are intimately linked to language. Therefore, the notion that we might uncover why our brain (most brains, not mine, but everybody else's) finds it an interesting question to ask, Why are we here? might be a question accessible to science through cognitive research.

McGrath. I'm sure that's right. But take someone like Bertrand Russell, who says that once we've learned how to survive, we then start asking the really big questions. In other words, when we were struggling for existence, maybe we haven't the time to ask why are we here because if we start asking that question, we won't be here much longer because we'll be eaten by a lion or something.

So Russell in many ways is saying that there may well be processing capacity in excess of what we are required to survive, but the questions that that raises are nonetheless important. For example, his classic example is, "What is the good life, and how would we lead it?"

That does seem to me to be a very important question. Now, if I can press this point, because I think it's a very interesting point: Dawkins himself, in *A Devil's Chaplain*, says science has no means for determining what is good and what is bad. I'm not at all imputing his views to you here, but it's interesting to note there that if we take this classic question, What is the good life, and how may it be lived? Dawkins seems to be saying that scientists can't really answer that question.

> *If I can press this point, because I think it's a very interesting point: Dawkins himself, in* A Devil's Chaplain, *says science has no means for determining what is good and what is bad.*

Now, that's no criticism of science whatsoever. But it is, I think, saying there may be questions that need to be asked which are not simply thrown up by excess brain capacity, which is redundant because we don't have to worry about survival, but actually might well be significant questions about what it means to be human.

Helfand. That, the second question—what is the good life, and how is it to be lived?—that I *do* find an interesting question. But I'm nowhere near yet despairing of the fact that science will have something to contribute to the answer.

McGrath. Well, shall we move on, then?

One of the things that I found very intriguing about Richard Dawkins's book is this whole question of religious violence. Now, again, it's something I touched on. That's one thing—if it's something you'd like to explore.

Helfand. No, I think I'm more or less fully in agreement with you, there. I think there is no doubt that religion has engendered and engenders today enormous amounts of violence. I think the lack of religion does the same, and I have no argument with your supposition, and it's only a hypothesis at the moment, that the complete obliteration of religion from society would not lead to the obliteration of violence. I do not agree with Dawkins on that at all.

McGrath. Well, then, I'd like to move on and talk about a question which Dawkins raises, which I sense is an issue between us. That is whether religious faith can be thought of as being evidence-based, or whether actually it orbits a separate planet.

Let me say what I think and then give you a chance to come back. I personally would base no faith on the Turin Shroud or anything like that. Nor would I want to go back to a very early understanding of, for example, natural forces.

My understanding of natural forces, I think, is entirely scientific. But I don't see that as actually impacting on belief in God at all. What I do find is that when I put it like that, religious faith is based on evidence, but evidence is notoriously difficult to interpret.

Really, what I'm finding is that there are so many things in the natural world that require investigation or interpretation that there are many possible competing explanations. If I can quote C. S. Lewis, who I think puts my side of things quite well, he says—and this is from an essay he wrote on theology and poetry: "I believe in God as I believe the sun has risen; not simply because I see it, but because by it, I see everything else."

In other words, he's saying it kind of gives us an explanatory framework, a lens or a prism, which allows us to see things and actually makes more sense of them than we otherwise would. So, I'd want to try and defend the position that faith actually does make sense of things, and that it makes sense in itself.

Helfand. But you used the word *evidence,* and I'd be interested to hear more about what "evidence" you find that supports your faith. Were you using the Lewis quote in that sense, as evidence?

McGrath. No, I was using the Lewis quote really to make the point that I think a worldview really has to be valued on a number of levels. One would be: how true it is to what may be observed. In other words, how evidence-based is it? My perception—which again, I'm very happy to argue with you—is that all worldviews actually at some point almost become faith, because they make assertions that cannot be proved.

It's not just that they have a basis in evidence. It is, rather, how much explanation, how much added value can they bring as they begin to engage with actually looking at the world?

Helfand. Yes. One interesting observation that one of my colleagues made today when I was discussing this lecture has to do with uncertainty, which is relevant to evidence. Scientists are extremely comfortable with uncertainty. We don't allow our graduate students to publish a graph unless it has error bars on the data points. We use probability in a very intuitive way, and the quantum mechanics, which you also cite in your book as somehow leading to uncertainty that leaves open the universe to God, we regard as the most precise of the physical sciences we have. It makes remarkably precise assertions. But it's made on a probabilistic basis, and we feel comfortable with that. I do get the feeling, without going too far into your definition of *faith*, that most people are not comfortable with uncertainty, and I wonder if that's not the basis for where faith arises.

McGrath. The view I take is that I am a Christian. I believe in God, but I'm aware I cannot prove that with absolute certainty. But then, if I were to have an argument with an atheist philosopher, I would find the same thing—that actually he or she would also say, Well, this argument seems to take me in that direction, but I realize it doesn't take me all the way.

The end result of our discussion would be that both of us believe we are justified in taking our positions, but we realize we can't actually prove them with absolute certainty. And yet, we believe that the case is good enough to commit ourselves existentially, so to speak, and say, "This is good enough for us to actually base ourselves on."

The end result of our discussion would be that both of us believe we are justified in taking our positions, but we realize we can't actually prove them with absolute certainty. And yet, we believe that the case is good enough to commit ourselves existentially, so to speak, and say, "This is good enough for us to actually base ourselves on."

Helfand. Yes. Well, I'll have to make a disclaimer, here, that as a scientist I think I'm not in the majority, but I don't believe it's possible for science to *prove* anything. We can only prove things in mathematics where we set all the rules, and then we can prove something true or false.

Science, to me, is not a mechanism to prove what's true. It's a process, a very social process, by which we build models that attempt ever more detailed and more predictive explanations of nature. And for me, that process is more than sufficient to lead my unexamined life.

McGrath. Well, and I'm very happy with that view of science, which I think actually is right, although we may find people in the audience who want to challenge both of us on that point. But again, because you and I seem to have an agreement here, I'd like to register a disagreement with Richard Dawkins.

Dawkins does seem to take what I would have to describe as a very simplistic view of science. Science proves things with certainty. And therefore, that kind of way eliminates the conceptual space for God. And again I find that to be a misstatement of what the sciences actually do, and I find that what you've just said actually resonates very strongly with what I think is the case.

But, of course, that doesn't have metaphysical implications, but it does, I think, help us to be realistic about what the sciences are and are not.

> *Science, to me, is not a mechanism to prove what's true. It's a process, a very social process, by which we build models that attempt ever more detailed and more predictive explanations of nature. And for me, that process is more than sufficient to lead my unexamined life.*

Helfand. Yes. I completely agree. But you do make a point of what you call radical theory change, or something like that, in science as being important. I just have two things to say about that. One is that radical theory change in science is discussed much more by philosophers of science who don't *do* science. In fact, the process of radical theory change in science, which our newspapers tell us every Tuesday occurs in one or two or three or four sciences, is not the way science proceeds at all. In particular, you mention in your book the period of 1870 to 1900, when physics sort of decided it was all done.

That's the way the historians of science write it. I think it's really far from the truth. There's a very interesting book I've read, *Einstein's Clocks and Poincare's Maps*, about precisely that period, in which it shows there was tremendous intellectual ferment among admittedly a small community that something was fundamentally wrong, that things had to be fixed.

So science evolves. It's a highly social phenomena, and it evolves not in Steven Gould's punctuated equilibria but in a continuous way. And sometimes it evolves at different rates. But I'd have to say that if radical theory change does occur in science, it's a tribute to the great strength of science.

We're perfectly capable of, willing to and enthusiastic about abandoning totally our concept, say, of Newtonian gravity and replacing it with Einsteinian relativity. But I have to say—and correct me if I'm wrong—that theology as a subject is immune to radical theory change because if it underwent a radical theory change, it would not have a subject to discuss anymore.

McGrath. Well, let me begin by saying that I think that's a very good statement for science and certainly for me. A radical theory change perhaps isn't quite as radical as made out, but simply part of the ongoing scientific process, and emphasizes the provisionality of where we are. In other words, this is the way things seem to us today, but we're aware that it may develop in future directions as we go on.

But on the theological point: I'm a Protestant, and you have heard of the Reformation? The Reformation corresponds very well to what Thomas Kuhn would describe as a radical paradigm shift. And the key thing about Protestantism is it proposes not simply one such reforming event in the past, but an ongoing process of constant reevaluation and revision to try to ascertain that we have the best possible handle on our knowledge of God, and we want a sort of biblical anchor for that.

In his letter to the Thessalonians, Paul talks about putting everything to the test and holding fast to what is good. And so, I represent a strand of Christianity that is always saying we've got to keep examining things again and checking things out. And that means responding to criticisms.

I happen to disagree with Richard Dawkins's book very much. But I respect his right to write it and my obligation to respond to it, and I think that's part of this process of trying to be responsive to these challenges I see coming my way and asking whether I need to rethink as a result of the challenges it raises.

Helfand. Yes, I guess I was equating Newton's theory of gravity to God and Einstein's theory to not-God, and you were taking a narrower view, which is fair. I think it's possible this audience would like to hear more about your transformation from seventeen-year-old atheist to twenty-three-year-old Christian, and I could share my opposite transformation, if you like.

If I may say, I truly find it deeply mysterious as to how someone like you could have made such a transformation. So, I would like to hear about it. I'm curious.

McGrath. Well, I'm very happy to talk about this. I mean, it puzzles me, as well. I prided myself, and probably still pride myself, as being a free thinker. In other words, no one tells me what to think. I think I would have been astonished if I knew where my process of free thinking was going to take me. But to highlight some of the issues, when I was an atheist I was a rather dogmatic atheist who actually, I think, had a very simplistic understanding of the sciences. Now, the understanding of the sciences I had then is very similar to the understanding Richard Dawkins has now. Your [Helfand's] much more nuanced understanding, if I may say so, I think is right. I want to be very clear about that. I had this very simplistic take on things, that science, atheism and so on were just locked together. That seemed to me to be the way things were, and I looked forward to developing my science and becoming a much more intellectually robust atheist.

Then, I began to find a number of things happening. One of them was reading something about the philosophy of science, and I began to realize that we were talking not so much about absolute proof but rather having good reason to believe that and being prepared to keep revising things. It actually began to suggest to me a most interesting option, namely, that we might be able to hold certain views which we believe to be right, we believe to be relevant, but nonetheless are not actually capable of being totally proved. That really began to make me see religious faith in a very new way.

I think another thing which really began to impact me around that time was the whole idea of a worldview. It was something that I was just discovering at that time. In other words, not just this idea and that idea, but a network of ideas which gave me a way of seeing things. I began to realize that atheism itself was a worldview, and hence one which actually went beyond the available evidence to make certain claims. Then I began to realize that all worldviews were actually very much in the same boat. Therefore, there might be a case to be made for considering others. And so, I began to reconsider the Christian worldview, and a number of things happened.

I think, if I can just single out two, because time is not totally in our favor:

One of them was a great interest in history. In other words asking, what actually happened in the New Testament? This was in addition to kind of the philosophical kind of reflections I was having, trying to ask what actually was the significance of Jesus of Nazareth. If I could write him off as simply an interesting teacher from the past, well, that's that. But it just seemed there was rather more to it than that.

And then there was something else, which is a very difficult thing to explain. Basically I was beginning to realize that something could be right, and yet have no discernible impact on the way in which we live our lives. Then I discovered that if Christianity were right, it actually had the capacity to transform. If I could make a distinction between being true and being real, it was real as well as true. That really had a very big impact on me. So, that was really how I began that journey of faith, which is still ongoing because I keep discovering more and finding myself very excited by that.

It is interesting that my pilgrimage has been in the opposite direction to what some people might have expected.

Helfand. Yes. Well, I guess a cynic would say that a dogmatic belief in atheism would easily transform itself into a dogmatic belief in God. But since you clearly demonstrated . . .

McGrath. Well, I shall watch Dawkins with great interest and see what happens.

Helfand. One never can tell when one gets very ill, for example, and I think that's right. Einstein once said that good young physicists turn into bad old philosophers, which may be relevant here. Well, all right. Because the audience may be interested, I'll give you a briefer explication of my transformation.

I grew up in a very small and very boring town. I had a mother who was British and a Methodist in Britain, but in our little town, there were no Methodist churches. So, she became what were then called

Congregationalists, and is now called United Church of Christ, which is sort of on the left side politically of American Protestantism.

My father was Jewish, but he was the kind of Jew that cooked the bacon for Easter breakfast at the sunrise service. However, he did fast on Yom Kippur every year, even after his mother died at the age of ninety-nine. So, I was brought up in a somewhat, you might say, ecumenical home—I mean, I'm sure my father was the only Jew in the town we lived in. It was not a very big town. We didn't go to synagogue; we went to church. I went to church every day. I sang in the choir. I played the organ. I was president of my church fellowship in my junior and senior year.

But I guess I never had a deep feeling (well, my wife would say I could stop there: I've never had a deep feeling); I didn't have a deep emotional response to this. It was all nice ritual, and actually I like rituals, so that's nice. I can't reconstruct this because of my lack of examination of my life, but the battle of Jericho played a role here. I think I was learning about sound waves at the time in physics in high school and, for some reason, the lesson had to do with the battle of Jericho: you may recall that Joshua circled the walls and blew the trumpets and the walls fell down, and the battle was over.

I have found it extremely comfortable to live my life without any reflection on the notion of whether God should exist or not. Until it's thrown in one's face, as it is constantly in this country through its influence on the political process, which I find deeply scary.

I started thinking about these sound waves and what the intensity of these sound waves would be to knock down walls of thick of rock. And I sort of thought, *This is silly.* By the time of my second semester of my freshman year in college I found the whole thing sort of irrelevant (though because I was in the glee club, I still had to sing in the local Episcopal church every Sunday morning). I'm not sure that I made any large transformations from one side to the other, but I have found it extremely comfortable to live my life without any reflection on the notion of whether God should exist or not. Until it's thrown in one's face, as it is constantly in this country through its influence on the political process, which I find deeply scary.

It's for that reason that last week I gave a press conference in Washington about the influence of religion on our supposedly secular government. I feel that it's important to take a more active stand than I otherwise might, not perhaps to the extent of Dawkins's polemics, but nonetheless from a rather firmly rooted belief that faith, at least as practiced in this country, is irrational and dangerous.

Moderator: Thank you.

6

A SCIENTIST WHO LOOKED AND WAS FOUND

Hugh Ross
The Veritas Forum at the University of Michigan, 1995

I'D LIKE TO TELL YOU TWO STORIES: a personal story of how I came from a secular scientific background to faith in God, and a story about what's happened in the astronomical community over the past few decades, especially among those doing research in cosmology. You may see some parallels.

I was born and raised in Canada. I did not meet anyone who took the Christian faith seriously until I was twenty-seven years old. So you could say I come from a secular background. Nobody seemed interested in God in the neighborhood I grew up in. But I got involved in science at the age of seven. Though it rains often and intensely in Vancouver, I remember walking down the street with my parents one night when the rain wasn't so intense and noticing the stars. I asked my parents whether or not the stars were hot. They said, "Yes, very hot." I asked why, and they told me to go to the library.

That evening's walk was my first exposure to astronomy and physics, and after my first visit to the library I knew I had found my future career. At the age of fifteen, I was persuaded by those weekly studies in the library that there had to be a God who or that was responsible for the existence of the universe. Of the several different theories to explain the structure of the universe, the big bang theory was clearly ahead of the pack. Following the same line of reasoning as Albert Einstein, I concluded that if the universe is a big bang—that means it's exploding—then there must be a beginning and, therefore, a Beginner.

But I was highly skeptical that this Beginner would pay enough attention to human beings or would bother to communicate with us. I felt that if there were a 100 billion, trillion stars out there, surely the Creator of the cosmos wouldn't be too interested in events taking place on an insignificant speck of dust we call planet Earth.

EXAMINING WORLD RELIGIONS

In my last year of high school, I thought that for the sake of intellectual honesty I should at least look at the different holy books and religions of the world to prove to my personal satisfaction that they were indeed what I assumed them to be, humanly crafted frauds. The scientific method of analysis was familiar. That's the approach I took.

I figured that the Hindu Vedas would be the place to start, given the ancientness of Hinduism. Indeed I didn't have to read too many pages of the Vedas before I discovered several scientific absurdities. The general rule of thumb I was using is that when we look up at the cosmos—in fact, when we look out in any field of scientific endeavor—we discover consistency, beauty and harmony. There's freedom from contradiction. So my assumption was that if the God that created the universe decided to communicate with us human beings in a direct fashion, that communication would have those same characteristics. But for things of human origin, we can expect human feelings and ideas to creep in, and that's what I looked for. I looked for those human perspectives.

In my last year of high school, I thought that for the sake of intellectual honesty I should at least look at the different holy books and religions of the world to prove to my personal satisfaction that they were indeed humanly crafted frauds.

So when I read about civilizations of humanity on the surface of the sun, I just chuckled to myself and thought, *Well, I guess the Hindus of three thousand years ago weren't aware of how warm it is on the surface of the sun.* When they spoke about time being eternal, while the big bang theory was telling us that time was finite and had a beginning, and when they made incorrect statements about the moon and the planets, I thought, *Well, I don't have to consider this any further.*

I was most interested, however, in what the Buddhists had to say, because I grew up in Vancouver's Chinatown, and outside of atheism or agnosticism, Buddhism was the dominant religion of my neighborhood. But it didn't take very long for me to discover that the Buddhists borrow their cosmological content, their doctrines about the origin of the universe, from the Hindus. A big ball of verbatim. So I said, *If that's Buddhism, then that cannot be from a divine source, either. It must be of human origin.*

The next holy book I decided to examine was the Qur'an of the Islamic faith. When I got into the Qur'an I began to see a common denominator among holy books. They seem to be written in esoteric poetry. They're written with a veneer of intellectual elitism, so that if you were one of the great "enlightened ones" you'd understand the meaning. Otherwise, forget it. From my experience in studying astronomy from age seven, that characteristic didn't fit. In the record of nature, everything is open, direct and ready for investigation to anyone who cares to look. It's not esoteric. So the fact that I saw this vagueness gave me some concern.

My greater struggle with the Qur'an was how much of it I had to read to find something stated specifically enough that it could be put to the test. So I probably read more of that document than of the Hindu writings. Finally, I did find some testable statements, such as one to the effect that the stars are closer to us than the planets. I knew that was incorrect. More frequently, the Qur'an places historical events in the wrong geographical location. I had studied enough geography to see that some statements were off by one or two thousand miles. So I put the Qur'an aside.

The next set of books I began to look at were the Mormon texts.

Mormonism is similar to Islam: it rests on a latter day prophet and a latter day set of books. In examining those texts I found that the book of Mormon claimed supernatural inspiration based on its ability to predict future history. It was marginally impressive that Joseph Smith predicted a future civil war, and yet in the context of 1830, others were making the same prediction. They were newspaper reporters. But what he said in detail about the coming civil war was clearly incorrect. For example, he predicted that all the European nations would participate in that war as belligerents. The truth is, not one of them did. From my assumption that the One behind the cosmos wouldn't make any errors, I rejected that book from consideration.

SEARCHING THE BIBLE FOR ERRORS

Finally, I picked up a Bible. It had become mine when two businessmen in dark suits came into my public school classroom, placed two boxes on my teacher's desk and left without saying a word. In those two boxes were Bibles. I still pack around that gift from the Gideons I picked up at age eleven.

Maybe it's just as well that the book stayed in my bookshelf for six years. It was written in Elizabethan English. If I had tried to tackle it at age eleven, I might have treated it as a foreign language. But in the Canadian school system Shakespeare is part of the junior high and high school curriculum. I had read more than a dozen plays and memorized hundreds of verses before I had a chance to pick up the Bible. So when I started reading through it, it wasn't a foreign language, and immediately I could see its uniqueness.

This was not esoteric poetry. There was no hint at "hidden" meanings. Unlike other holy books, in which I had to read for hours and hours to find something that could be put to the test, virtually every page had six, seven testable statements—in fact, the first page, Genesis 1, gave me more than thirty different statements that could be put to scientific and historical testing.

That possibility encouraged my scientific bent. In fact, that first night I spent three-and-a-half hours studying Genesis 1 because of the wealth of data that could be put to the test. As I ran down the page I found eleven creation events and three initial conditions, all put in the correct chronological sequence, and all correctly described from a modern scientific perspective. Having studied astronomy since I was seven, I had been exposed to numerous creation myths from around the world, and I was able to recognize that the Bible was far ahead of the slightly realistic *Enuma Elish* of the Babylonians. That account mentions thirteen creation events, and two of the thirteen are correct. The Bible scored fourteen for fourteen.

The other thing that impressed me was that the Genesis creation account reflected the scientific method. It begins with a statement identifying the frame of reference. Then it lists the initial conditions. Next it lists a sequence of events, and it concludes with a statement of final conditions. I was amazed by its structure until ten years later when I read the writings of a Scottish theologian, Thomas Torrance, who explains that the Bible is the source of the scientific method.

I was deeply impressed by that fourteen-for-fourteen score; in fact, I calculated the odds of any ancient author's placing various creation events in correct chronological order would be less than one chance of six billion. That improbability motivated me to commit at least an hour a day to reading the Bible until I found a provable error or contradiction. I figured if I could find even one provable error or contradiction, that would be enough to establish this book is not of divine origin. I thought this would take me maybe six weeks. Instead, it took me eighteen months, and that's because I skipped a few portions of the Bible on my way to Revelation 22.

My amazement grew as I encountered page after page like Genesis 1, filled with half a dozen or a dozen statements of history, geography or science that could easily be put to the test. So I kept plowing my way through. At the end of those eighteen months, I recognized that I had been unsuccessful in finding a single provable error or contradiction. I found lots of pages I didn't fully understand. But I thought, *That's really no different from astrophysics.* There are areas of astrophysics I don't yet understand. I also found problems I couldn't solve, but that is also true of astronomy and physics. Unsolved problems remain to this day.

However, in that eighteen-month time window I experienced what we witness in science: as time goes on researchers solve more and more problems they couldn't solve before. And so, during that eighteen-month period, problems that I couldn't solve in the first month I was able to solve in the fourteenth. This is just the pattern we see in studying the record of nature—it's the same kind of result in terms of what research study provides. That experience helped convince me that this book indeed must have come from a

My amazement grew as I encountered page after page like Genesis 1, filled with half a dozen or a dozen statements of history, geography or science that could easily be put to the test.

divine source. It couldn't possibly have come from a human source. No composite of human endeavor could possibly provide such a reliable record.

By the time I got to the New Testament, I found additional surprises, statements by the apostle Paul urging people to put their beliefs to the test. The other holy books seemed to say, *"Avoid* testing." The Bible's encouragement to exercise testing really appealed to my scientific mind: Don't believe something until you first verify it, until you first put it to the test.

By this time I was attending the University of British Columbia, and I was no longer seventeen. This campus had a reputation back in the late 1960s of being hostile to beliefs in God. Even though I was convinced the Bible is true and trustworthy, I felt I didn't yet have a strong enough case to convince my fellow students and professors. So, I went through the book a second time, and what I decided to do this second time was to make note of the passages that accurately predicted scientific discoveries.

After a few weeks my list included such things as the sphericity of the earth; the law of gravity and the first and second laws of thermodynamics; identification of the only star clusters visible to the naked eye that are gravitationally bound.

I calculated from this list the probability that someone living as long ago as the prophet Isaiah would be able to predict these scientific discoveries by chance, and what I saw became an impressive piece of probabilistic evidence that this information could not have come from a human source.

TESTING HISTORICAL ACCURACY

I did the same type of review with history in mind. Unlike the Mormon scriptures, the Bible made hundreds of forecasts thousands of years in advance. Joseph Smith was able to look ahead maybe twenty years, but the prophet Moses, for example, was able to make predictions that reached thirty-four hundred years into the future. And the

And the Bible writers named people by name, even before they were born.

Bible writers named people by name, even before they were born. I was impressed with a prophet who could name the future king by name three hundred years before that king was born and predict exactly what he would do, where he would do it, and the exact year in which he would do it. So I began to check these predictions and calculate the probabilities that they would be fulfilled by chance.

The prophet Isaiah said there would be a future king by the name of Cyrus who would rule over an as yet nonexistent kingdom, the kingdom of the Medes and the Persians, and would conquer yet another nonexistent kingdom, the Babylonian Empire. Isaiah went on to predict that this Babylonian empire would conquer the land of Judah and carry off the people of Judah to serve as slaves in Babylon for seventy years, at which time King Cyrus would set them free and give them money to rebuild their city, their kingdom, and their temple—even to finance their religious services.

All this happened.

What's the probability that it would happen by chance? What's the probability that you could correctly guess somebody's name eighty years before he or she is born? First, figure out how many names could possibly be assigned to such an individual. That's one, divided by the total number of possible names. What's the probability that you would get the year right? Again, how many years of history could such an event possibly be fulfilled? Take one and divide it by the total number of possible years.

But those are two independent events, so the probability you would get the year right and the name right would be one divided by the total number of possible names times one divided by the total number of possible years. Then you've got eight more details to work out. The bottom line is there is less than *a chance in a trillion* that what Isaiah predicted about this future king would come true exactly as predicted.

When I was studying all this, some scholars still debated whether the book of Daniel was really written by the Daniel of Nebuchadnezzar's court. Then the Dead Sea Scrolls were discovered, and they included all the chapters of Daniel. That ended the debate: it must have been written by a man living before 200 B.C., and Daniel was the only viable candidate for authorship. The fact that Daniel predicts historical events taking place *after* 200 B.C.—including the breakup of the Greek Empire and various intrigues impacting the royal courts of both the Greeks and Romans—means that we really do have an astonishingly precise prediction of future events.

I also found prophecies being fulfilled right before my eyes. I had the fun of going to the university library to read newspapers from the late 1940s onward and comparing them with predictions about the second rebirth of Israel. I saw remarkable details, such as the international reaction of horror and despair upon discovery of the "valleys of the dry bones." Indeed, you can look up old newspaper photographs of Auschwitz, with its huge ravines filled with hundreds of thousands of skeletons, and on the same page of the newspaper read, "Zionism is now finished, with the death of six and a half million Jews." Yet within a few years the world witnessed the rebirth of the nation of Israel.

As King David predicted, the rebirth of the nation would be orchestrated by those who escaped the death camps, those who had the "sentence of death upon them," written on their wrists. He predicted these same people would fight the key battles that would make it possible for Jerusalem to be part of the new Jewish nation. Those words were written three thousand years ago. That's exactly what happened: the key battles in the war for Israel's independence were fought by two regiments made up of survivors from Hitler's death camps, who still had their numbers on their wrists. They suffered the greatest number of casualties as they opened up the corridor between Tel Aviv and Jerusalem, but as David Ben Gurion said, "If it weren't for their shed blood there would be no nation of Israel today." King David accurately predicted these events.

Take a dozen such predictions, calculate the probabilities that they would be fulfilled by chance as opposed to divine intervention. (I later had these probability figures checked by colleagues at Caltech who were not Christians, and they came up with much more remote numbers than I did.) The number I calculated was less than one in ten with more than a hundred zeroes after it that all thirteen would be fulfilled. It's all those zeros that give me a point of argument because now I could demonstrate that this book has a higher degree of reliability than some of the laws of physics.

At nineteen years of age, at the same time I was coming up with this probability number, I was assigned problems in physics classes for determining the reliability of the second law of thermodynamics. For those who are not in engineering and science, let me give you an illustration: Think about an auditorium filled with air molecules. Not all the molecules are the same temperature. Some are very cold, some are very hot. Their average temperature gives you the room temperature. However, there's a finite mathematical possibility that all the air molecules in the auditorium below the freezing point of water will wander in the next second into the vicinity of someone sitting here and freeze him or her to death. That probability we can calculate to be about one chance in 10^{80}.

It's such a small possibility that no one in his or her right mind worries about being zapped by what would

> *No one in his or her right mind worries about being zapped by what would be described as a sudden reversal of the second law of thermodynamics. I just don't wake up in the morning with that on my mind. What I realized at the age of nineteen is that I had demonstrated the Bible has a much higher degree of reliability than that second law I gamble my life on, second by second, every day.*

be described as a sudden reversal of the second law of thermodynamics. I just don't wake up in the morning with that on my mind. What I realized at the age of nineteen is that I had demonstrated the Bible has a much higher degree of reliability than that second law I gamble my life on, second by second, every day.

RESPONDING TO THE EVIDENCE

That's when I responded to the challenge spelled out by the Gideons. My Gideon Bible included a couple of pages explaining exactly what to do once I became convinced of the Bible's reliability. First they reminded me I was not perfect. I realized that was true. But they revealed something else that really caught my attention: the harder a person tries to live a morally and ethically perfect life, the more his or her conscience acts up, and the more miserable he or she feels.

I said, *That's me.* During that eighteen-month period of research into the Bible I had done everything I could to lead a perfectly good life, and the harder I tried, the more miserable I became. The Gideons explained that's God's way of telling me he's perfect and requires perfection, but I can't produce it. The only way to acquire it is to accept Jesus Christ's offer of forgiveness. I said, *That's right.* I had read a lot about what Jesus Christ had accomplished and suffered in my place, and so at that point I made a commitment of my life to him, saying, *I want that forgiveness. I want to be on the pathway toward becoming like you.* So I signed my name and asked Jesus Christ to be in charge of me.

OTHER SCIENTISTS' RESPONSES

Since then I have seen changes not only in my own life but also in the thinking of other scientists. Back in the early 1980s, physicists were writing books promoting atheism, saying, "God doesn't exist because physics explains everything." One of the more famous was Paul Davies's book *God and the New Physics* (1983). Just one year after he wrote it, he published another book, *Superforce*, in which he asserted that "the laws of physics themselves are so exquisitely and elegantly crafted that that by itself demands a need for a divine creator." But he still credited the laws of physics with every cosmic development beyond.

Three years after *Superforce*, Davies published a book called *The Cosmic Blueprint*, in which he described the latest design evidence observed in the universe in the solar system. He details various characteristics of the universe that must be exquisitely fine-tuned in order for any conceivable form of life to exist. And he concludes his book saying that the evidence for design has become so "overwhelming" there must be Someone behind it all to explain why it's all here.

Ed Harrison, a British cosmologist, states the reasoning this way:

> Here's a cosmological proof of existence of God, the design argument of William Paley updated and refurbished: the fine-tuning of the universe provides prima facie evidence of theistic design. Take your choice— blind chance that requires an infinite amount of universes, or design, that requires only one. Many scientists, when they admit their views, incline towards a theological, or design, argument.[1]

Allow me to explain why these scientists, aware of this evidence, opt for a divine design conclusion rather than an infinite number of universes all taking different characteristics so that life may be possible, by chance, in one universe. To accept the latter alternative would be to assume the benefit of an infinite sample when we have direct evidence for only one. In other words, it would be like watching a coin being flipped ten thousand times and coming up heads ten thousand times in a row and still concluding it's a fair coin. Suc a conclusion would only be rational if there were *evidence* that a nearly infinite number of identical coins had been flipped and come up with different results.

Without that evidence, the rational conclusion to draw is that someone "fixed" the single coin so that it always comes up heads. By that same reasoning process, some researchers have come to conclude Someone designed our universe so that we could be here today. Some have come to share my commitment to become Christ-followers.

At this point I'd like to clarify the line of reasoning that leads from the finite beginning to a Beginner to the person known as Jesus Christ.

A paper published by Stephen Hawking and Roger Penrose back in 1970 provides a good starting point. Their theorem states if the equations of general relativity reliably describe the dynamics of the universe, then not only are we faced with the ultimate beginning for the matter and energy of the universe, but also with a beginning for the space-time dimensions along which that matter and energy are distributed. As Hawking himself declared, "We've proved that time has a beginning." That seemed a bit of a boast back in 1970, but thanks to Nobel Prize–winning confirmations of general relativity since then, it's no longer a boast; it really does follow.

If cosmic time has a beginning, if time is finite, time must have been created. Space must have been created. Matter and energy must have been created. By definition, time is that dimension (or realm) in which cause-and-effect phenomena take place. So, the fact that time is finite and has a beginning means that the cause of that time dimension must be some entity unconfined by that dimension capable of operating outside of length, width, height and time.

One of the unique attributes of the Christian God is that he is a transcendent Being, capable of acting through cause and effect independent of length, width, height and time. In comparing these different holy books, the Bible is the only holy book that portrays such a God. In the other religions, we see god or gods creating within time. In the Bible, God creates independent of time.

One of the unique attributes of the Christian God is that he is a transcendent Being, capable of acting through cause and effect independent of length, width, height and time. In comparing these different holy books, the Bible is the only holy book that portrays such a God. In the other religions, we see god or gods creating *within* time. In the Bible, God creates independent of time. So that piece of evidence is enough to establish that of all the gods of religions of the world, the only one matching reality with scientific precision is the God of the Bible.

The next step is to look at the personal characteristics of that Creator as revealed in both Scripture and nature and establish how these characteristics demonstrate creativity, power, intelligence and care for humanity. When we get that far down the road, we really have isolated the God of the Bible, and specifically the person of Jesus Christ. In his life and miracles he demonstrated divine power over nature, including power over life and death.

The approach I recommend for linking personally with Jesus Christ is this: reach the mind first by checking out the evidence for the reliability of the Bible. Really, I'm just following the pattern of Psalm 2 by King David, who states that we must first come to God with our mind "instructed"; second, we must submit our will to God. Then and only then can we enter in to an authentic relationship with our Creator. That's the step-by-step process: the mind first, then the will, then the emotions. Many people want to jump in to the emotions right away, but that's not the best way to build a secure and growing relationship. And that's the relationship our hearts truly long for.

7

THE PSYCHOLOGY
OF ATHEISM

Paul C. Vitz

The Veritas Forum at the University of Florida, 1995

TONIGHT, WE'RE GOING TO talk about the psychological reasons for unbelief. Before I begin, I want to say that this does not mean that I think there are no rational arguments on the side of people who are atheists or agnostics or skeptics. It's just that this evening we're going to look at another topic. We're going to be looking at what I consider, or will propose and give some evidence for, psychological reasons that lie behind people's rejection of belief in God.

And so, we will not be talking about philosophically rational arguments. We will not be talking about the way to interpret the big bang or constants in the physical world. We will be reflecting on our own understanding of our personal psychology. In this case, many of you are probably experts, perhaps even more so than I am, since we all are reasonably aware of our own interior life and that of those we know well. With that as a prelude, let me begin.

The title of my talk, "The Psychology of Atheism," may seem strange to some of you. Certainly, my psychological colleagues have found it odd, and I might add, a little disturbing. After all, psychology, since its founding roughly a century ago, has often focused on the opposite topic, namely, the psychology of religious belief. Indeed, in many respects the origins of modern psychology are bound up with psychologists who explicitly proposed interpretations of belief in God.

Given the rather close involvement between the founding of much of psychology and a critical interpretation of religion, it should not be surprising that most psychologists view with some alarm an attempt to propose a psychology of atheism. At the very least, such a project puts many psychologists on the defensive and gives them at least a small taste of their own medicine. Psychologists are always observing and interpreting others, and it is time that some of them learn from their own experience what it is like to be put under the microscope of psychology theory and evidence.

SOME QUALIFICATIONS

Regardless, I hope to show that the psychological concepts used, often effectively, to interpret religion are two-edged swords that can be used also to interpret atheism. Before beginning, however, I wish to make two points bearing on my basic assumptions:

First, I am assuming that the major barriers to belief in God are not rational but in a general sense can be called psychological. I do not wish to offend the many distinguished philosophers and scientists who might disagree with that, both believers and unbelievers. But I am quite convinced that for every person strongly swayed by rational argument, there are countless others more affected by nonrational, psychological factors. The human heart: no one can truly fathom it or know all of its deceits, but at least it is the proper task of the psychologist to try.

> *I am quite convinced that for every person strongly swayed by rational argument, there are countless others more affected by nonrational, psychological factors.*

Thus, to begin, I propose that psychological barriers to belief in God are of great importance, and what some of these might be I will mention shortly. One of the earliest theorists of the unconscious, St. Paul, wrote, "I can will what is right but I cannot do it. I see in my members another law at war with the law of my mind." Thus, it seems to me, sound theology as well as sound psychology that psychological factors can be impediments to belief and also, of course, to behavior. In addition, I think they may be unconscious as they apparently were for St. Paul.

Further, as a corollary, it is reasonable to propose that people vary greatly in the extent to which these factors have been present in their lives. Some people have large numbers of barriers to belief in God, others have very few. So, my first point is that because of this, we are not to judge others with respect to their beliefs. We are, if we can, to try to understand others.

My second point as qualification is that in spite of serious psychological barriers to belief, all of us have a free choice to accept or reject God. This qualification is not a contradiction to the first. One person as a consequence of his or her particular past or present environment may find it much harder that most to believe in God, as I said. But presumably, at any moment, certainly at many times, a person can choose to move toward or away. One person may start with so many barriers that even after many years of slowly choosing to move toward God, he or she may still not be there.

Some may die before they reach belief. We assume they will be judged, like all of us, on how far they traveled and how well they loved others, on how well they did with what they had. Likewise, another person without any serious psychological difficulties is still free to reject God, and no doubt, many do. Last, although the ultimate issue is one of free will, it is still possible to investigate those factors that predispose someone to unbelief and make the road to belief in God especially long and hard.

SIMPLE PERSONAL MOTIVES AND SOCIAL MOTIVES: MY CASE HISTORY

So, let's now begin with some reasons of a psychological kind, and I begin with what I call simple personal motives and social motives. There seems to be a widespread assumption throughout much of the intellectual community that belief in God is based on all kinds of irrational, immature needs and wishes, but that somehow or other skepticism or atheism is derived from a rational, no-nonsense appraisal of the way things really are.

To begin a critique of this assumption I start with my own case history. After a rather wishy-washy Christian upbringing, I became an atheist in college in the 1950s and remained so throughout graduate school and my first years as a young experimental psychologist on the faculty at New York University. That is, I am an adult convert, or more technically, a *re*convert to Christianity, who came back to the faith (much to his surprise) in his late thirties, in the very secular environment of academic New York City.

There seems to be a widespread assumption throughout much of the intellectual community that belief in God is based on all kinds of irrational, immature needs and wishes, but that somehow or other skepticism or atheism is derived from a rational, no-nonsense appraisal of the way things really are.

I'm not going into this to bore you with parts of my life history but to note that through reflection on my own experience it is now clear to me that my reasons for becoming and remaining an atheist from about age eighteen to thirty-eight were intellectually superficial and largely without a deeply thought basis. Furthermore, I am convinced that my motives were, and still are, commonplace today among many intellectuals, social scientists and probably college students, which is where I began my atheism.

The major factors in my becoming an atheist, although I wasn't really aware of it at the time, included one factor I call general socialization. An important influence on me in my youth was a certain significant social unease. I was somewhat embarrassed to be from the Midwest, for it seemed to me terribly dull, narrow and provincial. There was certainly nothing romantic or impressive about being from Cincinnati and from a mixed German-English-Swiss background. Terribly dull and middle class.

Besides escape from this background (which was, according to me, somehow rather an unworthy one), I wanted to take part and be comfortable in the new, exciting, glamorous, secular world into which I was moving at that time at the University of Michigan as an undergraduate. I'm sure that similar motives have strongly influenced the lives of countless upwardly mobile young people in the last two centuries. Consider all of the secularized Jews, for example, who have fled the Jewish ghettos because they wish to assimilate and get away from the strange and embarrassing behavior and characteristics of their parents.

Or consider the latest young arrival in New York City embarrassed about his or her fundamentalist parents. This kind of socialization pressure has pushed many people away from belief in God and all that this belief is associated with for them. I remember a small seminar in graduate school where almost every member there at some time expressed this kind of embarrassment and response to the pressures of socialization, that is, to become part of the modern secular world. One student was trying to escape his Southern Baptist background, another a small-town Mormon environment, another was trying to get out of a very Jewish Brooklyn Ghetto, and the fourth was me.

Another kind of socialization, and the major reason for me wanting to become an atheist, was that I desired to be accepted by the powerful and influential psychologists in my field. In particular I wanted to be accepted by my professors in graduate school. As a graduate student I was thoroughly socialized by the specific culture of academic psychology. My professors at Stanford, as much as they might disagree on psychological theory, were, as far as I could tell, united on really only two things: their intense personal ambition and their rejection of religion. As the psalmist says, "Those greedy for gain curse and renounce the LORD. . . . All their thoughts are, 'There is no God.' " In this environment, just as I had learned how to dress like a college student by putting on the right clothes, I also learned to think like a proper psychologist by putting on the right, that is, atheistic or skeptical, ideas and attitudes.

Finally, in this list of superficial but still very strong irrational pressures to become an atheist, I must list probably as the most important simple, personal convenience. The fact is, it is quite inconvenient to be a serious believer in today's powerful neo-pagan world. I would have to give up many pleasures, some money and a good deal of time. I didn't have enough pleasures, I didn't have enough time, and I didn't have enough money to do any of that as far as I was concerned.

Without going into details, it's not hard to imagine the pleasures that would have to be rejected if I became a serious believer. And then the time—there would be church services and church groups and prayer and Scripture reading. All these things that these people did and time spent helping others. I was too busy trying to help myself, and becoming religious would be a real inconvenience. Perhaps you think that such reasons are restricted to especially callow young men like I was in my twenties. However, such reasoning is not so restricted. In fact, just the other day I heard a very clear statement by Aldous Huxley of the same reason for why he wasn't a believer.

In this list of superficial but still very strong irrational pressures to become an atheist, I must list probably as the most important simple, personal convenience. The fact is, it is quite inconvenient to be a serious believer in today's powerful neo-pagan world.

But I'm going to turn to another intellectual that maybe some of you know about, his name was Mortimer Adler, a well-known American philosopher, writer, intellectual and professor at the University of Chicago, who spent much of his life thinking about God and religious topics, and also writing about it. One of his books is titled *How to Think About God: A Guide for the Twentieth-Century Pagan*. In this work Adler presses the argument for the existence of God very strongly, and by the later chapters he is very close to accepting the living God, yet he pulls back and remains among the vast company of the religiously uncommitted. But Adler leaves the impression that this decision is more one of his will than of his intellect.

As one of his reviewers notes, "Adler confirms this impression in his own autobiography, *Philosopher at Large*. In this book where Adler is investigating his reasons for twice stopping short of a full religious commitment he writes that the answer 'lies in the state of one's will, not in the state of one's mind.' " This is a philosopher, not a psychologist. Adler goes on to comment that to become seriously religious "would require a radical change in my way of life" and "the simple truth of the matter is that I did not wish to live up to being a genuinely religious person." There you have it, a remarkably honest and conscious admission that being a genuinely religious person would be too much trouble, too inconvenient. I can't but assume that such are the reasons behind many an unbeliever's position.

In summary, then, because of my social needs to assimilate, because of my professional needs to be accepted as part of academic psychology, and because of my personal needs for a convenient lifestyle, atheism was simply the best policy. Looking back on these reasons, I can honestly say that for me a return to atheism has all the appeal of a return to adolescence.

DEEPER PSYCHOLOGICAL REASONS FOR ATHEISM

Now I would like to stop and approach the deeper psychological reasons for being an atheist. Although I consider the just-noted superficial reasons to be the most common ones, there are people for whom these are not the issues. I want to look now at deeper reasons for people being an atheist.

And here I have much more sympathy with these people, even though they often are the most passionate of the atheists. These are not just casual atheists, but people for whom it makes a big difference and who are often very aggressively pushing the atheist position.

Freud's ideas about belief in God. Before I begin, I want to say a little bit about Sigmund Freud's own interpretations of belief because we're going to use Freud—Freud of all people—as our theorist for coming up with a psychology of atheism.

Freud was the first prominent psychologist to propose that people's belief in God could not be trusted because of its origins. In other words, what Freud did was take the ad hominem argument and make it a very popular and influential one. He didn't argue the truth value of the beliefs; he just argued that you couldn't trust the source of those beliefs. And he proposed this position most thoroughly in a book, a rather short one, called *The Future of an Illusion*, in which the illusion is religion, as far as Freud was concerned. He didn't consider religion true or false, he just considered it a psychological illusion that arose from our primitive needs for protection. Our basic, infantile, unconscious needs for a father who would look after us, and therefore an illusion.

This argument is not very convincing if you look at it carefully. First of all, Freud said that these sources were equally applicable to all of the contributions of civilization, including science and literature and psychoanalysis. So if the origins of a belief make us no longer accept its truth value, then according to Freud, we shouldn't accept the truth value of all the other accomplishments of civilization that he said arose from the same kind of motivation.

He also claims that one of the oldest psychological needs of the human race is this need for a loving, protecting, all-powerful father or divine providence, and that's unconvincing because many religions don't have that as the understanding of God at all, particularly many of the pre-Christian or pre-Jewish religions in the Mediterranean area. Some major religions either have no God or their understanding of God is quite different. So, his assumption that there was a universal need of this kind that explained the Christian and Jewish belief in God isn't very convincing on those grounds, or we'd all be finding the same kind of religion everywhere we looked.

Freud's projection theory. But let's put these two intellectual weak points aside and look at his projection theory. We can say two initial things about it. First, Freud didn't invent it at all. It was well known— and I don't think Freud would have challenged this interpretation— that a German philosopher-theologian named Ludwig Feuerbach had first made this argument in the 1840s. When Freud was writing his *Future of an Illusion* in the 1920s, he was updating Feuerbach.

Second, Freud's interpretation is not part of psychoanalysis. Many people think that somehow Freud's deep understanding of psychology was what he was distilling this theory from. But Freud is on record as saying that his projection theory is not part of psychoanalysis, and it doesn't relate to psychoanalysis in terms of its usual language and conceptual framework.

The thing to keep in mind is this: *Freud had very little experience, maybe none at all, with the psychological study of people who believed in God.* Not one of Freud's published case histories was that of a person who believed in God at the time of his or her psychoanalysis. His close friend and colleague Ernst Jones stated that he'd never had the pleasure of meeting even a believing Jew in his whole life. None of these men in psychoanalysis were believers.

So Freud was really not an expert on the unconscious psychology of people who believed in God. Perhaps most of you are better experts in terms of your own intuitive psychology of what might be going on. Freud didn't give us a good theory of belief, as far as I'm concerned; it isn't psychoanalytically rooted, and it isn't based on a lot of personal experience with believers. What he gave us was a well-developed position of an earlier theorist, the philosopher Ludwig Feuerbach.

Strangely enough, however, Freud has inadvertently given us, I believe, a basic theory for understanding why people would *not* believe in God, why people would be atheists! And here I'm going to have to remind you a little bit of perhaps Psych 101. We're going to have to look at some of Freud's ideas, and the one idea that we're going to look at is what he's very famous for. It's central to his theory; it's called the Oedipus complex.

Strangely enough, however, Freud has inadvertently given us, I believe, a basic theory for understanding why people would not believe in God, why people would be atheists!

Freud and the Oedipus complex. Now the interesting thing about the Oedipus complex is that Freud said it's universal. There's no reason to believe this, but Freud argued that it is universal, that it is unconscious, and in the case of the male child, the unconscious desire is to reject or remove and kill his father and to have some kind of erotic possession of the mother. Now, I don't happen to believe this is a universal description of our psychology. I don't, in my own counseling work, find it even that common. It is, I think, adequate for occasional people. That is, every now and then we run into somebody who seems to have this psychology.

In any case, Freud also linked our understanding and attitudes of our own father to God. He said God is a father figure and that our attitude toward God and our father are very similar. So what does this mean in terms of the young male child, in terms of the classic Oedipus explanation? It means that every male child should have an unconscious intense need to kill his father, either in dreams, fantasy or in fact, and to possess his mother.

Since Freud proposed that God is a father figure, this suggests that we should all have an unconscious desire to kill God, to be independent of God, to have the world the way we want it. In a sense, what he's saying is that an atheist has an unresolved Oedipus complex because normally the child discovers that the father is too big to kill and the child can't get away with it. And so, instead of killing his father, the child identifies with the aggressor, his father, and represses these aggressive and sexual desires, which then remain unconscious.

Freud is suggesting that we should *all* have a desire to kill God. Actually, I think he's on to something here. I would propose, first of all, that atheism is an example of Oedipal wish fulfillment. That is, it's an unresolved Oedipus complex in the person. But as I said, I don't believe that the Oedipus logic is very universal, so we've got to move away from that particular formulation to a little bit deeper one, a little bit broader and, in fact, simpler one.

Theory of the defective father. What I'm going to propose is something I call "the theory of the defective father." Freud himself stated this in the following way:

> Psychoanalysis, which has taught us the intimate connection between the father complex and belief in God, has shown us that the personal God is logically nothing but an exalted father and daily demonstrates to us how youthful persons lose their religious belief as soon as the authority of their father breaks down.

This statement makes no assumptions about unconscious sexual desires for the mother or even about universal competitive hatred focused on the father. Instead, it makes a simple and easily understandable claim that once a child is disappointed in and looses his or her respect for the earthly father, then belief in a heavenly father becomes impossible.

There are, of course, many ways that a father can lose his authority and seriously disappoint a child. Some of these ways, for which clinical evidence will be mentioned shortly, are when the father is present but obviously weak, cowardly or unworthy of respect even if he is a rather pleasant, nice guy otherwise. The father can be present but physically, sexually or psychologically abusive. The father can be absent through death or by abandoning or leaving the family. Very young children usually interpret the death of a parent as abandonment. One- to three-year-olds often see death as the person choosing to go away. Taken all together, I call these proposed determinants of atheism "the defective father hypothesis."

To support this approach I will conclude by providing a fair amount of case history material from the lives of prominent atheists, for it was in reading their biographies that this hypothesis first struck me.

Freud's own defective father. We begin with Freud's relationship to his own father. Freud's biographers agree that Freud's father, Jacob, was a deep disappointment, or much worse. There are many biographers on this. Specifically, Freud's father was a weak man unable to financially provide for his family. There's no record in Vienna, where Freud grew up, that Jacob had a job in the formal sense that required paying taxes. Instead, money for the family seems to have been provided by his wife's family and others.

Furthermore, Freud's father was passive in response to anti-Semitism. Freud recounts an episode about his father that is famous to his biographers. In this episode Jacob allowed an anti-Semite to call him a "dirty Jew" and to knock his hat off. Young Sigmund, on hearing this story, was mortified at his father's failure to respond, at his father's just taking it and walking away. Sigmund Freud was a complex and, in many respects, ambiguous man, but all agree that he was a courageous fighter and that he greatly admired courage in others. Sigmund as a young man several times physically stood up again anti-Semitism, and of course he was one of the great intellectual fighters.

Jacob's actions as a defective father, however, could go deeper than his inability to support his family and to confront anti-Semitism. Specifically, in two of his letters as an adult Freud writes that his father was a sexual pervert and that his father's own children suffered from this. There were other possible moral disasters involving his father as well, but I think we've provided enough evidence for Freud to want to get as far as he could in many respects from his father.

One other thing, his father was clearly associated with religion, especially Judaism, because as Freud got older his father began to read a good deal of Jewish scripture and things like that. So for Freud his father stood for religion, specifically for Judaism, and he also stood for weakness, incompetence and perhaps perversion. With a father like this—a rather passive nice guy, a *schlemiel*, as they might say in New York, with a serious lack of courage and other weaknesses—it's no wonder this was painful for Freud. The only other relative of Freud's father was an uncle, a brother of his father, who was in Vienna when Freud was growing up. This uncle was arrested for counterfeiting Russian ruble notes and put in jail, and it was in the Vienna newspapers. So there were lots of reasons he wanted to distance himself from his father, whom he found a serious disappointment.

Karl Marx, Ludwig Feuerbach and Madalyn Murray O'Hair. As for Karl Marx, the evidence is not as clear, and I'm still exploring it in some detail, but there is a fair amount of evidence that he probably didn't respect his father. In an important way, this came from the fact that his father converted to Christianity, not out of any religious conviction but out of a desire to get ahead in life as a member of the capitalist class. He assimilated for convenience, and in doing this Marx's father broke an old family tradition. His father was the first in his family who did not become a rabbi. The Marxes were from a long line of rabbis on both sides.

Now let's turn to Ludwig Feuerbach, who was really, in some ways, one of the first very prominent atheists. A German scholar born around 1800, he had very clear reasons for feeling intensely hurt by his father. When Feuerbach was thirteen, his prominent father left his family and openly took up living with another woman in a town not too far away. At that time such a public rejection would have been an incredible scandal, and young Ludwig of course would have felt deeply rejected.

Let us jump one hundred years or so and look at the life of one of America's best-known atheists, Madalyn Murray O'Hair. She was the woman who brought the lawsuit in the 1960s to get prayer taken out of the public schools, and she was a militant atheist. Here I will quote from Madalyn's son, William's, book *My Life Without God* on what life was like in his family when he was a child growing up. The book opens when this boy is eight years old. "We rarely did anything together as a family. The hatred between my grandfather and my mother barred such wholesome scenes." He writes that he really didn't know why his mother hated her father so much, but hate him she did. The opening chapter of the book records a very ugly fight in which she attempts to kill her father with a ten-inch butcher knife. Madalyn failed to do this, but screamed, "I'll see you dead! I'll get you yet! I'll walk on your grave." Now, whatever the cause of Madalyn's intense hatred of her father, it is clear from this book that it was deep, that it went back to her childhood, and at least psychological and possibly physical abuse is a plausible cause.

Other examples of the defective father. I would like to mention some other examples, more recent ones. My wife has said I can mention this one, which concerns her. She was a relatively religious child, grew up in the Midwest and was especially close to her father, particularly because she would go to church with him (apparently her mother didn't go all the time). She enjoyed very much going to church, sitting by her father and singing hymns with him. She attended since she was a child up through her teenage years.

When she was sixteen years old, she was at school one day and got a message to come home quickly; her father had killed himself. He had committed suicide, and she was totally unprepared for this. Her mother was in grave psychological condition as a result, and my wife sort of rallied around her mother. She was the only daughter in the family, and it was a year and a half later in college that she recognized that she had become an atheist. When she and I met, we were both atheists. I was sort of a skeptic, I guess. We got married in the 1960s: we made up our own vows with no reference to God at all, and she wore a little white

miniskirt with long green stockings. Our children look at those pictures and really crack up now.

It has only been since she came back to belief in God that she recognized that the blow caused by her father's suicide was the reason for all
of this. She couldn't associate God except with her father. It was so
deeply painful, such a rejection. She didn't know that her father suffered from very severe depressions, which could today be much more
reliably treated. This experience, as you might imagine, was a shatter-
ing blow for their family life. All sorts of things changed dramatically
after that event. She recognized that it had precipitated her atheism.
She got blown pretty far away from belief in God, but not too far away.
She still majored in the Middle Ages and studied religion as it had been
a thousand years earlier, or something like that.

Another example concerns Albert Ellis, a famous clinical psychologist. Ellis developed an approach using behavioral techniques called
Rational Emotive Therapy. He has an institute in New York City. A
few years ago, I was at a conference with him where I outlined my present theory about atheism in my talk. It was a lecture series where the
sponsors had a theist and an atheist paired for different disciplines (e.g.,
two biologists, two sociologists). We were the two psychologists—one
atheist, one theist. Well, he gave his critique of religion from a psychological point of view first; he's very critical of religion, very harsh. He
used coarse and often gutter-level language to describe believers. (It
was not rhetorically effective because he was talking to a largely Baptist
audience.)

In any case, he's an intelligent man, he's made major contributions to
psychology, and he heard me give this interpretation of the defective
father. Afterward, as we walked back after our mutual presentations,
we had to walk next to each other, so we looked at each other and said
hello or something like that. He looked at me and said, "Well, I got
along fine with my father." And I said, "Well, a psychological theory
can't be right all the time." We're lucky in psychology if we're right, say,
60 or 70 percent of the time—that's doing very well. I didn't think
much more about it.

When I got back to New York City I was talking on the phone with a friend of mine who was an editor for a small publishing company in New York, and I mentioned my talk, this paper. He happened to be a believer, so I sent him a copy of my talk. About a month or so later he called me again about something else, and we were chatting and he said, "Did you know, Paul, by the way, your theory fits Albert Ellis perfectly?"

And I said, "Oh come on, the paper you were reading was what I used as my talk, and he heard me read it and then told me it didn't fit him."

But my friend said, "Well, we're publishing his biography, and last night I was reading the proofs."

"Well, what was the deal?" I asked.

And my friend replied, "Well, Ellis grew up in New York City in the 1920s and 1930s. His mother had some emotional problems, and his father philandered around a lot and then abandoned the whole family. There were two boys, Albert and a slightly older brother. The mother was unable to provide for them because of her mental condition, and these two kids survived on their own on the streets of New York in the 1930s. Every now and then, he ran into his father in New York City at a party or on the street or at some gathering, and the relationship there was pleasant."

But can you imagine how a child that old would feel? We're talking about the 1930s; everybody else had a family or father, as far as Ellis was concerned. But Ellis and his brother were struggling to survive, earning their own money, earning everything on their own, and this guy was around and doing nothing for them. I can't believe that even to this day Ellis is in denial about this. This is a man who has devoted his life to Rational Emotive Therapy. I think this explains the incredible energy and personal venom he expresses toward God in his own understanding of religion.

There are some other pieces of evidence; we'll go very quickly:

- The first public atheist is a French philosopher, a rationalist, named Baron d'Holbach; he was born Paul Henry Thierry. He was apparently orphaned by thirteen and living with his uncle. He rejected his father's name and took the name Holbach. So, we assume that there is some basis for his being upset with his father.

- Bertrand Russell's father died when young Bertrand was four years old, and he never had a substitute father. It's somewhat complicated, but his case still supports the bad father dynamic.

- Friedrich Nietzsche was the same age as Russell when he lost his father. He also never had any father substitutes, and his life fits the theory about as well as any.

- Jean Paul Sartre's father died when he was only fifteen months old, and yet all his life Sartre was fixated about fatherhood and his father. His biographers explain this was an ongoing preoccupation, in all kinds of strange ways, all of his life.

- Camus, the French existentialist writer, lost his father when he was one year old.

Here's another case. I was told about an atheist philosopher who is still publishing. Another philosopher and friend of mine was at a convention of the American Philosophical Association, I believe. After the lectures there are lots of parties in the various hotels, and my friend walked into one room and this atheist philosopher was there, a little drunk. He was down on the floor, pounding the floor saying, "I hate my father, I hate my father." His father was a well-known theologian and religious writer.

There are lots of examples of this type, but I think you've got the point. The psychology, I hope, is reasonably clear of how a dead or nonexistent father could lay an emotional basis for atheism. If our own father is absent or weak or abandons us, even by dying, or is so untrustworthy as to desert us, or is so terrible as to abuse and to deceive us in various ways, it's not hard to put the same attributes on our heavenly Father and reject God.

I recently heard the same thing about somebody else, the author of *Star Trek*, Gene Roddenberry. He had a fundamentalist father—a very bad, very hostile, very harmful one. Scripture is filled with admonitions about the sins of the fathers being carried by the later generations;

it doesn't say anything about the sins of the mothers, just the fathers.

Here's another example of how atheism might take place. This doesn't explain it at all, but it gives a sense of its psychology. This is taken from the autobiography of *New York Times* writer Russell Baker, who was usually on the editorial page with a humor column. In his autobiography, he writes that his father was taken to the hospital and died there very suddenly, when Russell was five years old. He wept in sorrow, then spoke to the family housekeeper Bessie:

> For the first time I thought seriously about God. Between sobs I told Bessie that if God could do things like this to people, then God was hateful and I had no more use for him. Bessie told me about the peace of heaven and the joy of being among the angels and the happiness of my father who was already there. The argument failed to quiet my rage. "God loves us just like his own children," Bessie said. If God loves me, why did he make my father die? Bessie said that I would understand some day, but she was only partly right. That afternoon, though I couldn't have phrased it this way then, I decided that God was a lot less interested in people than anybody in Morrisonville was willing to admit. That day I decided that God was not to be trusted. After that, I never cried again with any real conviction, nor expected much of anyone's God, except indifference, nor loved deeply without fear that it would cost me dearly in pain. At the age of five I had become a skeptic.[1]

Let me conclude by noting that however prevalent the superficial motives are for being an atheist, there still remain, in many instances, the deep and disturbing psychological sources as well. However easy it may be to state the hypothesis of "the defective father," we must not forget the difficultly, the pain and the complexity that lie behind each individual case. For those whose atheism has been conditioned by a father who rejected, denied, hated, manipulated or physically or sexually abused them, there must be understanding. Certainly, for a child to be forced to hate his or her own father or even to despair because of the father's weakness is a great tragedy. After all, the child only wants to love his or her father and to have a father who loves back.

For any unbeliever whose atheism is grounded in such painful experience, the believer blessed by God's love should pray most especially that ultimately they both meet in heaven. If so, perhaps the former atheist will experience even more joy than the believer. For the atheist will have that extra increment that comes from the surprise at finding him- or herself in, of all places, our Father's house.

Q&A

Questioner 1. Dr. Vitz, I would like to say that as an atheist, I have enjoyed your presentation very much. And I would also like to say that your theory fits me to a "T" in terms of my own background, having been abandoned by my father when I was about a year old, and searching all of my life for a father figure. I've very consciously recognized the psychological component in my own atheism, but I'm wondering, wanting to keep the lines of communication open between atheists and theists, I'm wondering what your recommendation might be to a person in my position who recognizes in fact that psychological explanations are important. A very important component. Where would you, as a believer, recommend that I go from here?

Vitz. Be the father to other people that you never had.

Questioner 1. I accept that answer. I think that's a good one.

Vitz. You may already be doing it. So, keep on.

8

NIETZSCHE VERSUS JESUS CHRIST

Dallas Willard

The Veritas Forum at Stanford University, 2002

TONIGHT, I'M GOING TO TALK about some things that have come to a head in our time. I've used the names of Friedrich Nietzsche and Jesus Christ to try to represent that. I really want to emphasize that I'm not here tonight to attack Nietzsche, or for that matter, Jesus Christ, but rather to try to give them voice as it concerns fundamental matters for the contemporary world.

It's not easy to think about Nietzsche. And it's not easy to think about Jesus Christ. It's amazing how names and personalities and concepts become encrusted so that sometimes the very thing that they were concerned to get at is lost. But this evening we're going to try to put a sympathetic face on both Nietzsche and Christ and try to hear what they had to say.

NIETZSCHE CATCHES A WAVE

So let's begin with Nietzsche. Nietzsche has become very important on the campus and in our culture today because he has come to stand for something that was coming to a head in his own day, though he himself did not see much of the success that was to come to him later. He has become successful in culture generally only after World War II. The views that Nietzsche expresses are not particularly his own. He was not a driving force in culture then, nor is he today, but rather a symbol of something much deeper than himself.

Nietzsche, we might say in California language, "caught a wave." And that wave was the reaction of the world of art and intellect against something that we can only loosely call Christian culture. And Nietzsche experienced it deeply, not only in his own family life but as he prepared himself as a young scholar and then later as he became a member of the faculty at the University of Basel. At that time there was a great wave of reaction against the power of a Christian ideology that was without real spiritual vitality. That perhaps came most clearly to a head in England in the form of the controversy over allegiance to Thirty-Nine Articles of the Church of England, to which people had to swear fealty if they were to be a faculty member at Oxford or at Cambridge.

> *Nietzsche, we might say in California language, "caught a wave." And that wave was the reaction of the world of art and intellect against something that we can only loosely call Christian culture.*

The institutions of Christian society and government were to a large degree not based on what they professed—the reality of God. Everyone said, as we say on our coins today, "in God we trust." But it was clear that they did *not* trust in God. They trusted in their own abilities, in their capacity to form cliques and power groups and move in ways they wanted to, often about very trivial matters. And Nietzsche saw that.

The culture professed to live for a love of God and a neighbor. It's very hard for us today to recapture the extent to which the discourse of the university, up and well into this century—not only in Germany and France, but here and in England—was so explicitly and thoroughly Christian. It's difficult for us to capture that now, but that's the way it was, and Nietzsche looked at it and saw the irrelevance of God to what was actually being done to knowledge, to morality, to academic and cultural life. It was really his revulsion against a system of hypocrisy, even hypocrisy about inquiry and truth, that dominated his development.

He was, I think, the youngest man who had been appointed to a professorship such as he held, but within a few years he resigned. He gave as his reason health. But Walter Kaufmann and others who have studied this are quite sure that health was not the reason. Rather it was a revulsion against a system—a social system that he simply could not bring himself to be a part of.

Knowledge in this period was more and more divorced from theology, the church and God. There is a very interesting story about Noah Porter, the president of Yale in the 1880s, and William Graham Sumner. Sumner decided to use a book by Herbert Spencer in his course on sociology that had absolutely nothing to say about God. Porter read the book (presidents in those days read the texts) and went to Sumner and asked him why the book didn't mention God. Here's the reply Sumner gave, and it's deeply revelatory of the deep structure of academic life at the time and the change that was coming, "The reason that the book has nothing to say about God is because God has nothing to do with the subject matter."

Take a moment and think about that phrase. I suspect it doesn't sound shocking today. But that's because we are now acclimated to the idea that we can be the best educated and best informed person in the world and know nothing about God. I suspect that many of us resist the idea that God has any relevance to the subject matter. But up until this period of change, it was simply assumed, as the medievals said, "Theology is the queen of the sciences." Those of us who have read Descartes's *Meditations* know how he also says we can't know anything until we know God, because the only way we could possibly know that even our clear and distinct ideas are true is if God guaranteed them. This was the assumption.

Nietzsche recognizes that this change has happened and that people are not being honest about it. This is the meaning of his famous phrase that "God is dead." Nietzsche was not declaring that he had killed God or proven that God was dead. He was saying rather that as far as our culture goes, if God were dead, it wouldn't make any difference.

NIETZSCHE AND CONSTRUCTIONISM

Nietzsche stands for a certain representation of academic life and knowledge that came out of that period, and now in our campuses and in our culture it is almost automatically assumed by many. And that view of knowledge I shall call *constructionism*. It is the view that the world as we know it is a construction of the human mind, of language, of social structures. And the identities and terms in which we think and live are products of certain processes of living; they have a history. We count things as the same or different, we classify them in the way they do, because it enables us to realize our purposes.

Nietzsche was not declaring that he had killed God or proven that God was dead. He was saying rather that as far as our culture goes, if God were dead, it wouldn't make any difference.

Nietzsche thought that this was also an oppressive thing, and we're very familiar with that today, aren't we? The idea that the constructions that are formed are then oppressive to individuals. And the lines that are drawn between things give expression not to truth but to power.

Once we abandon the capacity of the mind to grasp a real world (which is what was really coming to a head with Nietzsche, though it had been developing for a couple of centuries, even from the time of Descartes), then what is to determine how the mind organizes its world and its life? Power.

There is just a show of appearances, and we rearrange them and rearrange them in terms of our will. And so for Nietzsche the will to power becomes the ultimate principle of everything, including the academic and, of course, the spiritual, ecclesiastical, historical, government or whatever else. I will read one or two lines from Nietzsche's *The Genealogy of Morals, Essay Three*. It's in section seven:

> In every animal, including the philosophical beast [which is his name for human beings], strives instinctively for the optimal conditions under which it may release its power. Every animal instinctively and with a

subtle flair that leaves reason far behind abhors all interference that might conceivably block its path to this optimum. [And he says in parentheses] The path I am speaking of does not lead to happiness but to power.

This is very crucial for Nietzsche. He called the form of ethics that was most prominent in England, namely hedonistic utilitarianism, "a pig's philosophy." Happiness is not what life is about, power is. Now this is his general theory: The path that we're leading to, for anyone, is simply realizing our power. Anything we do is simply a manifestation of that same instinctual drive. And this is what he calls "the will to power." What people want is the exercise and the use of their power; everything else they do, whether they call it "truth" or "holiness" or whatever, is actually an expression of this drive for power.

Out of that, then, comes *constructionism*, which is merely an exercise in constructing a world that will be suited to the use of our power. Nietzsche has a whole account of how the Judeo-Christian ethic became dominant. It was a power play on the part of weak people who were resentful and clever enough to dupe the strong people into thinking that they were wicked because they were strong, and that actually, people are better if they're weak. And so, "blessed are the poor," "blessed are they that mourn," they'd say. No, says Nietzsche, blessed are the strong. The "slave morality" of the Bible, as he called it, is simply a clever device of the exercise of power. Nietzsche recognized among the ascetics, the monks of the Christian tradition, some of the greatest exercises of the will to power, because to forgo life and to pledge oneself to poverty and to obedience and to celibacy exercised a great will to power.

You may sense that's a very contrived explanation, but you see, once we have accepted the view that the mind is not capable of grasping a reality that exists independently of itself—and that is what came through the history before Nietzsche—then there is nothing left but some sort of internal principle to try to explain why we think and live as we do. So, cognitive constructivism and moral and social constructivism are perhaps a way of answering the question.

NIETZSCHE AND PHENOMENALISM

The version of the mind that Nietzsche accepts is actually what we call *phenomenalism*, which is a way of saying that all there is that we can grasp consists of appearances. Nietzsche likes to use the word *perspective*, saying that all we have are perspectives and that there isn't anything more to "reality" than the will to organize them in a certain way.

Those who have read David Hume, and perhaps John Stuart Mill, Ernst Mach, A. J. Ayer or Nelson Goodman, will recognize Nietzsche's position. So then, all that is left is the perfection of the individual will. That means life lived with a will at its greatest strength, its most intense integration of self-aggrandizement. Only that gives a point to life. Some of Nietzsche's most characteristic sayings are derived from that.

For example, he says, "Build your house under the volcano." Think about that, now. That would do something for your will, wouldn't it?

But that sort of defiance of the individual will against the whole world, and finding in the individual will the only value, does not make Nietzsche a nihilist, as he is often called. He had a very healthy form of values. It was all tied to this idea that the degree to which one succeeds in bringing the whole of the individual life under the will is the degree to which one is a healthy person. We may recognize in this things that are similar to writers such as Søren Kierkegaard, Fyodor Dostoevsky or others in the nineteenth century. Indeed, the nineteenth century was a period in which, along with the growth of science and technology—though it doesn't look like much perhaps compared to what we have today—was an increasing sense of the loss of individuality.

In reaction, then, people said, "I will defy the whole world. I will defy causal law." Dostoevsky says in *The Underground Man*, "What are the laws of arithmetic to me?" If all you know are these general truths, and your will is shriveled, then you're nothing. This is a general tendency that comes out of constructionism, which locks the mind into its own little world and leaves the will with nowhere to go except to turn back on itself and find fulfillment in its own self-assertion.

Do I need to tell you that Nietzsche won? Watch where the focus is when you watch commercials on television. It will be almost 100 percent on the realization of self-will. How, if you will buy this kind of car or that kind of smell-good or whatever, you will be unique—along with several million other people.

Nietzsche leaves us in a position where, for example, in a university setting, about the only thing that we can appeal to in recommending our university is the degree of personal success someone may have if he or she studies with us. A few remarks may be made about community. Almost nothing will be said about family. But a lot will be said about individual creativity and the capacity to exercise judgments that will be valued, and how people will pay a graduate a lot of money to work for them. That's a natural outcome of the picture of the enclosed mind and the will turned back on itself that naturally comes out of Nietzsche.

Nietzsche leaves us in a position where, for example, in a university setting, about the only thing that we can appeal to in recommending our university is the degree of personal success someone may have if he or she studies with us.

I don't want to dump on Nietzsche. He was not so much an instigator as a person who expressed what had already come to realization in his culture. He was ahead of his day, so he was regarded as dangerous or loony for a long while. But he really comes into his own, especially after World War I because the first and second world wars were a revelation of a culture which Nietzsche had already decided was hopeless. And his insight into that is something that we really do need to treasure.

NIETZSCHE AND MODERNISM

So, what we see in Nietzsche is a natural outworking of what we've come to know as *modernism*. Now, modernism stands above all. It's a very complicated concept, and please forgive me for being overly simple-minded, but I will put it this way: *modernism comes to stand for the rejection of the past as a guide to the present.*

Once it is clear that knowledge cannot find a basis in the individual consciousness—and that is the outcome of philosophy from Descartes to Nietzsche—we've gotten rid of the past. At least we've called it so seriously into question that it can no longer be used as a guide. We could spend a lot of time talking about how that happened, especially in relationship to the church, to the Bible, to the history of both the Jews and the Christians, and how history was lost and the modern philosophers tried to regenerate morality on the basis of eternal truths found by mere thinking. That is what modernism tried to do.

Modernism tried to get rid of the religion of the past with all of its history because that was divisive. This is so relevant to today. It was thought that the way around the divisiveness is to recognize that if we would just set the history aside and instead think about the moral truths history was supposed to illustrate in one way or another, then there would no longer be divisiveness. Of course, one of the issues that gave rise to modernism was an attempt to get out of the religious wars and strife of Europe.

So, we just have these moral truths that come up now. But then, once we begin to examine the mind and find that all we've got is our mind, then we begin to ask the question, where do these universal truths come from? How can we say we have universals when we can't even escape our own mind? Right?

Descartes didn't succeed with the project of universal knowledge, except to his own satisfaction, and that's one of the occupational hazards of philosophers—to be satisfied with their own line of reasoning, when almost no one else is. And so, through a period of time from Kant to Hegel and Schopenhauer, and then to Marx and Nietzsche, and then beyond that to Freud and others, the whole idea of "truths" upon which we could base our life was disappearing.

Through a period of time from Kant to Hegel and Schopenhauer, and then to Marx and Nietzsche, and then beyond that to Freud and others, the whole idea of "truths" upon which we could base our life was disappearing.

What then is left? Individual will. As Alasdair MacIntyre has portrayed so very well in his writings, especially a book called *Whose Justice? Which Rationality?* all of a sudden the basis of practical reason is shifted to the point that mere individual desire is a reason for doing what we want.

What then is left? Individual will.

I pause over that statement again because we're apt to say, "Well, what else?"

See, that's how thoroughly we have been formed by this. It's mere individual desire that's thought to serve as a basis for action. This was not so until this period of modern thought where we have this artifact of the individual on his or her own.

NIETZSCHE AND TRUTH

Nietzsche saw how this was working itself out. And he then went so far as to say it isn't just a matter of religion. Our philosophers themselves are actually fooling themselves when they talk about truth. And he used words like *anti-Christ, skeptic, nihilist* and so on to characterize the people who went about destroying beliefs in the name of truth.

And then he says, "What about these people themselves? What about these earnest scholars, philosophers, scientists of today?"

He says, "Well, it is they. *These* are the ones. The professors, the writers, the scientists—*they* represent the ascetic ideal today. It's not monks, it's not preachers, it's not holy books. They are the ones who deny themselves for the sake of truth."

"Ah," he says, "but these men too are a long way from being free spirits because they still *believe in truth.*"

Interesting. "They still believe in truth." But Nietzsche said they don't actually *act* that way because what they're pursuing is *really* their own self-will. And they use references to truth to hide that, to keep us from seeing what's really going on. (One of Nietzsche's favorite words for himself was *psychologist.*) He said, "When we really come to understand what they're doing, we see nothing but unvarnished will to power again."

Truth, then, simply becomes another passion. It too is no longer something that we can look at as a way of guiding ourselves, because it's just an expression of our self-will. And the twentieth century joins Nietzsche in affirming that "truth is nothing." We put the word in Latin here, *Veritas*, and it's much more dignified in that way. But if you say "truth" in most places on the campuses I'm familiar with, people will immediately say, "Whose truth?"

And this is the deepest revelation of how thoroughly Nietzsche won the first round of this battle against Christian teaching, or against Christ, if you wish. (Though I hope you pick up from this discussion that what Nietzsche was criticizing may have had very little to do with Christ. But at least that's how it was represented.) Nietzsche won the first round and truth is lost. Any sort of universal is lost. Pragmatism, existentialism, positivism, linguistic constructionism, deconstruction and hermeneutics, and probably several other things that I could mention as currently important for our discussions on the campus, become ascendant. There was now no accessible body of moral knowledge, just people—including Nietzsche—yelling about issues.

> *Truth, then, simply becomes another passion. It too is no longer something that we can look at as a way of guiding ourselves, because it's just an expression of our self-will. And the twentieth century joins Nietzsche in affirming that: "Truth is nothing?"*

And I pause again to let you think about this. There is no accessible body of moral knowledge that currently functions in our culture. If someone wants to know many things in mathematics or history or physics, we know where to send them. If someone wants to know how to be a good person, where do we send them? Would we send them to Stanford for that purpose? I hope you won't send them to the University of Southern California for that purpose. We don't have a department for that, nor does any university.

I want that to soak in a moment.

This is where Nietzsche comes in, because if there is no available body of moral knowledge, then all that is left is will. All that is left is impulse. Really, after a while, nothing that can be called in a very serious sense "will" is left. But now, the process is over. We are through off-loading all of this burden of the past. Call it Christianity or whatever you want. But we've been through that.

Now, we can have battles over whether or not we will post the Ten Commandments in a courthouse or something of that sort. But it isn't about knowledge; it's about symbolism, on both sides. No one would dare to enforce them by grading. You could never grade a student on whether or not they thought the Ten Commandments were true. And that's just a way of saying we don't treat them as knowledge.

TRUTH AND ITS RELATIONSHIP TO FREEDOM

The heart of the issue between Nietzsche and Jesus Christ is truth: I'm not going to try to split all the hairs that have to do with Christianity; I'll just talk about Jesus Christ. I'd like to ask you to try to think of him as a serious person in the area of information.

See, that's the burden of human life: to find an adequate basis for human action in knowledge. We accept that naturally in our courses— I hope we do, anyway. (Though in fact, I can't be too sanguine about that because I often ask my students, "Did you believe what you wrote on the test?" They laugh. We are a culture where what is important is to know the "right" answers, not necessarily to believe them.) Still, I think we need to simply say that the heart of the issue between Nietzsche and Jesus Christ is truth and its relationship to human freedom, well-being and fulfillment. Since this is a major turning point and we're heading for

The heart of the issue between Nietzswche and Jesus Christ is truth, and its relation to human freedom, well-being and fulfillment.

home, I'm going to say that again: The heart of the issue between Nietzsche and Jesus Christ is truth, and its relation to human freedom, well-being and fulfillment.

So, "Thou shalt not steal." What does that have to do with freedom? The assumption of Nietzsche and the modern tradition he completes (and then represents more effectively perhaps than anyone else after World War II) is that we are closed off individually and

socially—by our language, our culture, our history or just our mind—
so that we cannot find our way out to an "other" that is reliably there,
that we haven't somehow created by our own thinking and feeling.
The inability to do that is what turns us back on the individual will.
It turns us back on ourselves, and our will is then the ultimate reality
in our life.

Freedom then means only "freedom from." Descartes, in his mind,
found that he was free from a world. But then, how does he get to that
world? The declaration of freedom that we make in a mind that is
closed off and lost in itself is actually an imprisonment of a kind. In the
modern attempt to deal with the mind and its grasp of the world, the
consequence is the increasing emphasis on freedom as merely "freedom
from." So we are condemned to our aloneness. Self-preoccupation is
our only possibility. And doing what we want is our only conception of
human fulfillment and well-being.

Here is how the prison works: someone says, "What shall I do?"
And we reply, "Do what you want."
And the honest person says, "I don't know what I want."

What do you want? What do you really want? See, that's how Nietzsche and freedom traps us, because now we don't know what we want,
and in this structure, because as living beings we have to act, desire as
a *reasonable* human capacity defaults into impulse. Curiously enough,
we wind up in a world where we desire to desire.

We have a Viagra society. What is Viagra about? It is about desiring
to desire. And addiction, in its many forms, is an attempt to escape the
loneliness that is enforced by a will uprooted from a world of truth and
reality.

FREEDOM AND INTENTIONALITY

Representing a different tradition than the boxed-in mind, I read a
word or two here from a man named T. H. Green, who was writing at
the end of the twentieth century.

> When we . . . speak of freedom, we should consider carefully what we
> mean by it. We do not mean merely freedom from restraint or compul-
> sion. [That's freedom *from*.] We do not mean merely freedom to do as

we like. [It's irrespective of what we like.] We do not mean a freedom that can be enjoyed by one man or one set of men at the cost of a loss of freedom to others. When we speak of freedom as something to be so highly prized, we mean a positive power or capacity of doing or enjoying something worth doing or enjoying, and that, too, something that we do or enjoy in common with others. We mean by it the power which each man exercises through the help and security given by his fellow men and which he, in turn, helps to secure for them.[1]

That's an entirely different conception of freedom than the one usually thought today. That's a freedom appropriate to a mind that has a world—that is open to a world.

There is another tradition about the mind that existed long before the modern period. It is represented in the Old and New Testaments, in Saint Augustine and Thomas Aquinas, and comes all the way up to the present. And yes, there are people today, in the twenty-first century who represent it, people like Emmanuel Levinas and Edmund Husserl and even Martin Heidegger. The primary word that is used here, for those of you who are into these things, is *intentionality*. Intentionality *refers to the openness of the mind to what is there.*

It's a mind that doesn't create a world, but which the world inhabits through intentionality, and of course, in the Christian tradition, that God inhabits. So God is always already there. That's the basic Augustinian teaching about the nature of the mind: the inner light. The inner teacher is God, and the light is interacting with the mind, enabling it to reach out to a world which God, and not the mind, created. And to find in that world, with others who are there, the proper support of a will that is capable of moving to genuine freedom.

So, if we want to see freedom, we don't look at a kid jumping around with nothing to do. We see freedom when we see an accomplished artist sit down at a piano and play something so beautiful that we can hardly stay in our seat. That's freedom. When Pavarotti steps up and does what he does, the incredible magic—that's freedom. Now how did he get there? He didn't get there by turning in on himself. He took the step that is always first in freedom, which is to submit himself to reality. That's the first step in freedom.

If we want to see freedom, we don't look at a kid jumping around with nothing to do. We see freedom when we see an accomplished artist sit down at a piano and play something so beautiful that we can hardly stay in our seat. That's freedom.

To do this, we need truth because truth is what guides us to reality. Reality is what we run into when we're wrong, I said. Now, truth can help us avoid those unpleasant occasions. In other words, truth enables us to represent how things are without running into them, as we submit our will to reality, through truth. I don't think we need to have a hard time understanding that; just think about ordinary life.

I'm not saying all truth is easy to grasp, but the basic idea of truth is very simple. A child picks it up immediately. If you don't believe it, promise a child something, and then don't do it. See, children know what truth is. They know what falsity is, and they know how important it is to try to manage reality by falsehood: You ask a child, "Did you do that?"

"No. He did it." [*pointing*]

See, that's trying to manage reality, but the important thing to understand is that the real world *is* there, and that is the tradition that has developed out of the ancient world and up into the present—until the theory of mind that says our mind actually gets in the way of knowing the world, and makes it impossible. *That* theory of mind, coming to a head in Nietzsche and others, set aside the access to truth that made freedom possible.

FREEDOM IN COMMUNITY

Now, we need more than truth for freedom. We need community.

And just a word or two about this because it's so very important. A little child who comes into this world, for example, has to bond with another person. The theory of bonding is one of the deepest and most important things that has come out of recent studies over the last decades. Children who are not able to step into a world that is already there simply cannot start, and they die. If you're not familiar with this literature, you might want to look up "bonding," because we depend on it for life.

When a child comes into the world, it has to step into life that is already going. And if it doesn't, it will not live. It's just that simple, and it isn't just a physical matter. What goes on when the child looks into the eyes of the mother and the mother into the eyes of the child? That is very deep in terms of what that child is. And then as that child grows, it has to trust the world, and it cannot trust the world unless it finds truth. So, human fulfillment comes through community in which there is trust and truth, and the will is enabled to grow so that it takes in what is not a part of itself and makes that a part of its life.

Think just for a moment about Jesus, not as a kind of sanctified religious figure but as someone who knew what he was talking about. Here he is, with his little community of students, or disciples, and he's telling them, "Now if you live in what I say, then you really are my apprentices and you will come to know the truth about life"—and here we mean the kingdom of God, the reality of the world, what community is, what love is and all of those things—"and you will know the truth, and the truth will set you free."

Now, go back very simply. Think about freedom as the capacity to live fully in the world. How do you do those things?

THE TEST OF FREEDOM AND TRUTH IN JESUS

So now, this is the rematch. The rematch between Jesus Christ and Nietzsche is in life. It's in *your* life. You are the heir of a Nietzschean culture, and I am too. We have a Nietzschean world. The question is whether we can find freedom in that world. And another world over here is presented by Jesus Christ. Think of him now for a moment as an intelligent person who would be very much at home on this campus and probably could teach us a thing or two. He says, "If you put my teachings into practice, then you will be my apprentices and I'll be your teacher. And you will come to know the truth about life, and the world. And in knowing that truth, you will find genuine fulfillment as the human being you were meant to be."

That's the rematch. It isn't something that can be argued abstractly or proven by words alone. It has to be put into practice. That's the test.

I don't need to tell you what the outcome will be. No one has yet managed to find fulfillment in the way that Nietzsche recommended.

You are the heir of a Nietzschean culture, and I am too. We have a Nietzschean world. The question is whether we can find freedom in that world.

Nietzsche himself did not find it in that way. And I don't say that to dump on Nietzsche. I'm very sympathetic of Nietzsche. In fact, Nietzsche is one of the people that brought me into philosophy, because of the incisiveness with which he addressed real issues in life. And we need to be as incisive as he was. But we need *not* to be under the false assumptions about the nature of the mind and the will that he was under. And I believe the way we can escape that is to take the teachings of Jesus about life and—as critically, as skeptically as you wish—put them into practice and test them.

And if the test of life shows that Jesus wins the second round, then that's no shame on Nietzsche. That's our opportunity.

9

MORAL MAMMALS

DOES ATHEISM OR THEISM PROVIDE THE BEST FOUNDATION FOR HUMAN WORTH AND MORALITY?

Peter Singer and *John Hare*, *with moderator Eric Gregory*
The Veritas Forum at Massachusetts Institute of Technology, 2009

PETER SINGER

THANK YOU, ALL OF YOU, and thanks to The Veritas Forum for this invitation, and also for what you're trying to do to get these deep and important issues raised in a setting which encourages skepticism and discussion, but which I hope will lead to a serious and not overly polemical consideration of the issues.

Let's begin with a question that Dostoevsky famously raised: Is it the case that if there is no God, everything is permitted?

Why would any of us think that that is the case? For example, with some of the atrocities that we have seen committed around the world in recent years, most recently, the terrorists attacks in Mumbai or, before that, 9/11 or the genocide in Darfur or the Nazi Holocaust—why would we think that whether or not those things are permitted depends on our belief in a being who created the universe and has various other characteristics that we traditionally attribute to God?

Well, I suppose one reason, you might say, is this: If there isn't a God, then who is there to prohibit them? Or, for that matter, to permit them?

Someone might reply: "There's international law. We have international laws against genocide." But of course we're talking about morality today, we're not talking about law. So I think we should set that aside.

If you're a theist, perhaps, you can say these acts are prohibited by God. And it's true that if you're an atheist, you cannot say that. But the fact that a theist can say these acts are prohibited by God doesn't make it true that they *are* prohibited by God. If there is no God, then obviously that statement can't be true.

SUFFERING AND ATHEISM

It's not really our topic, but let me just take thirty seconds to say that I don't believe there is a God. I certainly don't believe that there is a God who meets the attributes traditionally given by Christians to God: omnipotent, omniscient and omnibenevolent. As I view the world, there is an immense amount of suffering in it, and some of that suffering is, I think, impossible to reconcile with Christian traditional views. A good, all-powerful being would not allow it to happen.

Some Christians may respond that human beings have free will, and therefore God must allow humans to inflict suffering on other humans. But that doesn't explain all the suffering in the world, because there is suffering caused by things that have nothing to do with human free will, such as drought or floods or fires caused by lightning strikes.

And even if you were prepared to say that you follow the Christian tradition that humans suffer because they bear the sin of Adam, and Adam or Eve's defiance of God (which I think is a morally horrible doctrine—that we should suffer because of what was done by our ancestors a long time ago), it's still impossible to explain why nonhuman animals, who are not Adam's descendants, should suffer. And yet they do suffer. I think it's obvious that they suffer. Descartes denied that they suffer, and actually his denial of their suffering was in part to avoid this very problem of evil that I'm talking about. But there are very few people who agree with Descartes now.

So animals do suffer, and some of their suffering is not at the hands of humans with free will but is caused by the fact that, for example, there's a drought. Right now where I come from, in Australia, there is a drought, and kangaroos die painfully of thirst because the water holes on which they depend dry up. This is neither something that you could attribute to human free will nor to inheriting Adam's sin, and I can't understand how an all-powerful and all-good and all-knowing God could possibly have created a world in which that exists.

That's why it seems to me that there is no such God, and that's why these questions are very real ones. And although it may be true that the theist can claim that without belief in God, we can't say that these acts are wrong because God prohibited them, nevertheless, it seems to me that given the way the world is, we have to accept that and understand the phenomenon of morality as best we can in a world without God.

Does this mean, though, if I say there is no God, that the atheist can't say that some of the acts I have mentioned are morally wrong? Well, let's ask again why anyone would want to say that—why anyone would want to say that if there is no God you can't say that some things are morally wrong. I prefer *morally wrong* to *prohibited*, because prohibited does have this notion of laws and a lawgiver, and that, perhaps, doesn't work well without a belief in God.

ARGUMENTS AGAINST GOD AS BASIS FOR MORALITY

But why would anyone think that you can't say acts are morally wrong without the existence of God? I'm going to mention three distinct reasons, three distinct grounds why some theists have suggested we can't say this.

1. Right and wrong are arbitrary. The first claim is that the terms *right* and *wrong* are meaningless unless you believe in the existence of God. They're said to be meaningless because something is right only because God wills it or commands it, and wrong only because it's contrary to his will. So the very meaning of the moral terms, some theists say, is bound up with the idea of a God who gives meaning to these terms by his commands.

The standard response to this is what is known as the Euthyphro argument, coming from Plato's dialogue of that name, and I must admit I'm a little tentative about discussing the Euthyphro with somebody who's written a commentary on it. I am certainly not a scholar of Plato or of the Euthyphro. So if I get some of the actual argument out of its context, I'm ready to stand corrected. But the important point of the argument seems to be this: if we say that right and wrong are meaningless without God, we have to say whether it's the case that something is right only because God wills it and wrong only because it's contrary to his will, and then this means that if God had willed something different, then different things would be right and wrong. So if God had willed us to torture babies, then it would be right for us to torture babies. And if God had willed us not to help the weak and vulnerable, then it would be wrong for us to help the weak and vulnerable.

> *If we say that right and wrong are meaningless without God, we have to say whether it's the case that something is right only because God wills it and wrong only because it's contrary to his will, and then this means that if God had willed something different, then different things would be right and wrong.*

We might say, of course, that God is the God of love, and God could not have willed that we torture babies and don't help the weak and vulnerable, but to say that suggests that we already have a notion of what is good. Perhaps we're saying that love is good and that the loving act is a good act to perform, but then this claim—that love is good—is independent of what God wills.

So this is the dilemma that we face: either there is no notion of right and wrong independent of God, and God could have willed us to do things differently, and they would then have been right or wrong, or God wills these things because they are good, but then we have to have the idea that there is some notion of good independent of God.

Thus, it doesn't seem to me that we can say the very terms *good* and *bad* are meaningless without God, at least not unless we're prepared to bite the bullet on this claim that God really was making an arbitrary decision in choosing to command us to help the weak and vulnerable, rather than in choosing to command us to kick them when they're down. So I find it impossible to accept that claim.

2. Knowing right and wrong. The theist might now say: "Okay, so let's admit that the terms *right* and *wrong* would have some meaning, even in an atheist universe. We could understand what they mean, we could talk about what was right and wrong, in some sense, but we wouldn't really *know* what was right and wrong without God's guidance shown through revelation—for the Christians this is shown through the Gospels and to some extent the Hebrew Scriptures. That's what tells us what is right and wrong."

But in fact if we look at what Christians actually do when they develop a Christian morality, they certainly don't simply take everything that is in the Gospels as the source of morality. There are many things Christians don't take very seriously. I've just written a book about what our obligations are with regard to world poverty. If you were to ask, What is the single most emphasized aspect of the teaching of Jesus as portrayed in the Gospels? the answer would have to be: To help the poor. That's constantly emphasized in the Scriptures, and yet it seems clearly not to be well-followed. Christian churches in this country generally do not say that if you're rich and have a lot of possessions you are not being a good person. They've not really emphasized giving to the poor—some of them do a reasonably good job of that, and others do a much less good job of it.

If we look at what Christians actually do when they develop a Christian morality, they certainly don't simply take everything that is in the Gospels as the source of morality. There are many things Christians don't take very seriously.

They're much more likely to emphasize as distinctively Christian morality things that are not really in the Gospels. Jesus says, for example, nothing about abortion or homosexuality, although opposition to those seems to be a central part of what is considered Christian morality in the United States. Jesus did condemn divorce very clearly, except perhaps in the case of adultery. Again, most Christian churches accept divorce even in circumstances other than adultery.

Some people might say, "Well, the remarks about homosexuality are not in the New Testament but in the Old Testament, and some remarks about abortion can be found there as well." But if we start to appeal to the Old Testament, we get into a real morass of injunctions of various kinds, including the idea that eating shrimp is an abomination to God, something that Orthodox Jews take seriously, but Christians generally don't. Or take a look at Numbers 31: God here explicitly commands the Israelites to commit genocide. And they do. That's in accordance with God's command as portrayed in the Old Testament. Not something, I think, that we want to take as a moral lesson.

If we were to take the Scriptures as our chief source of knowledge about what's right or wrong, we would be acting very differently from what we do. It's hard to know exactly how we would act, but clearly what thoughtful Christians are doing is using their reasoning and intelligence to select from this mass of different injunctions some that they can endorse. Sometimes they reject them because they're uncomfortable, such as the injunction to the rich man to give all he has to the poor, and sometimes they reject them because they just seem wrong or unimportant.

So I don't think that we can use the argument that we need religion to work out what is right or wrong, because even theists are already using their own judgment to do that.

3. Motivation for moral behavior. The third claim that I want to consider is that even though the terms *right* and *wrong* make sense without God, and even though we can use our intelligence and discernment to work out what is right and wrong, nevertheless, without God we wouldn't do it. God provides the motivation for us to do this. In the traditional Christian view, of course, this motivation is linked with immortality: the idea of reward or punishment in an afterlife. It's an explicitly self-interested motivation.

Some people don't like this. Some people think that, in fact, the motivation that religion brings should not be as nakedly self-interested as the one we get in the Gospels, where rewards and punishment in the afterlife are repeatedly emphasized. These theists prefer to regard the example of Jesus as a kind of inspiration to living a good life. But I think we can follow various examples as inspirational. We don't need to regard Jesus as divine to be inspired by him. There are many other morally virtuous people throughout the world, some of whom have been religious and some not. For example, we might be inspired by what Bill Gates is trying to do to reduce poverty in the world today—certainly a pioneering example, at least in the modern era, followed by Warren Buffett. Neither Gates nor Buffett is religious.

So it seems clear that we have many examples of ethical behavior among people who are not religious. It's also very clear that we have many examples of unethical behavior among people who are religious. We've have had a lot of them recently, a lot of scandals in various churches of various kinds among those who are religious. We all know about them. There doesn't seem to be any strong correlation between people being religious and people acting ethically. According to an article by Gregory Paul in *The Journal of Religion and Society* (2005), when we look at things like murder rates, abortion rates, teenage pregnancy and suicide, and compare prosperous societies and grade them on whether they're religious or relatively secular, we don't find fewer of these things in the religious societies. In fact, the United States, which is more religious than almost any of the prosperous democracies in the world, also has high murder rates, high teenage pregnancies rates and so on. So it doesn't really seem that in practice we need religion as a motivation for us.

I've rejected three major reasons why we might want to relate religion to morality. But, we might say, it's still a bit of a mystery, isn't it? Where does morality come from? What is it, really?

AN EVOLUTIONARY EXPLANATION OF MORALITY

I take an evolutionary view of our origins. That seems to be well-grounded in the evidence. I think it's clear that we are social mammals. It's clear that both in humans and in some of those other social mammals to whom we are most closely connected, we can find the development in evolution of forms of social behavior, which are similar to some of our moral principles. We find practices of caring for one's kin and caring for offspring among social mammals, which we certainly regard as a moral obligation, for parents to care for their offspring. We also find reciprocity developing in other social mammals, practices of cooperation and of repaying cooperation with further cooperation, and conversely, repaying a failure to cooperate with some kind of penalty or some kind of negative behavior.

We find this in many social mammals. It is well-described in evolutionary psychology and in ethology. Research on other primates shows that they have basic notions of fairness, that for instance if they and another primate, another companion in the same area, are given similar tasks, and the other one gets a much better reward for doing the task, then the primate who gets the inferior reward is likely to become angry and reject it, much as human children will do.

So I think it's reasonable to say that a lot of our moral instincts come out of our evolution. That's not to say that they are therefore right. On the contrary, I think we can be critical of our evolved instincts, and sometimes we should be. But that's where they come from.

On top of that, we evolved a capacity to reason, a capacity to think. We evolved that, no doubt, because it has survival advantages in the conditions we were living in, but it also gives us capacities to see our place in the universe, to empathize with other beings in the universe and to ask questions like, What would I think if someone were to do that to me? That's a very basic question, which I think is important, in taking morality beyond the stage of those instincts that I was talking about, to something that we can talk about and reason about.

Because we have that capacity, we put ourselves in the position of others and get something that corresponds to what we know as the Golden Rule: Do unto others as we would have them do unto us. We may think of that as something coming out of a religious tradition, but in fact it's not specific to any religious tradition. We find it in a whole variety of developed cultures that have thought about ethics.

Some of those cultures are religious, as the Jewish, Christian and Islamic traditions are. Some of them are not, like the Confucian tradition, where we find versions of the Golden Rule too. Similarly with the Stoic tradition. I believe that this is something that we come to as a result of thinking about the world and thinking about our position in it, if we reflect enough on it. Within a religious culture it will be expressed religiously; within a secular culture it will be expressed in a secular way.

If we want to know if something's right or wrong, we ought to put ourselves in the position of all of those affected by our action and ask, Is this something that I would want to be done if I were in the position of all of those who are affected by our action?

So if we want to know if something's right or wrong, we ought to put ourselves in the position of all of those affected by our action and ask, Is this something that I would want to be done if I were in the position of all of those who are affected by our action? And if we can say yes to that —of course it's a very complicated question, especially when we're talking about different beings, some gaining, some losing, some of them human, some non-human animals—we have the best answer we can give to such questions as "what is right or wrong?" It's an answer that needs no reference to the idea of a God or a creator.

JOHN HARE

THE LAST TIME PETER SINGER and I talked together in public, it was at my father's memorial service, at the University Church in Oxford. And the family chose Peter because we thought that of all my father's students, he had done the most to keep alive my father's ethical theory of universal prescriptivism. I'm not saying that Peter has taken over the theory hook, line and sinker—he's modified it in certain ways, and I have too. But there's nonetheless a common ground between us here.

We're not going to talk about our disagreements about, let's say, the infanticide of defective newborns. We're going to talk about our disagreements about an initial choice that Peter Singer makes, I quote, "to treat ethics as entirely independent of religion." That's the question. Can we do that?

We're not going to disagree about the meaning of the term *good*. Roughly, good is what draws us and deserves to draw us. We're not going to disagree about whether atheists can "know" the good. I think God's revealed enough about good and bad to every human being so that every human being can be held accountable. I'm also not going to say that atheists can't be morally good. I think there are atheists whose moral lives put the lives of many theists to shame, and I think Peter Singer might be one of those people.

But I am going to disagree about motivation and justification. So I'm going to make three points: the third point is about justification. The question is, Why should I take the moral demand as a demand upon me? The second point is about motivation. Motivation is what actually gets us to lead a morally good life. And the first point will be about the governance of the world, or of the universe.

1. GOVERNANCE OF THE UNIVERSE: MORALITY AND HAPPINESS

God has organized the world in such a way that our morality and our happiness can be consistent with each other. The problem here, as I see it, is that morality is so demanding. Morality requires at least that every human need should count equally, morally, wherever it occurs.

> *God has organized the world in such a way that our morality and our happiness can be consistent with each other.*

And that makes it very difficult, for example, to go to a movie, especially if you consider that at this very moment there are thousands of people in the world dying of starvation. I'm a Christian, so I think of it this way: Jesus said, "just as you did it to one of the least of these who are members of my family, you did it to me." So we could ask: Which would Jesus prefer? That I go to the movie or that the life be saved? That makes the moral life very difficult. If I'm concerned only with my happiness, then I'll go to the movie. I'll take a nice vacation. I'll buy the down jacket. How can I trust that the moral life and my happiness can be consistent with each other, so that I don't have to do what's morally wrong in order to be happy?

If I don't have that trust, then the commitment to the moral life becomes rationally unstable, because our experience of the world is one in which those two good things, morality and happiness, come apart. The most that we can justify by enlightened self-interest is being fairly good—at least, when other people are looking. But morality requires unconditional commitment to the impartial point of view, or the point of view of the universe.

Some philosophers react to this difficulty by reducing the moral demand, to make it easier. But Peter Singer is admirable, both in his writing and in his living, in that he does not do that. He's a utilitarian, that is, roughly, somebody who believes that the right action is the one that produces the greatest happiness for the greatest number.

Sidgwick's utilitarian solution. The greatest utilitarian was Henry Sidgwick. The argument I've just been making is from Henry Sidgwick. He says there are two basic principles that reason gives us: (1) egoism, that is, to produce as much happiness as possible for me, and (2) the utilitarian principle, which says, I should do this for every sentient being. But these two principles are in tension with each other.

He proposed two solutions, only one of which he thought worked. One solution—the one that doesn't work—is to bring in psychology, that is, our sympathetic pleasures, so that we get happy when we see other people happy. Sidgwick said that the problem with this is it's limited in its scope, because we care most about the people who are closest to us, our friends and our family. The problem is if we just take sympathetic pleasures into account, all our caring will end up being used up by our friends and family.

So Sidgwick said the other solution is to bring in God. God—who cares both about our morality, or moral lives, and about our happiness—cares about the happiness of every sentient being, and he holds us accountable to that standard. Sidgwick said, "That is indispensable to the systematic coherence of our beliefs." John Stuart Mill said very much the same thing (I'm quoting now from his *Three Essays on Reli-*

gion): "Hope about the governance of the universe and [life] after death is . . . philosophically defensible. [Without this hope,] we're kept down by a sense of the insignificance of human life—by the disastrous feeling of 'not worth while.'"

He meant here, the moral life would not be worthwhile. The same thing can be found in my father's work, who talks about the governance of the universe, about people like Hitler coming to a bad end. He quotes from Psalm 75:3, where God says, in the translation from the Book of Common Prayer which my father loved, "The earth is weak and all the inhabiters thereof; I bear up the pillars of it."

So this is a basic trust in the governance of the universe that I'm talking about, that the good is more fundamental in it than the evil, and that good will, in the end, prevail. As Martin Luther King Jr. said: "I still believe that one day humankind will bow before the altars of God and be crowned triumphant over war and bloodshed. We shall overcome."

The problem of evil. Peter Singer brings up evil, as he should. If good is so fundamental to the world, why is there so much evil? Why would a good God allow it? One possibility is there are good gods and bad gods fighting it out. But for three thousand years the monotheist religions, who believe in one God, have found ways to come to terms with the agonizing evil in their own experience. In fact, much of great religious art and literature has come out of this tension.

When I was writing about this last, I met with a woman called Eva, who had been in the concentration camps of World War II. She said that her experience was that those people who went into the camps with a strong faith came out, if they did come out, with their faith stronger than when they went in. Elie Wiesel, even though he has no answer to the problem of evil, says he became closer to God through his protest. We're tempted to say, looking at the Holocaust, "A good God couldn't allow that." But then, we need to take seriously and respectfully the witness of those people who were in those experiences, and in those experiences they found God.

We can say, also, the Holocaust is chosen by humans, not God, and God respects our human freedom even to do the most terrible things.

What about tsunamis or droughts, says Peter, not caused by humans. Tsunamis are caused by, I suppose, shifts in tectonic plates, and those are part of the regulation of the temperature of the earth, which is one of the characteristics necessary for life. Lions and antelopes—when they meet, the antelopes get eaten. But I think natural selection, though bloody, is also, to a surprising extent, cooperative. We should think of evolution as God's instrument.

But the truth is, I often don't know what God's reason is for allowing something. And rather than discussing those sorts of arguments that I've just mentioned, I want to suggest a different one. This is one particularly appropriate for somebody like Peter Singer and myself also— people who believe in the rationality of morality, because it's not just any evil that God couldn't have a reason for. We can imagine even humans having a reason to allow some evil. But how much evil would there have to be for us to say God couldn't possibly have a reason to allow *that*. In particular, it would, I think, have to be so great that morality would no longer be rational for us limited beings to pursue.

Suppose it was the case, for example, that whenever we tried to do good, what resulted was harm. That would be, I think, enough evil for us to say, "Probably the world is not run by a good God but by some evil demon who wants to make our moral lives absurd." Indeed, some philosophers do think our moral lives are absurd. Some of the existentialists thought that. But Peter Singer and I both think our moral lives are rational. So anyway, that's my first point about the governance of the universe.

2. MORAL MOTIVATION

My second point is about moral motivation. I think more of us will accept the claims of all sentient life upon us if we care about all sentient life. I don't mean just feelings of sympathy but the recognition of value. There are various ways this can go, for those who believe in God. God has told us not to take innocent human life and to be stewards of creation. And we want to obey out of gratitude for our own creation. Or we want to please God and receive God's "well done." That's how Immanuel Kant, the philosopher, thought that it went. He said, "Morality has universal validity, and as such, it must please the Supreme Being, and this constitutes the strongest motive force." Being motivated by wanting to please God because we love God is not the same as self-interestedly wanting to get into heaven or being afraid of hell. Or it might be we want to be like Jesus, a model for human life, who died for others, and cared for the marginalized in society. Or if we love God, we will want to love what is like God, what is in the image of God. In particular, we should value, morally, the capacity to value things morally.

It's an empirical question whether animals other than humans have this capacity to live morally. In my own reading of the literature I think that we can find kin selection, various forms of tit for tat, but we don't find in nonhuman animals this taking of the position of the universe, this completely impartial point of view, which both Peter Singer and I think is constitutive of the full moral point of view.

Religious belief has the power to change people's lives. For example, the rate of recidivism (of returning to prison after they leave) is changed for those who are strongly involved in religious programs while in prison. In twelve-step programs, religious belief has the power over addiction. There's an inverse correlation between people who take part in religious activities and are involved in religious networks and criminality—criminal behavior. People who are strongly religious give more; they're more generous.

Peter says to compare the United States with, say, Sweden, or some less-religious prosperous country. That seems to me the wrong comparison because there are all sorts of differences between the United States and Sweden. The important question is whether in the United States and in Sweden those who are more religious behave differently than those who are less. I think there's an increasing consensus that the data suggest a positive impact in the answer to this question.

Why would we want to remove that power from people's lives, or spread skepticism about it? Especially for a utilitarian, a belief should be welcomed that makes people happy, unless it can be shown to be false or is itself productive of harm. Why can't Peter Singer accept religious believers who have the same goals as he does, many of them. Why can't he accept them as allies and welcome the additional motivation that their faith gives to them?

I have noticed, recently, he is starting to be more generous in his appreciation. And I think that is to be welcomed. That's a very good thing. I myself am pessimistic about the degree to which most of us are committed to our moral duty when we perceive this conflicts with our happiness. I agree with Peter Singer about the strenuousness of the moral demand. I think most of us have some sense of this, and we suppress it, because it's just too uncomfortable. This shows there's a gap between the moral demand on us and our natural inclination.

The Christian picture is that God can help us change those inclinations. I know that there are conspicuous Christians who have failed spectacularly. But there are utilitarians that fail spectacularly too. I don't think, given the evidence that I've just given you about, say, increased levels of generosity and so on, that we should cast off religion, tar it all with the same brush. We should welcome it.

It's true that religious motivation has also produced evil: flying airplanes into skyscrapers, or the Crusades. I don't want to minimize that. The desire to please God has produced great evil. But perhaps in the twentieth century, the greatest evils were from regimes like Hitler's or Stalin's or Mao's or Pol Pot's, which were outside the world's great religions; but I think it's hard to calculate that, so I don't want to put too much weight on it. The truth is, human regimes bent on their own power can use any ideology for evil purposes. Utilitarianism itself has been abused, for example, in inner city urban renewal after World War II, what Bernard Williams used to call "government house" utilitarianism.

The principle is that the corruption of the best is the worst, and we shouldn't hold that corruption to the account of what has been corrupted. We need ethical constraints on the use of any ideology, whether religious or not. For example, if we wake up in the middle of the night and we think God is telling us to kill our roommate, we should say to ourselves, *That isn't God telling me to do that.*

And I think that was the point of the story of Abraham and Isaac. That is, God wanted to show that it is not the divine will that we should demonstrate our devotion to God by killing our children. Roughly the same is true with the passages from the book of Numbers

that Peter talked about—the genocide passages. We're told later on by
the prophets that God does not want us to hold whole households accountable in this sort of way. And Jesus tells us we should not merely
not hate, but we should love our enemies. My neighbor, whom I should
love, includes my enemy.

Someone may object that if we use ethical principles as a constraint
on religion, then that shows all we really need is the ethical principle.
That's a mistake, because constraints do not produce original motivation. They function to limit the exercise of motivation. In the case of
the great religions, the constraints such as the Golden Rule are internal
to the faith, which they constrain.

3. JUSTIFICATION OF MORAL DEMANDS ON ME

I want to go on to my last point, about justification. Why should I take
the moral demand as a demand upon me? For example, why should I
reduce my standard of living in the face of the world's poverty? Some
people think you can deduce this from the nature of reason or reflection. Singer, I think, does not think that, because he says there's nothing irrational about preferring my own interest or the interest of
my family. Second, we could try deducing the justification of morality
from self-interest, but, as I've said before, I think self-interest only gets
us part of the way toward morality. It doesn't take us to the whole moral
demand.

Or third, we could try membership in the community. The community accepts moral standards, so, because we belong to the community
we should also. But the problem here is the community doesn't seem to
have the right kind of authority to justify the demand, since actual com-
munities are so often morally suspect. Fourth, we could try saying it's
just self-evident, like the principle "I should trust the evidence of my
senses." But I wake up in the morning, and I don't distrust my senses,
whereas I do sometimes reject my moral commitment; I turn over and
go back to sleep. It's not because I don't really understand that morality
is telling me to get up. I think the best bet for the nontheist is to say
there is *no* justification for morality. Morality is not justified by anything outside itself, it's just a primitive or an axiom or a starting point.

The problem is, if morality is just a primitive, that leaves us exposed, without anything to appeal to when our will is weak, when it would be good to have something more, because it's difficult to sustain the moral life without justification. Religion is so pervasive in human culture, it suggests that we need something more than just morality itself, because morality does not provide sufficient justification from its own resources. This need may even be hard-wired into us, although the evidence on that is not yet clear.

CONCLUSION

So now I will tie these three points together: If there is this justification, that God calls us to the moral life, then this relation to God can give us motivation, although the motivation question and the justification question are different. If we care about our relation to God, then we will care more about how God wants us to live. But if there is this relation between God and morality, then we can reconcile this care that we have for morality with the fact that we also care deeply about our own happiness. God cares both about our justice and what the Scriptures call "our peace," or in Hebrew, *shalom*—a state of complete well-being and delight. And this means we can have the hope that in the end, under the supervision of God's providence, morality and happiness come together, or as the psalm puts it, "justice and peace embrace."

> *Religion is so pervasive in human culture, it suggests that we need something more than just morality itself, because morality does not provide sufficient justification from its own resources.*

DIALOGUE

Moderator. The format now will be Professor Singer will have five minutes to respond, and then Professor Hare, and then we'll have a sort of Charlie Rose-style discussion sitting up here. Okay?

Singer. Well, it's very hard to respond to something as thoughtful and deep as John Hare's remarks in five minutes, so I'm not really going to attempt to go over all of those very significant points that were made.

Let me say that I do accept that there are problems caused by the fact that I cannot believe in what John called the "governance of the universe." As I see it, we cannot appeal to God in order to produce the reconciliation of morality and happiness.

I share John's view that Henry Sidgwick was the greatest of the utilitarians; in fact, I would think that his work *The Methods of Ethics* is quite possibly the finest treatise on ethics that has ever been written. It ends with this problem called the "dualism of practical reason," that it is self-evident that we have reason to pursue our own interests, and yet, also self-evident that we should take an impartial point of view from which we would give equal weight to all of the beings in the universe. Sidgwick sees no way of reconciling them, unless we accept this hypothesis of religious belief. Whether he does accept that hypothesis himself is something that Sidgwick scholars still discuss. Certainly, in *The Methods of Ethics* he doesn't clearly come down and say, "Therefore we should accept it." In fact, he's somewhat negative about the view that the existence of this dualism is itself a reason for believing in God. He says, rather, perhaps it's a reason for hoping that there is a God, but not a reason for believing in him.

Yes, it would be nice if we could be sure that there is that harmony between morality and happiness. I can't believe it for the reasons that I've already given you. So, nice as it might be, I think we have to face the fact that we're in a world without that sort of harmony.

That certainly does give rise to the questions that Professor Hare mentioned at the end; that is, what is the justification, not so much for deciding what's right and wrong—which I think we agree we can discover by looking at what we would decide on if we take the point of view of the universe—but rather for saying, "Well, why do I do it when it becomes difficult, when it becomes demanding?"

I don't think that there's a single answer to that question. I think we can find partial answers in some of the things that were mentioned. We can find, as Sidgwick said, partial answers in the benevolent affections that we have for others. But they very rarely lead us to act completely impartially. We can find a kind of a self-interested answer in terms of finding our lives fulfilling or rewarding, what the ancients called "the paradox of hedonism," which seems to me to go some way toward showing that it is in our interest, broadly conceived, to live ethically. If we live in a narrowly self-interested way, pursuing our own happiness, our own pleasures, we're not actually likely to find the deeper satisfaction or fulfillment that makes us regard our lives as really good ones. Only if we aim for larger purposes, which may or may not be ethical purposes, are we likely to find that kind of fulfillment.

So I think that there is something in that as well. But I also have to agree with John that, yes, the nontheist might say that ultimately there is no answer to this question. We make our choices. We may decide to live ethically because that's what we want to do. We will feel better in ourselves. We will feel that we've lived up to our values, that there's a kind of a harmony in our life. But I can't give a more definite answer than that.

I see my time is already up—those five minutes go very fast. I'll make one final remark. Professor Hare asked: Why don't I, as a utilitarian, welcome a belief that makes people happy, unless it can be shown to be false or does harm? Well, the fact that it makes people happy may be a good thing, but religious belief does quite a lot of harm in the world, not necessarily of the sort that leads people to do what is wrong but rather to make conflicts between people of religious beliefs much harder to resolve.

Take, for example, the situation in the Middle East. Although no doubt there are nonreligious motives there, battles over territory, for example, questions about the status of Jerusalem, for instance, would clearly be easier to resolve if we did not have very entrenched religious beliefs that are part of that situation. So that's a small example of the kind of problems that we can have when we get locked into religious beliefs.

Hare. Well, thank you for agreeing with me as much as you did. I wasn't expecting that. So you agree, first, that there is this problem of reconciling morality and happiness, and on your view it would be nice to have an answer, but we just don't. Second, you agree that it would be nice to have a justification for morality, but you think ultimately we just don't. On my view, we do.

But now, how about the question of conflict? Religion produces conflict. This is true. What's the best way to get through the conflict? Is it to abandon the religion? Is it to try to produce a public forum of discussion, in which everybody leaves their religious views behind? I don't think so. This is just a personal anecdote, but at Yale we had a conference of Christians and Muslims, between those who had signed what was called the "Common Word" document, based on the principle that we should love our neighbor as ourself. I discovered that an

Peter Singer, Eric Gregory and John Hare explore the basis of morality at MIT.

Ayatollah from Qum, in Iran, who teaches at a large seminary there, had been reading my work and translating it into Farsi to teach his students. And he wants me to go to Iran and talk more. I think I'm going to do that.

That's the way, I think, we're going to understand each other better, by talking with each other as religious people—*as* Christians, *as* Muslims, not by leaving all of that, as it were, behind us, because this is so large a part of so many people's lives throughout the world. Thank you.

Moderator. We do have a time now for a moderated discussion. The first question is for Professor Singer: You mentioned that Darwinian evolution explains our moral motivation. On what basis can we judge those desires given by purposeless Darwinian evolution? You suggest using the Golden Rule, but why choose to apply that? So, maybe this question brings out the larger question of how your understanding of Darwinian evolution relates to morality?

Singer. That is quite a large question. So why use the Golden Rule if I think evolution is purposeless? That's true, evolution is blind in that sense. But it has created beings who have desires, preferences, needs, beings who are capable of suffering or capable of enjoying their life. And I think value comes into the universe when we have beings with consciousness, awareness, and preferences, so that their lives can go well or badly for them.

It's our capacity to reason that enables us to see that, to not simply act on our instincts, but to reflect on them, and also to see that there are other being like us who have similar preferences and needs. So again, I agree with John Hare when he said that although nonhuman animals may have things like reciprocity, be able to practice tit for tat and so on, they don't take this impartial point of view, the point of view of the universe. They're not capable of it because they don't have high enough cognitive abilities.

We are capable of taking that larger perspective. If the question is why we choose to use that perspective, then we get back into the question of justification, which is not easy to answer, beyond saying, Well, that's the largest perspective you can take, that's something which takes into account all the relevant knowledge you have about what the world is like. It's also something we can discuss with others and expect them to agree with us. If I say, "Well, *this* is what *I* want," and you say, "Yeah, but *this* is what *I* want," then we may have difficulty in reaching agreement about what we ought to do. But if we say, "Look, let's put ourselves in the position of everyone affected," and we really do that, then, at least in theory, we ought to be able to agree on what we ought to do.

Moderator. There's a number of questions that talk about the shared demandingness of both your views of morality, so a question for both of you: To what extent are either of your ethical theories, or for that matter, what Jesus commands, actually livable? Does it matter, or are they just ideals, and would a life that is fully lived according to your principles be a life well-lived?

Singer. One of the things that I do in the recent book is to both put forward an argument that has very demanding implications and then to suggest that because it is so demanding, and so few people do seem to be prepared to try seriously to live up to it, we might have lower public standards. So I think yes, at least at the level of public morality, we ought to have standards that are realistic. There's some discomfort in that idea, that we have to accept a different and lower, public standard than we really think to be right. But if what we're trying to do is to achieve the best outcome, then maybe that's really the way to do it.

Moderator. Professor Hare?

Hare. I think it's not just an ideal, something utopian, as it were, so that we don't actually have to regard it as an obligation. I think we do have these very high demands from morality on how we ought to live. But if we're theists, if we believe in God, and we think God is requiring this of us, we also think God will not require of us more than we can bear, and that our moral life and our happiness can, in the end, come together, that we can flourish. And that's something, I think, that's available to a theist that probably is not available to someone who is not.

Moderator. I'll pick up on that. Professor Singer, how do you deal with the problem of falling short of the demandingness, either in theory, or if you don't mind, in your own life? Professor Hare has praised you for shaming Christians in your commitments to the global poor. But you've admitted that you don't do all that you should do. Even if that does not contradict the claim that it is what you should do, how do you understand knowing that you do not do what you should do? Is there a secular analogy of providence, grace, forgiveness or an understanding of weakness of will that Christians call "sin," that you have?

> *Am I tortured with guilt for going to the movies instead of donating the price of the movie ticket to Oxfam? No. It's an acceptance that I am, at least partially, a selfish creature, that I don't live fully ethically because my selfish desires have greater weight than they would in someone who was acting in a fully ethical way.*

Singer. Okay, so let's say I accept the way you stated the facts. I certainly think that I would be a better person if I gave more to the global poor or lived more simply than I do, even though it's probably true that I give more than most people who consider themselves Christian. Am I tortured with guilt for going to the movies instead of donating the price of the movie ticket to Oxfam? No. It's an acceptance that I am, at least partially, a selfish creature, that I don't live fully ethically because my selfish desires have greater weight than they would in someone who was acting in a fully ethical way.

Moderator. And Professor Hare, is this an element of rational instability?

Hare. I think it is. But I think if you really care about a moral commitment, then you will feel guilty when you break it. And if you don't, then you weren't really committed to it. So we do have to have a way of dealing with this sense of failure. We have to have some way of being forgiven, and that's a deep feature of a religious point of view.

Moderator. Professor Singer, here's another question about evolution. If ethics is an evolutionary product, and if it is advantageous to help raise a neighbor's offspring because they would reciprocate to help me raise mine, would it be not even more beneficial for me to cheat? To pretend to help others, only to take advantage of others' help? Yet I think generally we would agree that this is morally wrong. How does evolution explain this phenomenon?

Singer. The premises are right. The theory is, there is selection for cooperation because we get rewarded by reciprocity that's beneficial for us. If we can get the benefits and cheat and not repay, we do better still, and we see examples of this. But of course, as we get selection for cheating, then we also get selection for detection and punishment of cheats. So it's like a kind of an arms race. They develop the missiles, and we develop the antiballistic missile system, and they develop something that will evade our antiballistic missiles, and so on. It's still quite possible that because cheats can often be detected, to be a genuine cooperator is a good strategy, because we'll be trusted.

Moderator. How do you understand the role of Jesus Christ and his life and teachings for an understanding of morality? In thirty seconds, please.

Hare. Jesus is a model for me of how human life should be, of giving

his life for others and reaching out to the weakest. But if it's just a
model, and this is Kierkegaard's point, it produces despair, because I
don't seem to be able to live that way by my own resources. So it's
important to me that with the model comes power to live that way.
God actually helps us to live the way God asks us to live. And God
forgives us when we don't. Those two things are very important: the
power and the forgiveness.

So to Jesus' life and teachings I would have to add his death and his
resurrection. And this is all now within the life of the church. I think
the life of the church is very helpful, because it's a community in which
we can be held accountable to the standards that Jesus showed for us.

Moderator. Professor Singer, there are a number of people interested in
what it would take for you to become a Christian. So maybe I will invite you to say maybe a little bit more about how you understand the life
and teachings of Jesus.

Singer. One of the things it would take for me to become a Christian is
to have a plausible answer to the problem of evil, which I don't. But
even if I did, I think I could not see myself becoming a Christian. This
leads to the answer to your question. I don't think that the life of Jesus
is the most admirable life one can imagine. I wouldn't really want to
take it as a model. There are some things in it that I admire, in particular, the emphasis on the poor. But there are some rather strange
things in it too, a couple of incidents that I find difficult to understand.
One is difficult from the point of view of someone concerned about
animals. That is the incident of the Gadarene swine, when Jesus took
out devils and cast them into a herd of swine, and the swine ran down
the hill and drowned themselves. Why did he do that? If he could cast
out devils, why couldn't he make them vanish into thin air rather than
drowning the poor pigs, not to mention the people who presumably
owned the pigs and were now bereft of a means of a livelihood.

Then there's the incident of the fig tree. Jesus saw a fig tree and
asked for some figs and was told that there were no figs. One of the
Gospel accounts says, "Because the time of figs was not." It wasn't a
useless, barren fig tree; it just wasn't the season for figs. But Jesus cursed

it, and the next day the disciples come past it and say "Look, it's died." That seems a very petulant act, I have to say.

Moderator. I didn't realize you were a supporter of a literalist reading of the Bible.

Singer. I'm not . . .

Moderator. You and Jerry Falwell share much in common.

Singer. You see, the question is, if we don't take these as true accounts, then what do we take? Then we're in the business of distilling the essential message, while leaving out the little stories. It's hard, then, to work out what exactly the essential message is. I mean, one of them certainly is that the world is coming to an end pretty soon, and some of you are still going to be around when that happens. So Jesus seems not to have been a very accurate prophet either. That's another problem.

If we're going to talk about some version which doesn't deal with these details, we obviously need a lengthy discussion as to what we do take from it, and I'm not even quite sure where we'd begin and end.

Moderator. Maybe I will turn the table to Professor Hare. If you discovered a better theory on how to moderate an understanding of happiness and morality, would you still be religious? I guess the question is, What would it take for you to be an atheist?

Hare. Hmm. I don't think belief in providence is just a tool. I think it's that my religion helps me to make sense of my experience of the moral life and of my own moral failure. It's not that I'm religious because I want to get into heaven, or something like that, where it would be just instrumental, just a tool. What would it take for me to become an atheist? I might, I suppose, not be a Christian any longer if somebody could prove to me that Christ didn't rise from the dead. That would be a pretty hard thing to do, but if somebody were to be able to prove that, then that would stop me believing that Christ did.

Moderator. Okay. We are coming down to our final minutes, so I'll just close with a broader question. Why does moral philosophy matter so much to you? And do we need a shared theory of morality? Forty-five seconds each.

Singer. Certainly, I agree that we need to have more tolerance and understanding across different beliefs, whether they're Christian or Islam or theist or atheist. That's one of the reasons why it's good to do something like this discussion. I'm interested in ethics and moral philosophy because I'm interested in thinking about how we ought to live. I can't see that anything can be more important than that. So that's really what I'm trying to do, to change our ways of thinking about how we ought to live so that we reduce the amount of unnecessary suffering in the world.

Moderator. Thank you. Professor Hare?

Hare. Moral philosophy is about ideas. Ideas matter. I worked for a bit in the House of Representatives, on the staff of the House Foreign Affairs Committee. And I saw ideas having impact on policy. It matters how we think, because that changes what we do. I care about moral philosophy because it's a way of being clear about what we think.

10

LIVING MACHINES

CAN ROBOTS BECOME HUMAN?

Rodney Brooks *and* **Rosalind Picard**
The Veritas Forum at Massachusetts Institute of Technology, 2007

THIS DIALOGUE BEGAN WITH four questions, which Rodney Brooks and Rosalind Picard were each asked to address:

1. How do you define *human?*

2. What are the necessary and sufficient conditions for a robot to be called "human"?

3. What is the state of technology today, vis-à-vis these conditions for a robot to be called "human"?

4. What are your personal thoughts?

RODNEY BROOKS

Thanks very much for the invitation tonight, and thanks to Roz for agreeing to have this discussion with me. I've been building robots for a long time. I started back in Australia building robots based on Grey Walter's machines, and then as a grad student. Once I got to MIT, my students and I started building lots of different robots, some of which ended up inspiring missions to Mars and so forth.

Since 1992, I've been working on humanoid robots with various students. I've also been involved in iRobot Corporation, where we've now sold literally millions of robots. So I've been very interested in robots for a long time.

I have an admission to make tonight. And that is: I am a robot, and I mean that in a serious sort of way in response to the question about living machines. I view myself as a living machine. I am made up of biomolecules. Those biomolecules interact in rule-like patterns and out of that emerges this thing you see before you.

I have an admission to make: I am a robot. And I mean that in a serious way in response to the question about living machines. I view myself as a living machine.

But I also claim to be a human. I claim I am both a human and a robot, and all of us humans are robots. And to me this question has nothing really to do with Zeus or Juno or Yahweh or Brahma or Shiva or Buddha—it's a separate realm. It has nothing likewise to do with Jesus or with Muhammad, or even L. Ron Hubbard. They are separate worlds. And I think we serve our science best by keeping those worlds separate. So I guess I'm a skeptic in that sense.

CAN ROBOTS BECOME HUMAN?

Now, to address the question of whether robots can become human. Some people would like to say that there are humans and there is everything else; they're separate. Others would probably like to say there's some gradation, that chimpanzees are a little closer to humans than fish may be in the way they operate. I've often wondered what our world would be like, and what we as humans would be like, if the Neanderthals had not been driven extinct. As archaeological digs look more and more at Neanderthals, we see evidence that they had language, maybe. They had tools, certainly. There is some evidence that they may have had religious sorts of beliefs in the way that they treated their dead. It's very hard to tell exactly what they had, but they were different from humans.

If they were still around, how would we treat them? I'd like to think we'd be nice to them, although evidence suggests from history that maybe we wouldn't have been. And maybe we weren't, and that's why there's none of them left. That would be a different world for us to be living in because dolphins really aren't human—they're far enough away to separate them as a separate category, but Neanderthals would be fuzzier.

As we see all these different animals, the question is where would we put various robots in this sort of spectrum. Different robots will have different things that are similar to some of these animals and dissimilar to others. So I'm not sure that the question When is a robot human? per se is quite the right question when thinking about when a robot would be as similar to us as a Neanderthal so that we'd have to take them seriously in some sense.

If we go down to viruses: are they living or not living? I'm not so sure. But it is interesting that in the last few years people have built viruses *de novo*, not from viral material but from biological material, building DNA strings. They've also built viruses without having the virus genome copied via genomic material, but instead it was copied by computer representation of that genomic material, and they built the virus from scratch. It's built out of atoms and molecules. An artificial virus, a real virus, and they're the same.

Now we haven't got that far with bacteria. People are working on whether they can build a bacteria *de novo*, either a copy of an existing bacteria or a brand new bacteria, by getting minimal genomes and mixing and matching using mycoplasms. We're not there yet, so I can't obviously say it's true, but looks to me like before too long, we will probably get to building bacterial copies.

STATE OF TECHNOLOGY

Then the question is: how long will it take to get to a fish, a mouse, a zebra or whatever. That's building copies, piece by piece, but I want to make a slightly different claim, and then two questions. To me, since it seems that we are machines—that all those biological systems are machines, in principle—it should be possible to build atom for atom copies. Though probably pretty damn hard. But in principle, it should be possible to build—this is my work, after all, this is what I do and what I aspire to—human-level beings from other materials. Silicon and aluminum are my current medium. To be precise, my claim is: in principle, it should be possible for beings made out of other stuff to exist.

Then there arises two questions, and this first one I got when I was coteaching with Patrick Winston. Patrick Winston liked to give the first lecture to get a little bit of humility into the subject of artificial intelligence by telling about when he was growing up. Patrick had a pet raccoon, and that raccoon was very dexterous. It could get out of cages, undo and untie things, and he said it never once occurred to him that the raccoon was going to build a robotic raccoon copy of itself. It just wasn't smart enough to do it. So, are humans smart enough to do this? In principle, I say it's possible, but are we smart enough to do it? My big worry is that there are these flying saucers out there from Alpha Centauri and there's all these beings looking down and, saying, "Look at MIT; look at that little silly Rodney Brooks. He thinks he's gonna build a robot copy of himself. Isn't that cute?" So maybe we're not smart enough to do this.

This second question was inspired by my student Cynthia Breazeal, who is now a faculty colleague at the Media Lab: Will we want to? She inspired me to this through the phrase "appliance or friend?" and I'd feel bad. I don't want to have to feel bad that my fridge works seven days a week, twenty-four hours a day. I don't want to give it that much feeling. So we may not want to build to a human level. We may want to build other things that have certain capabilities.

So, there are the questions for me. We've built lots of robots over time, and as we build them with more and more human characteristics, people start to feel that they're sort of living, they're sort of humanlike, and some people say, Oh, you're just fooling people. You're just fooling people by building these robots that appear to be human.

Kismet, a robot, is Cynthia Breaseal's thesis project. *[Shows a video clip of a robot interacting in conversation with humans.]* Am I just fooling someone? What if I fool them for a whole day? What if I fool them for a year? What if I fool them for their whole life? Is that real then?

PERSONAL VIEWS

I will finish with the two questions that reporters always ask me, because they've watched Hollywood movies. (That's where all reporter questions come from, ultimately.) Should we fear robots? Are they going to want to take over? I'm going to ignore those questions for the night. The other question is (and I think this is part of the other question), will we accept them? All these movies are about wanting acceptance as humans, and *Star Trek's* Data is my favorite of all these.

Why do I think it's hard for us to accept robots as even in principle having humanity? Well, I think history has played out this game again and again. Galileo challenged the notion some other people had that the earth is the center of the universe, which really upset people. What do you mean? God made the world for us, it must be the center of the universe!

When Darwin came along, animals had been one domain, humans another domain. He challenged that specisism and said, "Well, humans and animals come from the same place." That upset people very much. And as we've gone along, human thought is the same as computation enhancements on machines: Gary Kasparov, the world chess champion was beaten by Deep Blue, an IBM computer. He got beaten by a hunk of junk. He said, "Well at least it didn't *enjoy* beating me." And he was right, it didn't enjoy it, but he retained his specialness. He was still special. We like to be special.

Recently, we've seen a couple of cases of this. A few years ago when a meteorite was found from Mars, evidence was disputed as to whether there was biological material on it. Maybe we didn't have our own creation event here on earth. Maybe it was somewhere else. "What do you mean? We're good enough on earth to have our own creation event." Then, when the genome was sequenced, it turned out we have less genes than a potato, and people were really upset. We like to be special.

But I think we're not going to be so special. Actually there was a very underrated movie, *Bicentennial Man*, with Robin Williams, a robot who over time develops human attributes. Conversely, people are extending their life technologically (as a baby boomer, I'm gonna do it). We've already got cochlear implants, we're starting to get retinal implants, we're starting to get neural implants for controlling limbs, and so on. A lot of silicon and steel is going in our bodies. We humans are going to become more robot-like, and at the same time we're starting to use biological materials to build our robots, as did Robin Williams, and became more animal-like. And the finale of this movie is the dispute between who's more human—he or what had started out as a human.

So I think (and I talked about it in the book *Flesh and Machines*) that it's not going to be robots and us, we're all going to be sort of the same as we merge together with our technology over the next fifty or five hundred years.

ROSALIND PICARD

HOW DO YOU DEFINE *HUMAN?*

We were asked us to address four questions in fifteen minutes. These are really hard questions. They are comparable to our oral qualifying exams, so I'm just going to dive in here. First, when I tried to figure out how we define human, I went to Google and typed: "how do you define human." It came up with Wikipedia, which you know is a big, risky thing to look at these days.

Wikipedia said a human was a bipedal mammal. And I thought, *Hmm? Is that all? That's kind of simple.* So I typed in other bipedal mammals, and sure enough it's really not sufficient to describe us. There's an anteater, a giant pangolin, that's also a bipedal mammal. So that confirmed my suspicion that there might be something more.

I went back to a slightly more trusted, old source—the Webster Dictionary online. It basically said that we are "man." Or that we "have human form or attributes." So I thought, *Okay, well, I don't mind being called a man, actually. That's the old word that used to apply.* (People sometimes still write "Dear Sir" to me.) So I looked up *man* and *human being*, and Webster said there was no definition. So I thought, *This is really going to be hard.* Actually, I dug a little further, but it's not entirely that satisfying. Actually, in all fairness, under "man," buried down a bit further is a definition that starts to describe some attributes, and attempts to define us in terms of things that might be present in us but not in other animals: speech, abstract reason and interbreeding. Again, we see this bipedal theme and comparison to apes through our anatomical relation. I'm surprised it doesn't say anything about DNA yet.

But I hope you're troubled by this list like I am, because, in fact, when we make definitions, lists with these sort of functional, measurable attributes, somebody is left out. I can think of people who don't have two legs, who aren't bipedal, or who through some accident, or quirk of birth don't have anatomical similarity to apes. I work with people with autism who don't have articulate speech, who are nonverbal, and I am the adopted daughter of parents who were not able to have their own biological children. We all know people who don't fit some list that specifies these finite criteria. They're still people. In fact, if we think a little bit more over history, it's kind of troublesome when people have excluded large groups by defining them as not being human based on race or culture. So this is deplorable and very disturbing.

So, in fact, it led me to think maybe we need to go a little further and even conjecture that any such definitions based on a list of measurable, functional attributes—things we can measure and verify that we can do—will always omit some people. This is not proven, but I'm conjecturing it is true.

Rod didn't get to show you all his videos, but he shows in his videos that interacting with something makes you think that it's like a human. Like when the guy's interacting with Kismet for a long time, he treats Kismet as if Kismet is a human, but Kismet clearly is not human; he's clearly a robot. Although Rod thinks those are the same.

So I came up with a thought experiment. We all like to dress up on Halloween. What if I dress up as a pumpkin? In fact, pumpkins come really big. So conceivably, I could carve out a hole in the pumpkin, slip inside and seal up the pumpkin perfectly so that nobody looking at it can see that it is anything but a regular pumpkin. In fact, I weigh the same as a regular pumpkin—we're both mostly water—and because pumpkins don't talk, I wouldn't have to say anything, and I would roll the same as a pumpkin if I'm positioned in the middle. So basically, with this functional list of pumpkin attributes, I would be equal to a pumpkin, right?

But of course, that's silly, any more than a robot that satisfies a list of functional attributes is suddenly a person.

In fact actually there's one more definition in that old dictionary, for the word *spirit*, which brings up the spiritual image and likeness of God. A number of religious traditions describe humans as having a spirit. But I'm a Christian, and from Genesis I learn that humans are made in the image and likeness of God. What exactly does that mean? There are many interpretations, and I don't have time to get into them all.

But I want to comment just very briefly on the word *God*. I find that people often have connotations of "God" that are vastly less than what Christians and Jews refer to. If we think of God as somebody like a great cosmic Santa Claus or a bell boy—there to give us want we want when we ask—or (especially as Richard Dawkins seems to describe) as some being limited by space and time, that is not the God of the Old Testament, the One we are made in the image of.

And yet how can it be that we're made in the image of this being that transcends space and time? At MIT we think of an image as a projection down into a smaller space, so clearly when we project back up, it's something well beyond our imagination.

NECESSARY AND SUFFICIENT CONDITIONS FOR A ROBOT TO BE HUMAN?

All right, the second question is the necessary and sufficient conditions for a robot to be called human. Actually, I'm going to use this question to save some time because I have a very easy answer. I don't think there are any. I don't think we are the same. I don't think a robot is going to be called human, even though Rod thinks he is a robot. It might become possible to biologically engineer humans, like we're able to now biologically engineer some aspects of human tissue. Someday it might be the case that some brilliant findings ultimately lead us to engineer people: those would be people, not robots. I think when it's made out of something else, it has some very different properties.

And I'll just add parenthetically, who would want to *engineer* a whole human, Rod? I mean, there's a much more fun way to make new humans! *[Laughter]* I'm sorry, I know he has children. I'm sorry, Janet [Rod's wife]! Okay, I just couldn't resist.

THE STATE OF TECHNOLOGY

Next, what is the state of technology today vis-à-vis these conditions? I don't think a robot will be called human. I work in an area called affective computing. Our research is at the forefront of giving computers skills of emotional intelligence, the ability to sense and respond to emotional cues that help people with autism recognize the facial cues of those that they can't recognize, or to help the blind. We use it to help make technology less annoying, as well as a whole bunch of other uses.

But the most controversial question is, to what extent are we giving technology not just the ability to communicate emotion but to *have* emotion? We are working on methods that give machines what I say are *mechanisms* of emotion. These are mathematical functions and processes that provide some of the roles we believe emotion plays in animals.

But these do not provide the computer with feeling. They do not provide it with experience. They do not provide it with subjective aspects of emotion that we are so quick to think of when we talk about having emotions. We can make the computer smile and look like it's happy, act like it's happy and retrieve happier words. We can make a computer write poetry that's more iambic, but it doesn't have the same internal experience, or self, that we have.

So right now, the state of the art is that we don't know how to build feelings, subjective feelings. And along with that, moral feelings—feelings of right or wrong—are sometimes ineffable. The notion of free will, the soul, the spirit, the "life-giving juice," as Rod has described it elsewhere, are things we really haven't a clue how to build. We have a clue how to build more and more of these mechanisms of emotion, and how to build some self-awareness type of functions of consciousness and so forth, but we don't have a clue yet how to build these other things.

I say "yet" because scientists never—unless we can prove it can't be

The notion of free will, the soul, the spirit, the "life-giving juice," as Rod has described it elsewhere, are things we really haven't a clue how to build.

done—can say something can't be done. So I won't say these things can't be done. I'll just say we don't know yet. Also, even as a Christian, I do not invoke the "God of the gaps" for these things that scientists cannot show. I can't say that just because we haven't done it yet means only God can do that. I do believe God can do it, but it may be that God will allow us to have more and more understanding about that as well. So I remain open to our capabilities in this area.

PERSONAL VIEWS

I've already been telling you some of my personal thoughts about reaching these conditions, I'll actually point to a difference between me and Rod's here. I'm glad Rod mentioned his book *Flesh and Machines*. In it he writes, "If we accept evolution as the mechanism that gave rise to us, we understand that we are nothing more than a highly ordered collection of biomolecules. A central tenet of molecular biology is that *that is all there is*."

I mostly disagree with this, but I agree with part of it. I just want to be very clear of the parts I agree and disagree with. This "nothing more than" is not something that the tools of science can tell us. And following Ian Hutchinson, I think this is an example of scientism.

Science can show us the biomolecules inside, but it can't tell us that this is all we are. When somebody, even a very famous and important and accomplished scientist, says that this is all we are, don't believe him or her, because that's not a scientific statement. That is a statement based on a presupposition. That is a statement based on a worldview, and that worldview is not based in science. It is based on faith.

However, when we say an essential tenet of a field of science is that we basically need to assume that this is all there is, I agree with that when we're doing the science. While we're looking for scientific knowledge, we can't say, well, I have this favorite Sidney Harris cartoon that illustrates it. This guy is writing on the board, filling it with a lot of math. There's a whole lot of math on the left, and there's a whole lot of math on the right, there's this little gap in the middle where he writes, "—and then a miracle occurs." How to get the left side to equal the right? In science, we don't allow the "and then a miracle occurs." In science we only consider those things that are measurable, repeatable and clearly specifiable in some way that others can identify. However, while we make this assumption, we should not lose sight of the big picture. We should not be permanently narrow-minded scientists, but recognize that scientific knowledge is just one of many kinds of knowledge.

So Rod believes in aliens. That is cool, I didn't realize that. I have an alien example. Imagine that aliens discover instructions to build a radio. They find all the parts, put them together and it looks like a radio. It weighs as much as a radio and all

Rosalind Picard, James Bruce and Rodney Brooks discuss robots and life at MIT.

that kind of stuff, and they turn it on. Let's suppose for a moment that maybe there are radio waves where they happen to run this experiment. They turn the radio on, and what do they conclude? Music comes from a radio. Then they look inside at all the little pieces because this thing produces music. In fact, they replicate it, and it still produces music. They think they've figured out how music works. They've explained music.

The aliens use words like *emergent* to explain this. (When you hear scientists use a word like *emergent*, I hope a little red flag goes off in your head, because the way that actually translates literally is "we haven't a clue how it happens.") So they don't really know how the radio produces the music, but it emerges. But, of course, later they could learn about radio waves, and then they could learn about musicians and radio stations and all this kind of stuff, right? We have to be humble in science, because even though we've built something that produces a phenomenon, it doesn't mean we fully understood that phenomenon.

So even if someday we can bioengineer or produce machines that function like humans, just as the aliens did with the radio, it doesn't mean we have fully understood what it means to be human. Reproducing some functionality is not the same as understanding the waves of music, or the waves of life.

A lot of people are familiar with the first part of 1 Corinthians 13, the love chapter, which is written by the apostle Paul. We hear it read at weddings all the time. "Love is patient, love is kind," all that good stuff. At the end of the love chapter, it says something else that I find very inspiring when we think about how much we might fully understand someday. It says, "For now we see in a mirror, dimly, but then we will see face to face. Now I know in part; then I will know fully, even as I also have been fully known." A different translation says, "we see through a glass darkly." That's where that famous expression comes from.

I believe that we are fully known by this God that transcends space and time, and who is much greater than most of us are capable of imagining. However, because we're known fully, that which we are made out of is known fully. And we certainly don't know now—I don't know if we will ever know—but from reading 1 Corinthians 13, I'm inspired to think that someday we will know it, but that will be in a life after this one. And it is something that is fully known.

DIALOGUE

Moderator. Rod suggested that we might start the discussion by talking about the fact that the biologist's position is nothing but a set of molecules, and start the discussion there.

Brooks. Yeah, although I did want to say if we cooked the pumpkin, it wouldn't taste the same.

   [Laughter]

Picard. How do you know for sure?

Brooks. It will taste like chicken.

   [Laughter]

Brooks. I didn't hear Ian Hutchinson's talk, so I stand accused of scientism, happily. Actually, I was surprised by one thing you, Roz, said in your answer to the fourth question, where you admitted the possibility of building an equivalent system as a living system, and then being human, and then being living. You used the word *spirit* in your definition of man, the fifth definition, and that being missing from what was being built with robots. Also, indirectly, you are suggesting that there could be other things than just biomolecules in living systems.

So if that is the case, I see two possibilities: Either the spirit, or whatever it is that God puts there, has no influence on the biological system, or it does have some influence on the biological system. So if it has some influence on the biological system, then it becomes a scientific question because we can then look for that. In molecular biology—and maybe it's just because every molecular biologist has blinders on and is not seeing any of that influence—you could be looking for it. Then, that would be a key thing, which then might be a showstopper for building robots out of other materials, because there's something there that's happening that we can't control or duplicate, unless God very cleverly puts it in every fake bacteria that we build without letting us know, which is a further possibility.

But either it has an effect or it doesn't. If it has an effect, it's something we can look for that we haven't seen any evidence of, and in the absence of evidence of some phenomena the scientific method says, It's not there until we see some evidence of something happening. And that could happen. I've talked about the "juice of life" to sort of explain what we might be missing from a scientific point of view. So if it has an influence, we can go look for it, and we may fail because we're not smart enough to find it.

If it has no influence, then it doesn't matter as far as building artificial creatures. So that's my take on it, and I actually agree with you when you said earlier that science and religion are different spheres. I think they're different spheres and that they don't intersect.

Picard. I actually didn't say they were different spheres and don't intersect.

Brooks. Well, I'd like to think you said that. *[Laughter]*

Picard. It's very good to say back to people what you think they said so they can correct it. Gosh, I have a lot of thoughts on that. Well, have you ever read Edwin Abbott's book *Flatland?* There are creatures in this two-dimensional space, and while they have infinitesimal depth they can't move. So when a 3D or a 4D thing comes, along everybody thinks that's odd because you can't describe it in that 2D world, and yet it can have a presence in that 2D world.

Brooks. Yes, absolutely.

I think we're sort of like the creatures trapped in Flatland, where we really can only get a projection of what's going on and can't fully comprehend it until we are freed up to this greater reality.

Picard. So I think maybe humans having the image of God with a soul might be sort of like that. There's some aspect of it that has a presence in us. It also may be free for us to invite it to have a presence or more of a presence. I don't think we can measure all of it in our current world, in our current state. I think we're sort of like the creatures trapped in *Flatland* where we really can only get a projection of what's going on and can't fully comprehend it until we are freed up to this greater reality. That's my thought on that.

You also mentioned there's no evidence for spirit. I think people's experience is underrated, often. I've been thinking about how experience is evidence. For example, when we measure something scientifically—the height of this bottle or whatever—ultimately it's not just that you and I and all can measure this repeatedly, it's that our *experience* is that we measure it repeatedly. Ultimately, even our scientific measurements are subject to human experience. I think we often forget that human experience really is our ultimate judge of whether something is true or not.

So when enormous numbers of people—as with the Holy Spirit from God—report experience of this, and they come not just from the Western culture but from China and Korea and Africa, and every nook and cranny of the planet, then I think, while that experience is probably a very limited piece of what the reality is, it's real. And I think that counts as evidence.

Brooks. I want to go back to *Flatland* and then come back to what you have just said. Hans Marbeck has a great set of examples about *Flatland*. He says maybe we're cellular automata in someone's simulation where a program is running somewhere else. So his idea is to look for the bugs in the program because that will get you out—that we'll see the anomalies. It's like we're on the Holodeck and suddenly things go wrong, and we see the beams coming through.

Picard. That's how we know we're not in *The Matrix* right? Because it's working so well?

Brooks. But then the question comes down to the Flatlanders. Can they develop science and an engineering which is consistent within that world they are constrained in, which lets them understand the mechanisms that are there and duplicate them and build them? That's why I say that these are independent things, this spiritual world and this other world, because we can work within the system. Now either the system is consistent or it's not consistent, and then we would see evidence of it. Your argument is that lots of people have feelings that maybe it is. My trouble with that is that different people have different feelings about what it is, and I don't see a consistency. In fact, I see arguments against it. I agree that as scientists it ultimately comes to human experience, but what we're trying to do is look for consistency. We always look for patterns and consistency; that's what we do in science, and that's what we do in engineering. It's how consistent our engineering is that is the ultimate proof of the pudding. It doesn't mean that we may have missed something. So, the engineers of the nineteenth century built wonderful systems, but they didn't know about quantum mechanics, and so there was some phenomena that came along that they couldn't explain within the system. They had to build a more complex system. And I'm not for a minute saying that we have understood the materialist, scientific reality yet. But it's the worldview that I take that that's where science and engineering are—

and these other things [e.g., religion] are different.

I'll give you one last little example. I also have multiple sets of beliefs, as I think religious people who are scientists do who work in different domains. I think of myself as a robot, as a bag of skin full of biomolecules, and if I step back, that's what Janet is, that's what my kids are. But I have this completely different way of interacting with them, with unconditional love, which is not part of that scientific view. So I have multiple views I operate under every day.

Picard. I don't just call those multiple views, I call those inconsistent views.

[Laughter]

Brooks. I was being kind to you.

[Laughter]

Picard. Well, I'm referring to yours. I don't see mine as inconsistent. Tell me how mine are inconsistent.

Brooks. No, I was being kind—my own personal belief is that religious views are inconsistent with science, but since I have my own inconsistent views on various things, I'm content to let everyone have their own inconsistencies, and not to get too worried about them.

[Laughter]

Picard. Yes, but you keep referring to everybody having this need to be special. Where do you think that comes from?

Brooks. Well, then I'm going to get into Dawkins's land and say it is a mechanism that evolution stumbled upon that has helped us beat the crap out of those Neanderthals.

[Laughter]

Picard. But that's not what the selfish gene does. It's supposed to make us have more children, so . . .

Brooks. And save the resources for our own genes and our own children rather than the others. It's a mechanism—an emergent property, by the way.

Picard. I knew that was going to come.

[Laughter]

Brooks. I really didn't like your definition of an emergent property. If someone thinks scientists use "emergent property" for something they don't understand, that person doesn't understand the emergent properties. One can have emergent properties at different levels, and yet understand them fully. We've been doing that for hundreds of years—the gas laws come out of models of molecules hitting each other and out of that comes pressure, which is an emergent property from the mechanics of the molecules hidden. It's in a different realm from the molecules.

Picard. But there are still different things to be learned about bridging those gaps between those.

Brooks. Yeah, and that's what science is about—figuring out how those gaps are bridged.

Picard. I'm curious, too, about your view that we're just this collection of biomolecules that evolution produced, and typical of this view is that evolution operates with random mutation, natural selection. So there's no purpose, there's no meaning, there's no free will.

Brooks. That's why I said I have a set of inconsistent views that I live under, because that's really desolate, but it's the truth.

Picard. Yeah, that does seem really desolate, and I wonder how you —why you care?

Brooks. I live in a fantasyland. That's the fantasyland I've chosen to live in, where I treat you very nicely.

Picard. I don't think you have to treat me nicely. And I don't think you have to live in a fantasyland. Even physicists talk about the big bang (and there's probably some of them here who know a heck of a lot more about this than I do), about a time before there was time and space, as we know it. So it's not a fantasy to ask about a Being that transcends, and things that transcend space and time within physics.

Brooks. Actually, I want to be clear. I didn't come here to debate the validity of religion, and I don't want to do that. But what I do think is that we all have sets of inconsistent beliefs all the time. We are very confused beings, we muddle through, and somehow we get through life with our sense of inconsistent views. Science is about trying to isolate an area where we can get a consistent set of views about something. Engineering is about taking those scientific views and building predictable mechanisms based on those ideas. That, I think, is the fun of science and engineering and technology, and it's why I'm here at MIT.

Picard. Well, I share that fun.

Moderator. The question I'd like to turn to is how your worldview informs or doesn't inform your research work?

Brooks. Clearly my worldview is very materialist. There is matter and it interacts in certain ways, and at some level we're able to understand it. It may be too complicated for us to understand completely. I'll take Roz's argument that maybe there are things outside the plane, and that's why we can't understand. I sort of prefer to take the view that we live in the plane, and we're just dumb. We just don't have enough mechanisms. I don't think that my dogs are going to start talking about calculus to me. I don't think they have the mechanisms in their brain to understand it. I can understand calculus at some level, but there may be phenomena in the world that I—all humans—are incapable of understanding. Now some scientists say okay, then we'll set artificial evolution going to evolve something that's smarter than us. As we get more and more computational power, we'll get the crank going and we'll still win because we'll build this machine that can build even smarter machines. Then we'll have the singularity. We're going to download our brains into the machine, and we can live forever without being religious. But I'm prepared to think that we are limited, and we will be limited.

Picard. So, my worldview: sure there's material stuff, and that's the stuff I deal with when I have my science hat on. I'm still a Christian, even when I have my science hat on. I don't inject God explanations into the material stuff.

Brooks. Why not?

Picard. Because, again, I think we're fully known. We are a projection of that reality, so I want to understand this greater reality. I want to understand what is in this world that can be understood, and that's what the tools of science let me do. So I enjoy that, and there's plenty of riches there, and when I look at that, actually, I keep finding there's more and more and more. We start to understand one thing about a person, and it opens up more questions. It's more beautiful, more wonderful, and I see that as moving me toward even greater awe for the Mind that made this incredible world. So the beauty and the depth and the incredible brilliance of so much of what we encounter inspires this awe in me. And instead of me just feeling awe and thinking *Why do I feel awe for purposeless, randomless, directionless, meaningless stuff,* I think, *Wow, maybe this is pointing me to this great Mind that exists.*

Brooks. What I think is, *Boy, that's a great search space. Look what was in there.*

Picard. Well, I think that too, but I think there's a purpose behind that also, that we can know, and it brings incredible joy when I invite that in, because I've experienced it, and I don't want to go back to the way I lived before.

Brooks. That's why I never tried cocaine.

　[Laughter]

Picard. You asked why I don't just refer to God in these gaps. First, I think science has a way of filling these gaps over time because it's within the world, in this projection, and we have all this measurable stuff so we'll just keep discovering things. But I don't think it's the gaps that point to God. I think there are two things that happen. One is we look at all of science and see that it's ordered, it's reasonable, there seem to be laws. There's amazing fine-tuning and to believe that all of that is random takes a lot of faith. It's such a low probability event that even Dawkins has called it miraculous, and it just takes a lot of faith.

Brooks. I think Dawkins is a pessimist.

Picard. So, from our limited worldview, it takes this awesome faith to believe that things are the way they are. Things just don't seem so random and disordered (although sometimes my children's rooms are a little different). But the second is not bottom up, which is the way we're looking in our Flatland, but is top down. We've learned in science whenever we can get a top down view as well as a bottom up, we usually have a lot to learn from that. So, we have not only the reality that we can try to grab onto with our tools of science, but there's also a revelation, that is kind of a top-down message. And that is given to us through Scriptures, through recorded events in history that are described lots of times when God has revealed God's purpose and character and more to us.

When I was an atheist, I just assumed all that Scripture stuff was bunk, and religious people were weirdoes, stupid and all kinds of other things. I'm sorry if I'm offending anybody, but this is what I thought. One day, somebody challenged me to actually read that Scripture and that revelation. I thought, *I guess I really should read it since it's such a famous book, and I shouldn't just be the kind of person who throws things out without having looked at them.* So, I actually sat down and read it, and I was just amazed at what I found inside. It very gradually transformed me. I read it like four or five times privately before I ever could 'fess up that I was starting to believe in it, because I just couldn't believe that I *could* believe in this. But it did a number on me, and I started to actually change and . . .

Brooks. You should be glad you didn't try cocaine.

Picard. I don't plan to try cocaine.

Brooks. Sorry, couldn't resist.

Picard. After the joy and pleasure of cocaine, supposedly it's just hell. That's not my experience with this.

Brooks. You've kind of evoked me into fighting with you over religion. And I really didn't come to fight over religion. People have their beliefs, but I'll leave it at that.

Moderator. OK, thank you.

11

THE SENSE OF AN ENDING

Jeremy S. Begbie

The Veritas Forum at the University of California at Berkeley, 2001*

*This was a multimedia lecture-performance, with integrated images,
sound clips and illustrations at the piano.*

"THE SENSE OF AN ENDING." English majors will, of course, recognize this phrase. It was about forty years ago that the British-born critic Frank Kermode completed a book with that title. He pointed out that in a lot of narrative fiction, the ending gives the whole story a unity, gathering the strands together, resolving the discord and dissonance into what he calls a "grand temporal consonance." What would otherwise be sensed as mere events occurring one after another are then felt to belong to a greater whole. And he thinks that this is a model for the way we find pattern in successive events. To make sense of what would otherwise be mere successiveness, we "read" history as a story with a plot, a story unified by its ending.

TENSION, RESOLUTION

Even more than literature, music lives with a sense of endings. It oper-

---

*This Veritas Forum was held exactly one month after the 9/11 attack on the World Trade Center in New York City.

ates in a kind of permanent sonic future tense, always pushing toward endings. That, at least, holds for the music we know best, "tonal music" or "Western tonal music." This kind of music first came to flower in the seventeenth century and has dominated Western music since. Whether Mozart, Beethoven, symphonic, grunge, chamber, funk, be-bop or hip hop, it will be tonal. And two of its strongest devices are *tension* and *resolution*.

Remember what it's like to wake up at 7:00 in the morning. You're deep in a dream, and suddenly the alarm goes off. Your head explodes and you ram your hand down on the bedside table, shoving off your favorite novel, or whatever. And eventually you get your sleepy hand on the right button. Tension . . . resolution.

It's one of the fundamental patterns governing our lives. And if we're going to compose music in the Western tradition, we need to know how to handle tension and resolution. One of the most basic types is called "harmonic" tension and resolution. We hear an "unresolved" pi-ano chord, and we want—and expect—a "resolved" chord.

A large part of the skill in writing effective music is handling the dynamic "space," as it were, between tension and resolution. Every-thing depends on how and when we resolve our tensions.

HOME—AWAY—HOME

Tensions and resolutions are of many different types, operating at many different levels. Harmonic tensions and resolutions are by no means the only type. We can have them, for example, in meter, rhythm, attack, timbre and volume. But let me stay with harmonic tension and resolution for the moment. A tension, of course, assumes something before it that isn't a tension: an equilibrium before the tension comes along. You were asleep before the alarm went off—that's the equilib-rium. So the fuller picture is equilibrium-tension-resolution, or home-away-Home.

Thousands of pieces of music are built out of this pattern, as in the Van Morrison classic "Whenever God Shines His Light"—a fairly straightforward example. The process can be very subtle, very stretched out. If you go to one of the operatic dramas of Richard Wagner, for instance, you'll probably find yourself away from home about four-and-a-half hours.

All the tension-resolutions of music combine to give it a forward-moving feel, a sense of the incompleteness of the present. It pulls us into a dynamic of desire, giving us an appetite for closure. In short, we sense endings. And even if we don't stay with it long enough to hear the final ending, there's an overall sense that it's oriented toward a home, a resting place.

Notice two things. First, we're not dealing with a circle. This is not circular time, in the sense of exact return and repetition. When you stop the alarm, you don't go back to sleep again—or at least, that's not the idea. You don't return to equilibrium. In music, even if the destination is a note-for-note repetition of the opening, it marks the culmination of a journey, so it will *feel* different. It's not so much like going around the block; it's more like finding a home at the end of the street, which is like our home, only bigger and with much better furniture. It's like the home we left, only more so. (Hence the capital *H* in "home-away-Home.")

Second, final endings come in weak and strong forms. In the majority of popular music there's a sense of home, but the actual end of the song may not be a flag-waving climax. The music might just fade out. On the other hand, in other music there's not only a flag-waving climax but a huge sense of battle beforehand, as in much of the music of Beethoven, for instance. But even in music with weak final endings the sense of orientation to a stronger, bigger ending is usually there.

"HOME-AWAY-HOME" IN THE JUDEO-CHRISTIAN SETTING

What's all this got to do with Christianity? The Christian Bible tells the story of the world, from God's first "Let there be . . ." to the world recreated at the end of time. The Bible doesn't tell of a circle; it tells a story of hope, directed to an ending. And it can be told as a threefold story:

- Home. At the beginning is the equilibrium of the good earth and the Garden of Eden, when the first humans live in harmony with God and delight in each other.

- Away. Then tensions enter in: humans rebel, they say no to God.

- Home. So God gets to work on a resolution, beginning with a character called Abraham, climaxing in Jesus, and finishing with what the last book of the Bible calls "a new heaven and a new earth." Like the music, the final home isn't simply a return to how things were but to a universe remade.

And also like the music, the big story has lots of smaller stories nested in it, smaller tensions and resolutions. Jesus told one about a young man who told his father, in effect, to drop dead, and who then went off into a far country. When he returns, the father runs out to meet him and welcomes him home. Home—away—and Home.

So it's not surprising that tonal music has arisen in a predominantly Judeo-Christian setting. We need to be very careful about pressing this point because many other factors were involved in the development of this kind of music. But it's hard to deny that the Jewish and Christian faiths have had a part to play. To live in this story is to live with a sense of an ending. As the spiritual puts it, "We're on our way to glory."

A Suspicion of Metanarrative

But are we? What kind of a sense of ending or endings do we detect as we glance across the modern and postmodern landscape of our culture? The people we study with, go to classes with, have a coffee with—would we find in them any belief in an ending in Kermode's sense, like the ending of a great novel, when all the strands are gathered together and we see the sense of it all? Can we really believe in a final fulfillment to life and a spectacular climax to world history, a glorious gathering together, when the broken themes are at last pulled into one?

A belief in that kind of ending has become not only much rarer but deeply suspect today in many parts of the West. We might even say we're witnessing the ending of hope in final endings. Talk of grand finales has fallen on hard times in postmodernity. The huge stories of the world leading to a glorious future, total accounts of the world from beginning to end were the big "metanarratives" of Marxism, Judaism, Christianity. These, say the pundits, are waning. An "incredulity toward metanarratives," to use the jargon, has been setting in.

Especially now. I started preparing this talk earlier in the summer, and I couldn't have imagined, back then, what new and dark weight the words *sense of an ending* would have by now. After September 11, 2001, the air seems thick with a sense of ending. I don't mean a sense that the world's going to grind to a halt in a week or two. (That's a minority view and a pretty shaky one, I think, considering that for thousands of years, every prediction that the world's going to stop in a fortnight has turned out to be wrong.) No, I mean the ending of a confidence that great futures are possible, that we can build a new and great age, that we are basically omnipotent through technology, and can bring civilization to some kind of glorious climax, or at least bring it much closer. That confidence does seem to have been severely dented.

Of course many tell us that confidence has been waning for some time. Cultural commentators say that one of the marks of contemporary European and North American society is a lack of shared vision of what the goal of human life is. Zygmunt Bauman, the sociologist, has said: "One may say, paradoxically, that the post-modern idea of the good life is the lack of definition of the good life." What is our vision of the good life? What kind of society do we want? It's hard to find a consensus.

Some of you may know the writings of Alasdair MacIntyre, only one of many philosophers who have been exposing in our time the lack of any particular vision of the future, a lack of any shared sense of a desired end.

And why this waning of confidence? Why this hesitancy about naming and claiming a great future? Well, for many, the Christian form of it, at least, sounds like escapism. Many attack Christianity for that reason. They think that it's escapist, that Christians are focused on an end utterly beyond this world—heaven beyond the bright blue sky. And that's delusion, that's deception, so it's said. What Bruce Cockburn calls the "sweet fantasia of the safe home" is just that—a fantasia, a fantasy. What's more, this way of thinking avoids coming to terms with our life here and now in any constructive way. It certainly won't bite in today's world for the man who's just lost half his company in the World Trade Center. Escapism is the last thing he needs.

All right, you say that's not authentic Christianity. Quite right, but the rumor that it is still haunts our world.

But even if we do deal with the escapist objection and want to speak of hope for *this* world, talk of a grand future is still going to have a rough ride. For many today it sounds like naive optimism in human nature, captured in that famous photo of a worker on the Empire State Building in the 1930s: the belief that human beings are ascending to ever greater heights through rational, scientific, technological and economic advance allied to the imperialist's dream of spreading these advances worldwide, the progressivist's vision of a vast upward crescendo of human improvement toward some blazing climax. As I needn't tell you, for millions this kind of confidence has brought a trail of destruction. Yes, thank God for medical advances, telecommunications, the microchip revolution. But not for the weapons of horrific destruction, mass starvation and the ecological devastation which these very advances have so often brought in their wake.

What's more, behind the rhetoric of grand futures, the postmodernist will sniff manipulative power, a desire to dominate and exploit. Nietzsche told us long ago to be wary of people who hold out long-term hope. The much-vaunted "hermeneutics of suspicion" has made us wary of talk of hoping in climactic culminations. As the cynic will remind us, hopeful attempts to create the new heaven often end up with the old hell.

Think of the way so-called Western development has violated other cultures. Think of that word *resolution* I used earlier and how closely it echoes the ominous phrase "Final Solution," used of the death camps of the 1940s. And think of the way Christians have often used their story of hope as a dehumanizing weapon against women, Hispanics, African Americans, and so the list could go on. Talk of happy endings, so many say, is most likely to be a kind of political aspirin, handed out by those in power to keep the downtrodden quiet and to give the rest of us an excuse to do nothing to help them. "Hang on for heaven," the slave owners sung to their slaves as they pulverized the life out of them.

MUSICAL SUSPICION

Escapism, naive optimism, oppression—the postmodernist suspects them all behind talk of grand endings. And that suspicion has at times been played out in the world of music, sometimes unconsciously or half-consciously, sometimes very consciously—and long before the word *postmodernism* was invented!

As we turn to music, it's worth keeping in mind that having a sense of a destination will often involve assuming three other things as well: first, a sense of direction or orientation (that although there will be twists and turns, there will be an overall sense of heading or traveling somewhere); second, a sense of continuity, a sense that events can be related at some level, whatever the cracks and breaks; and third, a sense of origin, a sense of having come from somewhere.

Some musicians have found themselves questioning all of these, not so much verbally but musically. Many musicians have been asking, "Why resolve the tensions?" And what if we loosened the sense of origin as well? Many experimented with this through the nineteenth century. Beethoven, in many respects the archetypal heroic musician, the musical "modernist self" (so many have said), in his late works at the start of the nineteenth century seemed to be engaged in a kind of critique of that very phenomenon, playing with endings, nonendings, deferred resolutions and the like in quite extraordinary ways. A little later, Frédéric Chopin could write pieces of remarkable daring, loosening considerably the sense of a stable home.

Some of you will know the work of Roger Lundin and his fascination with the theme of the "orphan" in nineteenth-century literature, which he takes as symbolic of the orphaned self of the modern age, without origin or home. In the last of Claude Debussy's Préludes for piano, "Feux d'artifice" or "Fireworks," written soon after the ending of the nineteenth century, the resolutions (insofar as they *are* resolutions) are weakened; sound colors are enjoyed for their own sake, not pressed into the service of going *from* somewhere *to* somewhere. The "froms" and the "tos" are local, modest, unpretentious. The result is both delicious and disturbing, nudging this home and that, but never settling down for a long-term relationship, shifting from one temporary condo to another. One deferral of closure slides into another. There is a settling at the end of the piece, but only just. Origin, destination, even direction now loosening, the old modernist stabilities dispersing like the after-image of a firework.

In another place the process is extended yet further. Vienna, 1908. A time when so much was being questioned, so much unsettled. A culture rife with rumors of endings. Arnold Schoenberg experiments with music deprived of the gravity of a home key. In his second string quartet he uses a text with the words: *Ich fühle Luft von anderen Planeten*—"I feel air from other planets." His scores of this time evoke a sense of being rather than becoming, suppressing direction and goal orientation. In the fifth of his orchestral pieces (op. 16), we're given a complex tangle of musical lines, but with little to root the sound in origins or map them toward a destination.

Later, Schoenberg tightens things up, composing pieces carefully constructed out of a line of notes from the twelve notes of the chromatic scale, but arranged in such a way that no one note predominates, no one center serves as an orientation point or "home." It is some of the most carefully organized music ever written. Fiercely calculated to be permanently "away."

Now if you're a music major or former music major, you'll know I'm simplifying drastically. I'm not claiming for a moment that these composers were drowning in pessimism or had no sense of hope (anything but; just read Schoenberg!), nor that this illustrates a steady decline of music into some dark cul-de-sac of chaos. That would be crass as well as naive. But cautiously, I think we can say that these sensitive artists were caught up in complex turbulent cultural currents that often unconsciously or implicitly played out a questioning and uneasiness about closure, an uneasiness woven into much of the fabric of European culture, and that this playing out finds at least some traces in the medium of musical sound.

THE POSTMODERN SELF

And what of us today? As I've hinted already, in some circles, this suspicion or unease about Home would seem to be stronger than ever. It's not surprising that a wealth of literature has flooded out on the effects of these uncertainties on the human self. And most of that literature is a variation on the same theme: Say goodbye to the so-called *modernist self*, the individual self striving optimistically to create a better future on his or her own, the heroic, self-confident, self-reliant agent who's going to make a difference and carve out the New Jerusalem. Say hello instead to the "postmodern self."

This self comes in many guises. The commentators speak sometimes of the *disoriented self*. Without a sense of an ending or a shared stable set of coordinates in the future, it's not surprising if the result is a radical destabilization. A philosopher of the ancient world, Heraclitus, sketched what it was to speak of all things in flux, *panta rei*—"everything is in flux." And contemporary forms are not hard to find. Take the sound-track of Peter Gabriel's show for the London Millennium Dome. Although written two years ago, his words are chillingly apt in a way I couldn't have predicted when I first decided to use them:

> I looked up at the tallest building, felt it falling down.
> I could feel my balance shifting, everything was moving around.
> These streets, so fixed and solid,
> Ah, shimmering haze and everything that I relied on, disappeared.
> Downside up, upside down.
> Take my weight from the ground.
> Falling deep in the sky.
> And all the family looks so strange—
> The only constant I'm sure of is this accelerating rate of change.

A colleague of mine at Cambridge speaks of "multiple overwhelming" in our society, being pulled in a multitude of directions by the bewildering variety of options our culture offers: a plethora of TV channels to hop around, thousands of brands of goods, trillions of websites. Do you remember The Verve's chart-topping album *Urban Hymns*, with its multiple recycling of styles, and the line from "Bittersweet Symphony," "I'm a million different people from one day to the next"?

Commentators also speak of the *plastic self*. Without a sense of shared ends, the self becomes a product of roles and performances imposed by society and its own inner drives and conflicts. We learn to change very quickly, slip in and out of roles, reshape ourselves. Say goodbye to Jeremy Begbie as a self-integrating, rational agent with a central core that makes me me and endures through time. No, "Jeremy Begbie" is the name given to the decentered self, shaped by the multiple forces of culture.

And yet another image: the *fragmented self.* Without a sense of ending or endings, very often continuity will begin to dissipate; past, present and future will tend to fracture. Bauman, who I mentioned earlier, wrote a book a number of years ago about our times called *Life in Fragments*, about a society where jobs for life have all but disappeared, when professions have a habit of appearing from nowhere and disappearing without notice. This is the ethos of the weekend fling, fleeting and flirting, where we can only handle a night or a day at a time. Only microhopes, microendings, not megaendings.

I suppose it's not surprising if many of us will retreat into the present in these circumstances, the isolated moment, the moment of the fleeting sound bite, the photo opportunity, the flickering and transient image on the screen. Of course all this can be huge fun. There is the gentle amusement of multiple ironies, of hopping from one sexual experience to another, one dotcom to another, living like there's no tomorrow—as if there's no end. Why worry if it's a huge denial, a way of avoiding the ultimately unavoidable tough questions about ourselves, or the piercing eyes of a starving child in Mozambique, or the bewildered refugee on the border of Pakistan? Turn the music up louder—we don't want to spoil our day. From a band called The Beautiful South:

> The world is turning Disney and there's nothing you can do.
> You're trying to walk like giants, but you're wearing Pluto's shoes.
> And the answers fall easier from the barrel of a gun
> Than it does from the lips of the beautiful and the dumb.
> The world won't end in darkness, it'll end in family fun.
> With Coca-Cola clouds behind a Big Mac sun.

And to these I add two more images of the postmodern self: the *feverish self.* Steve Reich tells us about a fascinating piece of music he wrote: "When I first played a tape version of [a] section to . . . my publisher, I remember turning to him and saying, 'Out on the plain, running like hell.' And that's the image: it's as if you were in the desert and running as fast as you can." Feverish activity without direction. Not a bad sonic image of much in our own culture: without fixed coordinates, when we can't measure our progress or our direction (footprints get quickly blown away). Think of lost travelers in a desert—they tend to go round and round in circles. But they dare not stay still or they'll die. Feverish activity without direction. (Of course, I'm not saying Reich had all that in mind, but the music can serve as an effective sonic parable nonetheless.)

And a final category: the *timeless self*. In the midst of disorientation, plasticity, fragmentation and feverishness, one option is simply to pull out, to disengage into a supposedly timeless world. Over the last ten years or so we've seen an explosion of the popularity of music which in effect offers something like this, from chill-out music through monastic chant from Spain, to carefully processed Hildegard of Bingen. I'm certainly not claiming this or similar music represents bad art or that there's no place for it, or that all these composers would subscribe to what I'm saying. But I would suggest that a large part of its popularity is due to the fact it's been sold and marketed in a culture already deeply anxious about hoping for any rich ending (or endings) for themselves or this world.

I suppose with all this in mind, and in these troubled post 9/11 days, it's not surprising if thousands upon thousands have been flooding into churches, in England as well as America. And indeed, onto streets and squares to have services or quasi-services. I gather there were multitudes in a square not far from here in Berkeley, because with such a sense of ending, it's only natural that people should reach for the possibility that there is something or someone *which might not end*, and that the "end of the world" might at the same time be its *fulfillment*.

GOD'S IMMERSION IN OUR ENDING

Of course, to many that will just seem like good-old-time escapism, clinging at false straws. But suppose that the God they speak about in those churches and squares had actually created this world—and you and me—with an ending (fulfillment) in mind. And suppose that this same God wanted us to be part of that ending, and, what's more, wanted to give us a sense of that ending now. And suppose that in order to get our attention, he met us at our lowest point, when our own attempts to make grand endings failed dreadfully—not at the summit of our ambition but at the point where all our attempts to create the New World, all our purely human attempts to usher in the New Age, all our attempts to resolve all our problems had become murderous and destructive.

In the death of Jesus, God becomes the victim of our naive optimism. He becomes the victim of religious oppression: Jesus was crucified by a religion that, glorious as it was, had by this time become distorted by purely human hopes. And for many it had become cruelly oppressive. Jesus was crucified by the Roman Empire, which, magnificent as it was in so many ways, had in many parts become corrupt and viciously tyrannical. He is radically disoriented. Indeed, his very identity seems to be on the line: "My God, my God, why have you let me down?" (Matthew 27:46). His past, present and future feel as if they're disastrously fragmented. He questions his own past, present and future. He is torn in many directions by disciples, crowds, politicians, religious leaders. But God in Christ endures, bears it all, absorbs it all.

Would it be possible to hear something of this in music? Nothing I've ever heard or found comes quite as close as a piece by a pupil of Schoenberg, Anton Webern. It's a funeral march written after the death of his mother. The piece begins with about two minutes of murmurings on percussion, slow and low beating gongs, barely audible. And then in the last minute, the sound erupts violently from below, before suddenly disintegrating into silence.

Death, of course, is the reality hovering over everything I've been saying. The ending of all endings. The reality that threatens every hope of a rich closure. The reality that makes us hesitant about hoping for anything too keenly.

But *this* is how God gets our attention. He meets us here, where false hopes reach their abyss, where all purely human hopes die.

And from here also, a fresh kind of hope emerges. Three days pass, and the followers of Jesus find themselves with a new kind of hope in a new kind of ending. Rumors of an empty tomb, and then the man himself, nail marks in his side and hands and feet. Alive. Newly alive. More alive than before. What kind of ending can they now look forward to?

The raising of Jesus from the dead is God's great "Amen" to Jesus—to everything that's happened in him. In the raising of Jesus, God says to us, in effect, "You can trust this person, and he will give you a new sense of an ending, an ending for this world and for each of us, unimaginably greater than anything you could have dreamt of before." Here's an ending we don't create, but which *God gives*.

And with this ending in view, a new kind of self emerges—a new kind of human being. Not the modernist self, striving optimistically for an end he or she tries to build. Not the postmodernist self, destabilized and trying not to think about endings at all. But what I'm going to call "the musical self," a self I'm going to try to describe largely through music. I do this slightly tongue-in-cheek—I'm not saying that if you're not musical, you are somehow less than fully human! And of course, different types of music tell different kinds of story about the self. Nevertheless music can be incredibly powerful in helping us see what it means for humans to live with a sense of God's ending.

LIVING WITH A SENSE OF GOD'S ENDING

Let's hear from Paul in Romans 8:

> I consider that the sufferings of this present time are not worth comparing with the glory about to be revealed to us. . . . We know that the whole creation has been groaning in labor pains until now; and not only the creation, but we ourselves, who have the first fruits of the Spirit, groan inwardly while we wait for adoption, the redemption of our bodies. For in hope we were saved. Now hope that is seen is not hope. For who hopes for what is seen? But if we hope for what we do not see, we wait for it with patience. (vv. 18, 22-25)

1. A new creation. First, living with a sense of God's ending means heading for a new creation. What is the "ending" Paul envisions there? Not some completely separate "place" *beyond* this world but *this* world remade. That's the hope the raising of Jesus makes possible. A hope for *this world renewed*—not the unseen eternal world of Plato, not the hazy, unknowable noumenal world of Immanuel Kant, not a fairytale world beyond the bright blue sky, but *this* world, which God entered in Jesus to remake. This world, liberated from the things which devastate it, finally judged, freed from evil, purged of pain. This world, with a thousand dimensions added. This world, bursting with fresh color and cadences, new rhythm and riffs in a wild, ecstatic, endlessly expanding dance.

In one of his paintings the Indonesian artist Nyoman Darsane portrays the countryside of his own beloved island of Bali. He paints the fertility of that lush place he knows so well. But not even Bali looks this good in real life. The picture is deliberately exaggerated to evoke the new heaven and the new earth promised by God. It depicts a scene from the last book of the Bible, perpetual waters of the rivers of life flowing from God's throne, nourishing the fruit-bearing tree on the bank, the rich life of the multidimensional New World, overflowing, nourishing, endlessly abundant. Home, with a capital *H*.

So the end will not be like arriving at a giant rock concert in a foreign country. It'll be like finding that you can play the guitar without anyone being embarrassed, that the only three chords you know generate an entire dance, a crazy Irish dance, as it were, that never stops and never tires you out. And at the center of the dance will be the welcoming reality of Jesus Christ, raised from the dead, leading the celebration of his people. He'll be leading a community who find that they can at last be truly and *fully* human. As Paul says here, we can be adopted into his family—not dehumanized but *re*humanized. That's the hope for those who trust in him: re-creation.

2. A foretaste of the end. Second, living with a sense of God's ending means tasting that ending *now*.

In most stories the ending comes at the end. The gathering together comes at the temporal end of the story. But just suppose for a moment that the ending got injected into the *middle* of the story. Then you would get a foretaste of the ending ahead of time. The apostle Paul believes that in the raising of Jesus, the final resolution has come early. When Jesus was raised from the dead, that was a preview of the new world of the future. The great resurrection of Israel they expected at the end of time has happened in Jesus. Easter is a preview of the end.

But it gets better than that. As Paul tells us in many places, this risen Jesus sends his Spirit so we can start to taste and enjoy this new world here and now. We can, as it were, "get in on the act" in the present. That's the role of the Holy Spirit—to bring the future into the present.

Some of you may know Mozart's "Jupiter" Symphony. In the middle of the third movement, we hear this:

Figure 11.1. "Ending" in the middle of the third movement of Mozart's "Jupiter" Symphony

And what's that? Well, it's an *ending*, isn't it? An instantly recognizable gesture of closure in Western music. And if it wasn't for the suddenly reduced orchestration, we'd think all Mozart was doing was putting it in as a kind of period, or full stop, to what preceded it. But then what happens?

Figure 11.2. Trio, from Mozart, Symphony no. 41 in C Major, K. 551, "Jupiter," third mvt.

The "ending" (fig. 11.1) has turned out to be the first phrase of a new eight-measure phrase. So which was it? An ending or a beginning? The answer is: both. Mozart is playing on the ambiguity between closing gesture and opening process. An ending has come too soon, and marks a new beginning.

Likewise, the raising of Jesus from the dead was seen by the first Christians as an ending come early. But it marked a fresh start for the world, a fresh phase in God's dealing with the world—or should I say, a fresh *phrase?*

What's more, out of that little closing gesture—which, let's face it, isn't the most promising melody in the world, is it?—Mozart spins a whole series of developments.

Christ was raised from the dead, yes, but now the Holy Spirit will weave all sorts of new developments in our lives, out of that great ending-too-soon.

A couple of years ago I was preaching in a black South African township. I was told, immediately before the service, that a house just around the corner from the church had just been burned to the ground because the man who lived there was a suspected thief. A week before that, a tornado had cut through the township, ripping apart fifty homes; five people were killed. And then I was told that the very night before, a gang hounded down a fourteen-year-old, a member of the church's Sunday school, and stabbed him to death. The pastor began his opening prayer: "Lord, you are Creator and Sovereign, but why did the wind come like a snake and tear our roofs off? Why did a mob cut short the life of one of our own children, when he had everything to live for? Over and over again, Lord, we are in the midst of death." As he spoke, the congregation responded with a dreadful sighing and groaning. And then, once he finished his prayer, very slowly, the whole congregation began to sing, at first very quietly, then louder. They sang and they sang, song after song of praise— praise to a God who in Jesus had plunged into the very worst to give us a promise of an ending beyond all imagining. The singing gave that congregation a foretaste of the end.

Christian hope isn't about looking around at the state of things now and trying to imagine where it's all going. It's not about trying to calculate the future from the present. It's about breathing now the fresh air of that ending, tasting the spices and sipping the wine of the feast to come.

3. No escapism. Not so long ago, I heard the West Angeles Church of God in Christ sing "Let the redeemed of the Lord praise him," an eruption of ecstatic joy. I often go there when I am in Los Angeles because those Christians remind me that hopeful praise can intertwine with community renewal, the education of the disadvantaged, legal aid for the downtrodden, and a fight for better housing. It reminds me that authentic hope doesn't drive one away from the world but back into the world, where the world burns with pain.

Paul's vision that we heard in Romans 8 is of Christians *in* the world, *for* the world. Christians *in the midst* of a groaning creation, and indeed groaning themselves, to bring about (and witness to) foretastes of the end. Sentimental evasion has no place in Christianity. Again, I think of words from that same The Verve album I quoted earlier:

> I need to hear some sounds
> That recognize the pain in me.

4. Hearing between the notes. Of course, for thousands hanging on in the midst of dire circumstances seems impossibly and unbearably hard. So it is worth saying, fourth: living with a sense of God's ending often means "hearing between the notes."

A remarkable CD has recently appeared. It includes the playing of one of the most famous pieces every written for solo violin, the spectacular "Chaconne" from *Partita in D Minor* by J. S. Bach. A German professor of music has argued that intertwined with the notes of this chaconne are a number of chorales or hymn tunes that Bach had in mind when he was composing the piece. We don't hear these melodies, but she believes they are there, as it were, between the notes. The chorales are all related to death and resurrection, and as it happens Bach may have composed this piece in the wake of his first wife's sudden death. A group of singers called the Hilliard Ensemble has paired up with a violinist and made a recording in which they sing these chorale tunes alongside the violin part. We are made to hear between the notes. And somehow, the violin part seems to make so much more sense.

I had no active interest in Christian things until I was about nineteen. And one of my biggest fears in becoming a Christian was that all my interests, and particularly music, would suddenly be pushed to one side, and life would become far less interesting. The world would turn from color to black and white.

I can honestly say I have found just the opposite. Music is now far more fascinating and engaging, because I can "hear between the notes." I can begin to ask, In what ways does this music bear witness to the God who made it possible? Why did God allow (or even inspire!) this kind of music to be written? The notes sound somehow more alive. If you're a botanist, a medic, an economist, a mathematician or whatever, the skill is to hear between the notes, as to how God relates to this or that activity, what he might be doing in and through it, or what we might learn about God and God's ways with the world. When we can bring our discipline and the Christian gospel together in this way, the result will be a rich foretaste of the end, that eternal day when the "notes" of God's world will somehow make infinite sense.

5. Delay and silence. Fifth, living with a sense of God's ending means living with delay and silence. In Paul's words from our reading, "Now hope that is seen is not hope. For who hopes for what is seen? But if we hope for what we do not see, we wait for it with patience." Delay is part of the package.

Music has a great deal to offer here. As I said earlier, one of the crucial skills in writing music is negotiating the space between "away" and "Home." Music theorists have studied the ways in which, after expectations are set up, the "Home" can be deferred through a whole range of devices such as digressions, pauses, extensions. This is called "delayed gratification." Tensions can be resolved instantly or delayed, perhaps for long periods. This kind of thing is very common in music. But—dare I say it?—there's not very much deferred gratification in so-called Christian music. Christians need to recognize that much of their art has been embarrassingly full of quick resolutions, endings reached with a mind-numbing predictability.

In any case, a very interesting thing happens with deferred gratification. It pulls us in; we get drawn into the drama of the music more deeply until the resolution comes. The delay, in other words, becomes charged with hope, because we are drawn in and drawn forward. Hope lives in the midst of delay.

And that can happen even in silence. Why are we so petrified of silence? Because we think nothing happens in silence. We live in a culture frightened of silence. Our culture likes to fill every silence with sound. We're frightened by silence because silence means void, it means emptiness, it means blank space.

Music can tell us otherwise. If I introduce silences into a well-known hymn like "Amazing Grace," they will not be empty. They will be charged with hope, because you remember what *has* happened and sense what *will* happen. (There's more to music than meets the ear.)

Being a Christian means living with many in-between times, when nothing much seems to be happening, when it seems like God is on an extended vacation, when grace doesn't seem very amazing anymore. But into those meantimes can come the memory that God *has* raised Jesus from the dead as a promise of what *will* be. And the in-between times become charged with hope.

6. *Hope on many levels.* Sixth, living with a sense of God's ending means hoping on many levels.

I've talked about harmonic tensions and resolutions, but they are secondary to deeper patterns of tension and resolution called *meter*. Imagine you're living in a building where you're living on six stories simultaneously. That's what meter gets you doing.

Meter is the pattern of beats underlying music. In a score, it is indicated by a time signature (2/4, 3/4 or whatever). When we tap our feet to music, we are tapping to meter. A conductor, whatever else he or she does, is meant to beat meter. When we dance, the chances are we are dancing to meter (whatever else we may be doing as well). Metrical beats are grouped into bars (or measures). In a waltz there are three beats to a bar. These beats are not of the same strength—as anyone who has tried to dance a waltz will know. The first is strongest, the second is weaker, and the third is weaker still, "moving toward" what will be the first beat of the next bar. A wave of tension and resolution is set up, repeated bar after bar:

Figure 11.3. Metrical beats and bars of a waltz

Meter does not only operate at this one level. The successive down-beats of each bar are *themselves* of a different strength. In many pieces they are grouped in twos or fours—the first is strongest, the last beat of each group the weakest. Together, then, they build up another wave of tension and resolution at a higher level. And the downbeats of *that* wave are also of a different strength, which make up another wave and so on. The process continues up, level after level, higher and higher, until the whole piece is covered:

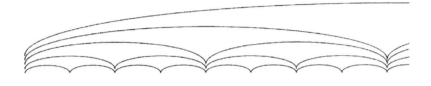

Figure 11.4. Build-up of tension and resolution at a higher level

This can be a highly complex process, but this basic multileveled pattern is present in one form or another in virtually all types of West-ern music, from Bach to Brahms, R.E.M to Eminem.

The key point we need to grasp is this: *Every resolution or ending on one level stimulates a wave forward at another level.* Put simply: there's always hope on another level.

Now slip the Bible in behind that pattern. What do we find? The God of the Bible moves not just in mysterious ways but in mysterious *waves.* God gives people hope by inviting them to live on more than one level.

The God of the Bible is repeatedly making promises. The promises get partly fulfilled, but at the same time the partial fulfillments make people hope all the more, and for more. The promise that dominates the Bible is the one given to Abraham, way back near the beginning, that God would create a people, a community. This is fulfilled. A small community emerges, eventually called Israel. But the people of Israel know there's got to be more. So the fulfillment that has come makes them hope all the more, and for more.

In the New Testament, one of the things the apostle Paul is saying is that Christ is, as it were, the great downbeat. Jesus fulfills the hopes of Israel, going way back to the promise of Abraham all those centuries ago. But does that mean we stop hoping? On the contrary! God's great downbeat, Paul tells us, should make us hope all the more, and hope for more, for a final fulfillment (a higher wave) of that first promise, when all the nations of the earth will be gathered into a new community, a new multiracial community in the new heaven and the new earth. The great resolution intensifies our hope.

Those first Christians had to learn to live on more than one level. If we hope only on one level, we'll soon stop hoping. Tune into the upper waves of what God is doing, and we'll never stop hoping.

Our so-called postmodern culture encourages us to live "in the flat," with only little short-term miniwaves—microhopes, a day at a time. But to be a Christian means we start hoping on many levels. Our life is set in the context of a huge hope stretching into eternity, but under that, there will be many different hopes on many different timescales. And very often out of the small ones, God builds large ones. Out of the short-term little routines in our life, perhaps, God may be crafting something wonderful which will make us hope again.

Stay on one level, and we'll soon stop hoping. Live on many levels, and we'll never stop hoping for more and more and more.

7. Improvising. Seventh, living with a sense of God's ending means improvising.

Maybe some of you can juggle. Jugglers tell us that one of the first things you've got to learn is how to let go. Your natural instinct will be to put all your energy into catching the balls. Paradoxically, the first thing you have to learn to do is *throw* properly, toss the balls without worrying about the catching. When we know the ending is assured by God, we can stop being held captive by our fear of failure, and we can be freed to improvise.

One of the most successful CDs of the last five years includes an ancient motet, written in the fifteenth century by Pierre de La Rue, sung by the Hilliard Ensemble. Over it and through it, a jazz saxophonist improvises. The ancient motet is brought alive by an improviser.

A great theme has already been played in Jesus, and the great motet of Scripture has been written around him. Now God, through his Spirit, invites us to sing with him and improvise on what we find there, always confident that the ending is assured.

Push the model further. Think of a whole group improvising on a single theme. What do we find? Improvising brings *newness*. In a good improvisation, we don't know exactly what's coming next. It tingles with contingency, with openness. Yes, there is the theme, or the chords—we know them. But a lot of the music will be unpredictable, new.

If we're locked into the past, if our future is just the unwinding of our past, that's a pretty grim prospect. Some worldviews turn on just this idea: we reap what we sow, and that's that. But the good news is that our future doesn't have to be set by what we have made of our life. Newness is possible at every moment. Here are words from the Irish poet Micheal O'Siadhail, from a love poem, but they could apply to a great deal of the Christian life:

> Suddenly, in the commonplace,
> that first amazement seizes me all over again.
> A freak twist of the theme, subtle jazz of the new familiar.
> Trip of surprises.

Improvising not only means newness, it means *we become more truly ourselves*. The singers in that motet on the CD become more fully themselves as they sing and listen to each other. In early medieval polyphony, the ideal sound was not a fusion but a mixture in which each voice stands out all the more clearly. And when the saxophonist comes along, the two styles of jazz and medieval music don't merge into one, they enhance each other in their difference.

The "modernist self" is the prima donna, who can only ever sing solo and who drowns everybody out with fortissimo confidence, before collapsing with exhaustion. The "postmodernist self" wonders whether her voice is anything more than the creation of her last singing teacher, because she's sung every part and still doesn't know who she is. The truly musical self lives with a sense of God's great finale, when every voice will be given a place and become more melodious, more real, more alive. And she knows she can start to enjoy that now.

A few years ago I was part of a group that organized a large celebration event in the University Concert Hall in Cambridge. In one item we asked the whole orchestra to improvise on a given melodic shape and chord structure, in the midst of a giant chorus of praise sung by a sizeable congregation. The majority of players were Christian. But some were not, among them a fourteen-year-old in the second violins. Normally, when she played in an orchestra, she would play exactly the same notes as the seven others in a second violin section. Here, for the first time in her musical life, she discovered her own "voice," but through trusting and being trusted by others—and in the context of praise. She came to faith during this extravagant extemporization. The Holy Spirit is not out to homogenize people into one but to enable them to become more truly themselves in relation to other people, "musical selves" in anticipation of their final fulfillment.

A last word—still under the heading of improvisation: *errors can be remade.* Sometimes when performing a hard piece, we stumble and make a major error. We can't, of course, erase the mistake. A piano has eighty-eight keys on it, but it doesn't have a delete key. The blunder has happened—it can't be undone.

We could throw a tantrum and run out, but that usually doesn't go down well. Instead an experienced player learns to improvise the wrong notes into the music which follows and make something of them. To use a technical term, she transforms the wrong notes into "passing notes." Passing notes are notes that don't really fit but can become fitting or even beautiful.

For me, one of the most breathtaking things about being a Christian is that God can take our worst mistakes and turn them into his passing notes. That's what God is promising to do for us in the end, and it can start now. And if you haven't heard that before, it's time you did.

12

SIMPLY CHRISTIAN

N. T. Wright

The Veritas Forum at Georgetown University, 2006

I'VE BEEN ASKED TO SPEAK about my recently published book *Simply Christian*. That's always slightly an odd thing to do, because I'm tempted to read you bits of it. And indeed I shall read one or two little bits just to give you a taste of what it's about. This was a fun book to write, because my assignment for it was the rather scary one of trying to do a *Mere Christianity* for the twenty-first century. This book really isn't a bit like that, with one exception, which I'll highlight as we go along.

What I've tried to do in the same tone of voice, as it were, as Lewis, is to say: this isn't about how to be an Anglican (which I happen to be) or a Catholic or a Presbyterian or anything else. It isn't about how to be a special variety of Christian. It's about what I see as the very central heart of the Christian faith. And, no surprises, the book is quite a bit about Jesus, quite a bit about God, and what that all means for us.

Let me set it in context right now. We are in the midst of quite a turbulent time in terms of the whole question of religion, faith in public life and integrating what we believe with who we are and what we do. We have at the moment in England several controversies—rather hot issues running in terms of how we do this religion in public life thing.

We have issues about Muslims in our society, whether Muslim women should have the right to wear the veil and to keep it on at all times. Some of our politicians have been saying that women who teach in schools should remove the veil, and some Muslims are up in arms about that. And this has backfired into the Christian community in that there are people who have either been threatened with losing their jobs—or have actually lost their jobs—for wearing a cross.

But the idea that in the United Kingdom, in my lifetime, somebody would be threatened with dismissal from a job—in one case with British Airways, in another case with the BBC—for wearing a cross in public, I find *quite* extraordinary. Even though I find it shocking, I find it more just a remarkable social phenomenon. That's where we've got. People are so uptight about Christianity and about how it relates to the world, and about religion in general.

My view is that we get into trouble about that sort of issue because neither our politicians nor our media have taken the trouble to study and understand what Christians actually believe and how that might relate to the public world. Though this book wasn't written to answer that question exactly, I do believe that what I'm trying to say about the Christian faith and its true nature should not only shake up some (I fear rather second-rate) ways of thinking about the Christian faith, but actually address some of those larger public issues. They are issues of really quite urgent importance in our world right now.

So, how are we going to talk about God and Christ in the world in ways that make any sense at all within the larger social and cultural community? Some people start by simply going straight for the question of Jesus, who he was, what he did, what it all meant. That's fine. That's one perfectly good way in. If we start off with that, we shouldn't go too far wrong, although there are voices in our culture that will push and pull us this way and that in our interpretation of Jesus.

But I wanted to start in a more oblique way and try and reach out to people who might be coming from a long way outside the Christian faith. They might actually ask:

1. Why should I even care whether this man Jesus even existed?
2. What's going on that might draw me in?

At this point, some Christians, some philosophers, have tried to start off by "proving" the existence of God. I'm not sure that you can actually do that in any way that makes sense to people today or in any other day. To prove something you have to accept some sort of framework of reference and then prove what you're proving in relation to that framework of reference. And then the framework of reference becomes the really important thing, and the thing you're proving is merely one function which it happens to have.

How are we going to talk about God and Christ in the world in ways that make any sense at all within the larger social and cultural community we are placed?

If somebody asks me, Can you prove that God exists? what they normally mean is: Granted that I am a late Western human being, or perhaps a postmodern person, or whatever, can you show me evidence for God within the framework of thought that I am assuming to be absolute? My answer to that is: If there is a God, and if this God is worth talking about with that word *God*—then this God must be greater than all our frames of reference. So, to seek to put this God into such a frame of reference really isn't going to do the business at all.

ECHOES OF A VOICE

So I start off rather differently. The first section of this book is what I call "Echoes of a Voice." The image that I'm using is of somebody who's in a room and can't see anybody outside but hears a voice. It seems to be saying something sensible. They can't be sure who it is or quite all of the conversation, but they're aware that there's something happening there. I track four voices of which I believe all human beings, to a lesser or greater extent, catch echoes from time to time.

1. Justice. The first of these—and this is where I pay homage to C. S. Lewis because this is where he started in his book *Mere Christianity*—is justice. To put it crudely, we all know that the world needs putting to rights, but we are all puzzled because we don't seem to be able to do it. This applies globally to politicians who see the great things that are wrong with the world and say, "Right, we're gonna sort that

242   A PLACE FOR TRUTH

out!" And then at the end of their lives they say, "Well, we have this program and that agenda and we passed these laws, but there still seem to be a lot of problems out there which we haven't sorted."

And this applies also to us as individuals. We know there are many things that are wrong in our own lives. And I don't just mean wrong in the sense of, Oh, there I go again, I keep on doing something that I know I shouldn't. There are things which are out of joint and need putting to rights about ourselves and the way our world is. And that's remarkably hard to do, and yet we know it ought to be done. We don't have to teach people that there is such a thing as justice.

Go to a playground where there are kids aged five playing together—and this was Lewis's point—and pretty soon one says to another, "That's not fair." How do they know that's not fair? Not because they've been to a seminar on the nature of justice. It's because we come hard-wired with a sense of fairness and unfairness, of justice and injustice. And the puzzle about it then is that we know there is such a thing as putting things to rights, but we don't seem to be able to do it. This constitutes one of these strange voices of which we all catch the echo. And I say all—Christians, Jews, Muslims, people of any faith and none, secularists, modern people, postmodern people—we all *know* there's something called justice.

2. Spirituality. The second echo of a voice that I talk about in this first section is spirituality. Thirty years ago if you'd put on a lecture called "Spirituality in the Modern World," probably no one would have shown up. Everybody knew that spirituality was what we got rid of with the brave new world of secularism in the 1960s and 1970s. Well, spirituality is back with a bang. So, whether or not people want orthodox Christianity, they certainly acknowledge that as human beings, we are multilayered, many-dimensioned creatures, and that there is far more to the life and the world and as a human being than we can put in a test tube or indeed in a bank balance.

But what is this spirituality? How can we tap into what seems to be "out there"? Spirituality is puzzling because some people spend their lives pursuing one spiritual path only to find that it doesn't seem to satisfy them. It doesn't scratch where they're really itching. The call to explore other dimensions to human life, which is again I think common to most human beings, exists in most societies, at most periods of history. That too leaves us often puzzled, hearing the echo of a voice but not being quite sure where it might be leading us.

3. Relationships. The third of these echoes that I track here is the question of relationships. To put it crudely, we all know that we are made for one another, but we all run into difficulties in making that work. This works at every level, even the global, where we know in our bones that we ought to be able to work together as a global family. It's crazy, all this business of wars and rumors of wars and cutting economic deals which cut out a third of the human race from prosperity or, even worse, from any prospect of prosperity. We know that we ought to be in better relationships with each other. Yet, however hard we work at it, it's jolly difficult.

Whether or not people want orthodox Christianity, they certainly acknowledge that as human beings, we are multilayered, many-dimensioned creatures and that there is far more to the life and the world and as a human being than we can put in a test tube or indeed in a bank balance.

Likewise, at the most personal and detailed level: friendships are hard to sustain. The most intimate, even familial, even marital relations can be very difficult to work at. Even though we say to ourselves when we get up, "I'm really gonna get this right today," we can still blow it. So relationships, like justice, like spirituality, are enormously important, and yet we find we're getting them wrong.

4. Beauty. The fourth of these is beauty. I invented a little parable to describe what I think is going on with beauty. I want you to imagine that one day somebody in an attic in Vienna is grubbing through some old papers and he or she comes upon a music manuscript, a piece of scrawled writing that looks as if it's meant for the piano. Somebody tries it out—strange, don't recognize this—the handwriting, wait a minute. This looks like Mozart's own handwriting—this is very exciting. Take it to the piano, play it through and it really sounds like Mozart too. And it's a piece that we didn't know before. That's wonderful! But what is it?

Then the puzzle continues, because there seem to be bits missing where the piano seems to be silent for a while, and then it kicks in again doing something else. It has wonderful bits that are building up to a climax, but we don't seem to have all of it.

And then the truth dawns: this is the piano part for a larger piece of writing, for maybe a string quartet with a piano accompaniment, or a string quintet. Maybe it's a violin sonata, and we've only got the piano part. It's beautiful, but it's haunting because it's pointing beyond itself, to something else. This is the position we're in when we're confronted by beauty:

> The world is full of beauty, but the beauty is incomplete. Our puzzlement about what beauty is, what it means, and what if anything it is there *for* is the inevitable result of looking at one part of a larger whole. (from *Simply Christian*)

Incidentally, I wrote this parable just a couple of months before a librarian in Philadelphia came upon a Beethoven manuscript which turned out to be Beethoven's own transcription of his *Grosse Fugue* for two pianos. Wonderful case of life imitating art.

The point is that beauty, like justice, slips through our fingers. We admire the wonderful sunset, and then it's dark. We admire the fantastic, beautiful flowers, and then they fade. We wonder at the beauty of the face of a child, or even the beauty through age of a wise old person, but we know that all that beauty is going to fade. And we know that ultimately there is this thing called death, which though our culture has tried to pretend isn't terribly important, we all know perfectly well is hugely important. It's one of the problems with all of those four things—justice, spirituality, relationships and beauty.

So there are puzzles, both about how we can get at them and what they are, and yet those echoes are persistent. One might at this point in the argument say, "Well here are the echoes of a voice and these echoes prove that there is a voice and that it's the voice of God"—but I'm not trying to go that route. I'm merely saying, as you hold those echoes in your mind, and reflect on them and what they mean, try listening to some stories about people who have spoken. Maybe listen to stories about a God who has spoken. And because this is a book about Christianity, I say: try listening to the story about Jesus.

STARING AT THE SUN

So the central section of *Simply Christian*, which I've called "Staring at the Sun," is about trying to talk wisely about God, and about Jesus within the context of God, and about the Spirit of God as the Spirit of Jesus let loose into the world. It's staring at the sun because if God is God, we shouldn't expect to be able simply to tell the exact truth about God. So when people ask, "Is God like this?" or "Is God like that?"— the answer of a genuine believer might be, "I really don't know and I don't think we can know." I'm not claiming that I can give you an exact account of God anymore than when I stare at the sun (not that I do, because it's bad for my eyes), I can see it clearly. You can't, actually, see it very clearly. It's blinding and dazzling. God is a bit like that; and, if God is God, that's what we ought to expect.

Which God? At this point we run into problems because of the way the word *God* functions within our culture. If you walk out onto the campus here and say to somebody, "Do you believe in God?" the proper answer ought to be, "*Which* God are we talking about?" Today people are more aware than ever that the word *God* is not univocal.

When I was growing up, it was assumed that we all knew who God was, and the question was did you believe or not in that God. The God referred to at that time was what I would call a deist God. Deism has a distant, remote, detached deity who may well have made the world in the first place and may well from time to time look down with a bit of a frown to see what sort of a mess we're making of this world. But probably this God doesn't get involved too much in the world, except occasionally to punish bad people and eventually to take good people away to be with him forever in a place called heaven. That's what many people thought you were talking about when you'd use the word *God*.

Equally, in our day and in some other generations, not least in the first century A.D., there has been the opposite view of God. This is the pantheist option. That is, God and the world, instead of being miles apart from one another, are pretty much the same thing. God is the soul of the world or the life of the world. So there is divinity anywhere, in anything—in you, in me, in the trees, in the flowers, everywhere. Everything is divine or part of the divine, or the divine is in and through everything, permeating it. That's actually quite a difficult position to maintain once you are faced with radical evil in the world. If something really bad happens, yet if everything is divine, what are you going to appeal to?

That quickly leads to cynicism, and in the ancient world, frequently for pantheists such as the Stoics, when bad things happened—well, the option was suicide. And actually, as pantheism has been on the rise in our culture, so the rise of suicide has often gone along with that. Not necessarily cause and effect, but it's an interesting phenomenon.

But those two equal and opposite ways of looking at God and the world are not the classic Jewish and Christian option of how to talk wisely about God.

The Jewish-Christian God. Within Judaism, the God who made the world is both "other than" the world and present in and with the world. The latter is very mysterious, because the world is in quite a mess, and yet God has not withdrawn the divine Presence from it. That's the paradox within Judaism, which comes out in institutions like the temple. The temple for the Jews wasn't simply a big church building on the corner of one street in Jerusalem. The temple was the place on *terra firma* where the living God had promised to live. So you've got a God who is transcendent, and yet has said that he's going to live with and among his people within the world. That's a paradox which neither option one (deism) nor option two (pantheism) can really cope with. It gets developed in Judaism in a wide variety of ways: God's Wisdom, which is his gift to humankind, so that we can be wise with God's own wisdom; God's Word, which is breathed out—a word is a vocalized breath—as a result of which things happen in the world, so that when God speaks, his word actually goes out and does things in the world. These and others are ways of talking about a God who is other than the world and yet present and active within the world.

But if God is present and active within the world, then what's it like being God but being present and active within the world? The answer is it's a matter of grief as well as joy, of sorrow and tragedy, as well as comedy and delight.

And so, in the story of Israel (I devote an entire chapter to the story of Israel because without it we won't actually understand who Jesus was and what it was all about), I talk about this people who were called to be God's people *for* the world. Not God's people away from the world but God's people for the world, to be God's light into the world. They too found this deeply puzzling because they kept on trying to do it and kept on getting it wrong. And yet the word kept coming to them, and through them.

In the story of Israel, we find again and again those four elements that we heard as echoes of a voice: (1) The passion for justice—the Jewish people have that ingrained in them over and over again, the need for justice globally and communally. (2) The sense of spirituality—because that's what you get if you believe that the living God is somehow present with you, gives you that extra dimension to your life. (3) The sense of relationships—the Jewish law is largely about how you relate to one another, how you can relate wisely and actually make it happen, even though they kept on getting it wrong. (4) And repeatedly, we get in Israel this sense of transcendent beauty nevertheless being glimpsed on earth, the temple itself being a good example. The temple in Jerusalem was one of the joys of the whole earth, in the way it was built. Then, particularly in the prophetic literature, there are those amazing pictures of an ultimate beauty, of a world put to rights, of joy as well as justice, where the wolf and the lamb lie down together with a little child leading them. It's an amazing, haunting, beautiful image carrying forward, and we can feel people saying, "Oh, I wish! Oh, if only."

> *If God is present and active within the world, then what's it like being God but being present and active within the world? The answer is it's a matter of grief as well as joy, of sorrow and tragedy as well as comedy and delight.*

Jesus, the coming of God's kingdom. Then, as the climax of the story of Israel (and that's how the New Testament writers see it), we get the arrival on stage of Jesus of Nazareth, himself.

> Christianity is about something that *happened*. Something that happened to *Jesus of Nazareth*. Something that happened *through* Jesus of Nazareth.
>
> In other words, Christianity is *not* about a new moral teaching—as though we were morally clueless and in need of some fresh or clearer guidelines. [Not to say Jesus didn't give a lot of moral teaching. He did, but that's not what it's basically about.] (from *Simply Christian*)

Christianity is not about Jesus offering a wonderful, moral example, as though our principal need was to see what a life of utter devotion and loyalty to God and goodness to one's fellow human beings is like and copy it.

Actually, if you had something like that it could be quite depressing. I'm a very bad golfer. (I enjoy playing golf, but I'm very bad at it, so people ask me why as a bishop you play golf. I say it's important to have something in my life that I can do really badly and I can enjoy it and it doesn't matter. Just about everything else I do, I'm supposed to get moderately right.) But if I watch Tiger Woods hitting a golf ball, that doesn't make me feel, *Wow, that's great, I can go out and do that.* I think, *Oh well, that's it, I'll never be able to do that.* And when I read the stories about Jesus, I sometimes feel that. In other words, yes he is a great example but it's actually not always terribly encouraging to those of us who find that our moral lives seem to be much more fragmented than that.

"Nor"—this is enormously important, and quite controversial—"is Christianity about Jesus offering or demonstrating or even accomplishing a new route by which people can go to heaven when they die" (from *Simply Christian*). It's a medieval notion that the name of the game of Christianity was to escape this world and go to a place called heaven.

Within the New Testament, again and again—and I'll come back to this, so please get your heads around it—the final destination of God's people is God's new heavens and new earth. Read it in Revelation 21. Look at it in Romans 8. See it in the way that the Gospel writers tell the stories of the resurrection. Jesus taught us to pray, "Thy kingdom come on *earth* as in heaven," not in *heaven* as in heaven.

The New Testament envisions the coming together in renewal of God's whole creation. In Ephesians 1:11, God's purpose was to sum up all things in Christ, things in heaven and things on earth. So I say to you, as I've said again and again in lectures over the last year or two: Heaven is important, but it's not the end of the world. Yes, when you die, if you belong to God's people, Paul says you go to be with Christ, which is far better. There is a greater future out beyond. I'll come back to this. The point of Jesus coming was not to show us how to escape earth and go to heaven. The point of Jesus was to say, "Kingdom of God—here. Now. Get on board!" We in the church have often falsified that.

Likewise, Christianity is not about giving the world fresh teaching about God himself, as though the main thing we needed was more information about what God is like and who he is and what he's up to. So what is Christianity all about then?

Christianity is all about the belief that the living God—in fulfillment of his promises and as the climax of the story of Israel—has done what we needed, finding us, saving us, giving us new life in Jesus. With Jesus, a great door has swung open in the cosmos which can never again be shut.

It's the door to the prison where we have been chained up.

> We are offered freedom: freedom to experience God's rescue for ourselves, to go through the open door and explore the new world to which we now have access. . . . [And] to discover, through following Jesus, that this new world is indeed a place of justice, spirituality, relationship, and beauty, and that we are not only to enjoy it as such but to work at bringing it to birth on earth as in heaven. In listening to Jesus, we discover whose voice it is that has echoed around the hearts and minds of the human race all along. (from *Simply Christian*)

HOW JESUS BRINGS THE KINGDOM

But it isn't just a matter of Jesus coming and saying, "Okay, kingdom, here now, that's all right, isn't it?"—because it isn't, because the world is a dark and tragic place, and has been for a very long time. Woven into the fabric of the Israel story and then reaching its climax in the Jesus story, right at the center of the Gospel story, we find that the evil of the whole world—the evil of power structures, the evil which is what we call natural evil, evil within people—is taken and focused onto the central figure, to the Jesus who ends up hanging on a Roman cross. And so:

> The meaning of the story is found in every detail, as well as in the broad narrative. The pain and tears of all the years were met together on Calvary. The sorrow of heaven joined with the anguish of earth; the forgiving love stored up in God's future was poured out into the present; the voices that echo in a million human hearts, crying for justice, longing for spirituality, eager for relationship, yearning for beauty, drew themselves together into a final scream of desolation.
>
> Nothing in all the history of paganism comes anywhere near this combination of event, intention, and meaning. Nothing in Judaism had prepared for it, except in puzzling, shadowy prophecy. The death of Jesus of Nazareth as the King of the Jews, the bearer of Israel's destiny, the fulfillment of God's promises to his people of old, is either the most stupid, senseless waste and misunderstanding the world has ever seen, or it the fulcrum around which world history turns.
>
> Christianity is based on the belief that it was and is the latter. (from *Simply Christian*)

What the resurrection means. Of course it didn't end there, and I and others have explored at length the question of what precisely happened on the third day after Jesus' death. I've argued elsewhere substantially for understanding the bodily resurrection of Jesus of Nazareth, not only as a real event within real space-time human history, but as the launch pad for something which many Christians have just not got on board with at all.

If you go into church on Easter Day and listen to sermons on the resurrection, again and again you'll hear preachers saying things like, "Jesus died, therefore there really is a life after death." Or "Jesus rose again, therefore we can be assured that we can go to heaven." Or "Jesus rose again so we can have a new life here and now."

All of those have truth in them, but it's not what Matthew, Mark, Luke and John say. They say, "Jesus has been raised from the dead, therefore God's new creation has begun and we have got a job to do." That's rather different from some of the escapism which we often get in Easter preaching. The resurrection is not about proving that there's a life after death.

The resurrection is the launching of God's new creation. And in fact the resurrection of Jesus is not so much a very odd event within the old world; it is the prototypical event within, and the launching pad for, God's new world. Believing in the resurrection from the New Testament's point of view is believing that it's about the new thing that God is doing. And God will not rest until, as the prophets foretold, the earth—not just heaven but the *earth*—shall be full of the glory of the Lord, as the waters cover the sea.

That's the promise. And we who live between Easter and the fulfillment of that promise are not to be passive spectators. We are not merely to be beneficiaries of God's new world—though, please God, we will be that—but we are to be agents of it. And that's what gives genuine biblical Christianity its central dynamic.

How can that come about? The New Testament says it is because God breathes his own life into those who follow Jesus in a new way. They become, often to their surprise, new creation people. And that is the foundation of it all. I have two chapters on the work of the Holy Spirit in *Simply Christian* in order to show how it is that as we breathe in the life of God, we are not only little by little (and often painfully) slowly transformed in ourselves, but more to the point, able to *be transforming people* in God's world.

That transformation is the point at which those "echoes of a voice" have to be translated into a voice we ourselves utter. We become people who can work for justice; who can develop and explore the riches of spirituality that are ours as free human beings; who can work at relationships (ours and those around the world); and who can be agents of transforming beauty, beauty which will lure people to glimpse the glory of God, even in unlikely places. So our task is to discover, through Jesus, whose Voice it is that we've been hearing. Then we discover what it would mean to follow that Voice, and become part of the project which that Voice has in mind.

REFLECTING THE IMAGE

The third and final section is called "Reflecting the Image," because the task of being a Christian is to be a genuine human being. A lot of people get this mistaken idea that to be a Christian, you're going to be somehow a shrunken sort of human being, a sub- or semihuman being, rather than a fully alive, glorious creature reflecting the image of God. And sadly, the church has often given quite a bit of credence to that, as many Christians have thought it was their job to live rather shrunken human lives. Not so.

Yes, of course, there is renunciation in the Christian life. There is fasting, there is taking up the cross, but ultimately the aim is to become more truly human. And that begins with worship and prayer. Worship for many Christians is, "Well of course I'm a Christian, of course I believe in Jesus, of course I read the Bible and of course I try and live a Christian life. Oh, and of course I go to church on Sundays and sing a few hymns."

But actually, worship is designed to be the living center of it all, because one of the great spiritual laws is that we become like what we worship. If we are made in the image of God, the God who made the whole world, then worshiping this God is the way to reflect God into the world. Notice how the "image of God" language works—it isn't just that being image bearers means we are rather like God in some way or other. The idea of the image is that of an angled mirror reflecting what's up there to what's out there and back again.

A lot of people get this mistaken idea that to be a Christian, you're going to be somehow a shrunken sort of human being, a sub- or semihuman being, rather than a fully alive, glorious creature reflecting the image of God.

When I lived in Oxford, we lived just down the road from one of the great classical museums in Britain, the Ashmolean Museum. I remember walking down a long gallery one day looking at all the statues of Roman emperors. (I was trained as a Roman historian before I became a theologian.) It just struck me, as I was looking, about where all these statues came from. Among the great, big statues of emperors and their children and their wives and their families, not one of those statues, as far as I recall, came from Rome itself. These statues were from places like Egypt and Turkey and Spain and France and anywhere else around the Mediterranean world except in Rome, because in Rome, they had the emperor and his family. They knew what they looked like. But the rest of the empire needed to have images of the emperor to tell the subject peoples who their lord and master was.

The point about being made in the image of God is that God has put into his world a creature—namely ourselves, human beings—whose purpose is to let the world know who its Creator is. We do that by the wise stewardship of creation. We at the same time reflect the praises of creation back to God the Creator. (Revelation 4–5 is all about that.) Thus, we become genuinely image-bearing human beings. Within that, I have various discussions about sacraments and other aspects of Christian worship which fit remarkably well once you understand how creation and new creation are designed to work together.

The Bible. That all inevitably leads to the question of the Bible itself. You have battles with the Bible in this country much more than we do in my country. People aren't nearly as interested in the Bible in the United Kingdom. I wish they were, actually. But often when I come to America and lecture about the Bible, I find there are huge controversies about what actually to say about the Bible. It's a shame, because the Bible itself, by simply diving in and starting to read it, is so absolutely stunning that it's much better just to let yourself get soaked in the story than to worry about particular theories. The theories matter, but they don't matter nearly as much as reading the text.

I'm going to read you another little bit from the first of two chapters of *Simply Christian* on the Bible. My parents are getting on now. My father is in his mid-eighties and reads everything I write. Bless him, he was a businessman who never read any theology until I started to write books. I'd sent my parents a copy of this book, and he said, "When anyone comes to the house, I read them this opening paragraph." So I'll read it to you:

It's a big book, full of big stories with big characters. They have big ideas (not least about themselves) and make big mistakes. It's about God and greed and grace; about life, lust, laughter, and loneliness. It's about birth, beginnings, and betrayal; about siblings, squabbles, and sex; about power and prayer and prison and passion.

And that's only Genesis.

In other words, go for it! Sometimes, after morning prayer with my chaplain in the little chapel we have at home, we've read a chapter from Kings or Jeremiah, and I say, "Supposing that book had been lost forever and then somebody had dug that stuff up in the sands of Egypt and had published it. We would all say, 'This is the most amazing stuff!'" I read ancient literature until it was coming out of my ears because I was a classicist by training, but this is just an amazing book, this Bible. We Christians actually don't take it nearly seriously enough.

How do we take it seriously? I talk about that quite a bit, but the point is this: This Scripture is not designed to be authoritative in the sense of having a textbook on the shelf so that you can go look up the right answer to your questions. There are lots of right answers to lots of questions, but that's not how the authority of Scripture works.

According to the Bible itself, God is the one with authority. At the end of Matthew's Gospel, Jesus doesn't say "all authority in heaven and earth is given to the book you chaps are going to write." Jesus says, "All authority in heaven and earth has been given to me. Go therefore and make disciples."

According to the Bible itself, *God* is the one with authority. At the end of Matthew's Gospel, Jesus doesn't say "all authority in heaven and earth is given to the book you chaps are going to write." Jesus says, "All authority in heaven and earth has been given to me. Go therefore and make disciples." So if you take the phrase *authority of Scripture* seriously (which I do—I take it very seriously), that must actually be a scrunched-down, shorthand way of referring to the authority which God has given to Jesus, somehow mediated through Scripture.

But as soon as we say it like that—and that is how the Bible comes to life when we take it like that—then we say, "But what is God up to in the world through Jesus?" The answer is, God is dealing with sin through the cross of Christ, and is launching his new creation through the resurrection of Christ. He is applying that to human hearts and lives, and to the whole wide world in the power of his Spirit. When we have the Bible in our hands, it is not so that we can be safe, sound, good little Christians. It is so that we can be energized agents for God's mission in the world. That's what the authority of Scripture looks like in practice, or ought to look like.

The church. For a lot of Christians today, not least young Christians, the church is—let's face it—a bit of a turn off. For a lot of people today, that stuff, like a bishop's regalia, is just yesterday's story. We want to do it differently today. I fully understand that. It's not actually so very long ago that I was young myself. I know that the church often presents itself as a very dull, very boring, very out-of-date, dreary, muddled, misguided sort of place.

And yet one of the great Reformers, John Calvin, said if God is our Father, the church is our mother, because when we become a Christian, we become a member of the family. It isn't just that if we believe personally in Jesus then it might help to go to church from time to time because there may be some people there who can help us on our way. It is that we belong to one another. And that belonging actually matters enormously in terms of what God intends to do in and through the church for the world. We can't do that by ourselves. We can't do it as isolated denominations. We need one another. Church unity matters, even though it's hugely difficult and actually hugely stressful very often (believe me, because I try to work at that).

Agenda of the new creation. Last, it's about new creation starting now. The challenge we have had ever since the resurrection of Jesus is to say God has launched this project of new creation. It's about justice and spirituality and relationships and beauty and a whole lot more besides, and what are we doing about it? It's about announcing to the world that there is a God, and he is its good Creator. It's about announcing to the world that Jesus is the Lord of the world, and so Caesar isn't—neither Caesar in the ancient world nor whoever "Caesar" might be in the modern.

It's announcing to the world that God's Spirit, who is the Spirit of truth, is let loose into the world, and that all our fumblings and mumblings about truth, not least within postmodernity, have to be rethought and reassessed in the light of that. What's that going look like? How do we actually go about that? What is the Way (the early Christians called Christianity "the Way"). It's a way that we have to go. It's because we are called to become, in the power of the Spirit, people through whom new creation can happen starting here and now. It's new creation deep down within people's hearts. It's new creation as wide as the world, where two thirds of the world is in hopeless, unpayable debt to one third of the world, and that one third is us—you and me. It's about working for new creation in places where global warming and other devastating things are happening to the environment.

Some Christians have a real difficulty about that. I suspect the agenda of new creation has somehow slid out of the back of their Bibles and got forgotten in the frantic quest for them simply to be rescued from the world and to go off to heaven forever and ever, amen. It's not what we find in the New Testament. Heaven is important, but God's eventual goal is new heavens and new earth. We are to become citizens of that and agents of it in the present time.

And so, Christian ethics takes its proper place. Think back to what I said about the different views of God. A lot of people think of Christian ethics in terms of that deist view—that there's a God upstairs somewhere who's made a list of rather difficult and arbitrary rules, and he inflicts them on us poor humans and gets very cross if we disobey them.

It reminds me (another first-century Roman story) of one of the Roman emperors who was particularly malicious. He used to delight in inventing odd laws at a moment's notice and having them carved in very small letters on stone tablets. We stuck them up high on buildings so that people could hardly read them. Then he would have an excuse to punish anybody he wanted for breaking those laws. A lot of people really do conceive of Christian ethics along that sort of model.

Equally and oppositely, some people have thought of Christian ethics much more in terms of getting in touch with the way the world is, and being true to their deepest feelings. The Romantic movement and existentialism have driven us quite a long way down that road. It's as though, because the world is God's world, whatever we find it in it is really good. So we just have go with that and find the way through somehow.

Neither of those corresponds to the God we know in Jesus and by the Spirit. Neither of them actually constitutes Christian ethics as such. Christian ethics comes when we take seriously the goodness of the God-given world, but also the radicalness of the evil which has infected the world, and also the dealing with evil that happens through Jesus and the Spirit and the birth of new creation.

In other words, when we map what it means to be human on the story that I've been trying to tell this evening, then we discover that, yes, of course there are rules. But it's not just a matter of learning the rules and trying to do them. It's a matter of those being the key guidelines which remind us what it means to be people of new creation. It's being people of the cross and the Spirit. Therefore, we're going to have to say no to some things deeply ingrained in our person and in our world, and also say yes to some things that seem (at least to begin with) completely counterintuitive. It's not easy. It takes wrestling and wisdom and struggle and, not least, fellowship with other people who are on the same path.

But as we do so, we discover again and again that those four echoes of a voice become more and more true to who we are. If you deafen your ears to the call of justice anywhere in the world—watch out. Think whose Voice it is you are squelching. If you fail to pay attention to the spirituality which is there in and through the whole of God's world, and you think it's only what happens when you kneel down and say your prayers—watch out, because you are belittling a key element. If you play fast and loose with relationships at any level, whether individual, communal, global—watch out. We are made for one another to reflect God's image together. And if you scorn or spurn the call of beauty, as though it's irrelevant, just a bit of pretty stuff around the edge, but we're going to get on with the reality in the middle—beware. This is God's lovely world. We have only heard the piano part of the music. One day we're going to hear the full quintet.

So let me read you the final paragraph of *Simply Christian:*

> Made for spirituality, we wallow in introspection. Made for joy, we settle for pleasure. Made for justice, we clamor for vengeance. Made for relationship, we insist on our own way. Made for beauty, we are satisfied with sentiment. But new creation has already begun. The sun has begun to rise. Christians are called to leave behind, in the tomb of Jesus Christ, all that belongs to the brokenness and incompleteness of the present world. It is time, in the power of the Spirit, to take up our proper role, our fully human role, as agents, heralds, and stewards of the new day that is dawning. That, quite simply, is what it means to be Christian: to follow Jesus Christ into the new world, God's new world, which he has thrown open before us.

13

WHY HUMAN RIGHTS ARE IMPOSSIBLE WITHOUT RELIGION

John Warwick Montgomery
The Veritas Forum at the University of California, Santa Barbara, 1999

EVERYONE IS IN FAVOR OF human rights. Human rights in many ways parallel motherhood, apple pie and the flag. No matter where we go in the world, we will find that the political leaders in power—including some of the very worst dictators—are nevertheless in favor of human rights. Human rights, as my head of school in England remarks, is a "sexy" subject. It's a subject which immediately elicits interest, and everyone presumably favors human rights.

And yet.

And yet a decade ago Claude Lelouch, the famous French film director, did a movie based on George Orwell's *Animal Farm*, the title of which, *Les uns et les autres*, was taken from Orwell's celebrated line: "All the animals are equal, But some are more equal than others." And the point of the film is that in reality—in practice—though everyone favors human rights, they favor human rights in their own terms. That is to say, human rights are employed as a device, very often, to justify what one's own nation is doing, to ensure that one's own nation receives favorable treatment, but other nations are not looked at in the same light.

The most important question in the area of human rights is certainly how rights can be justified. Very often in the field of human rights there is a confusion between rights, on the one hand, and wants and needs on the other. The fact that we want something, the fact that our life would be immensely better were we to have something, or the fact that we genuinely need something—do those matters equate with a right to have such?

Though everyone favors human rights, they favor human rights in their own terms.

How do we define rights? And after we've defined them, how do we justify them? That's what we have to address. And in order to do this I will take you on a little journey back in time to the nineteenth century.

HUMAN RIGHTS: FROM NATURAL LAW TO LEGAL POSITIVISM

In the nineteenth century the prevailing legal philosophy of the West was replaced by another legal philosophy. For some fifteen hundred years the prevailing legal philosophy in the West was known as *legal naturalism* or *natural law theory* or *juris naturalism*. That philosophy held that there is a higher or deeper standard, outside of the law, on the basis of which the law needs to be judged. When the positive law sets forth a particular statute or a particular series of case decisions, it is nonetheless, necessary to judge all of that from the outside by a higher ethical or moral standard.

In the middle of the nineteenth century that legal philosophy was replaced very largely in the West by a philosophy known as *legal positivism* or *legal realism*. (There's a slight difference between the two, but we won't worry about it.) In general, that philosophy came to prevail in legal instruction in the common law world, England and America, and also in the civil law world, the European continent.

According to the legal philosophy of legal positivism, law is the command of the sovereign. It is not to be judged by any standard outside of itself. It is impossible for such standards to operate within the law per se, and one must go to the positive law, to the law of the land, in order to find out what the law is. If it looks like law, tastes like law and smells like law, *it's law,* and we don't ask subsequent ethical questions in regard to it. If we are asking such questions, we're not asking them within the area of law at all.

Jeremy Bentham. Now this philosophy was developed by two English scholars. One of them is well known: Jeremy Bentham, the utilitarian philosopher. (The other is John Austin, whose work was solely within the area of jurisprudence, and he died quite young.)

The problem is that Bentham had diarrhea of the pen. He could not stop writing. He wrote a great deal, and most of it was not published during his own lifetime. Bentham, a utilitarian, had various ideas on social improvement, ideas that influenced the law, penal reform and the like.

(Parenthetically, one of his ideas was that it would be useful, utilitarian that he was, if great men were not buried. It would be better for them to be embalmed and set up in public places as models for the next generation. Fortunately, this idea was not carried out, except in the case of Bentham himself. If you would like to see Bentham, you can—he is stuffed in University College London. The embalming was not entirely successful, however; the original skull is between his legs and the head is wax, but in any case, this is quite something to see. And we understand that he is rolled out for certain board meetings at the University of London. His vote is not known, but that's true of the other members of the board as well.)

Anyway, the fundamental philosophy of the law set forth by these gentlemen is that once we have identified the political system in operation, and we've determined how law is made within that particular culture, whatever it happens to be, we cannot raise higher issues as to the legitimacy of the whole thing. The thing is legitimate by virtue of the fact that it follows from the commands of the sovereign. This doesn't require a monarchial system or an autocratic system. If we have, for example, a constitutional democracy and those procedures are employed, and we end up with a certain law, then that law is law. Period.

This, of course, means as a philosophy that there will be different legal systems with contradictory laws, as compared to other systems, and there is no ultimate way to resolve this, because though we can criticize the laws within a system as to their consistency, we cannot criticize the system per se. The system stands beyond that.

H. L. A. Hart and Hans Kelsen. And this carries us to the two most influential representatives of this position in the twentieth century, namely H. L. A. Hart, professor of jurisprudence at Oxford (who died just a few years ago) and Hans Kelsen. Kelsen, who was an Austrian fortunate enough to immigrate to the United States before he could be persecuted under the Hitler regime, spent his last years in California. He taught at the University of California at Los Angeles and also in the north, in the San Francisco area.

These two gentlemen refined legal positivism. We can't go into their positions here since that would carry us too far afield, but their positions, in spite of the refinements presented, are nonetheless classical positivism. They will not allow the law to be judged by an extrinsic ethic. Let me read you a fairly dense paragraph from H. L. A. Hart, and then I will translate from English into English:

> We only need the word "validity," and commonly only use it to answer questions which arise within a system of rules, where the status of a rule as a member of the system depends on its satisfying certain criteria provided by a rule of recognition. No such question can arise as to the validity of the very rule of recognition, which provides the criteria. It can neither be valid nor invalid, but is simply accepted as appropriate for use in this way.[1]

He employs the analogy of the meter bar in Paris. Let's say we're in Strasbourg, France, during the summer, and we go into a hardware store and buy a meter stick. But we suspect the owner of the hardware store is selling meter sticks that are not accurate. So we get on the train to Paris, clutching our meter stick in our hand, and we go to the Bureau of Standards, and there in a case is a standard meter bar. Now we can go up to that case and compare the length of your meter stick with the standard meter bar. But suppose the thought occurs: *How do I know that the standard meter bar is the right length?* So we ask the guard there,

"Is the meter bar the right length?" And he says, "You can't ask that question! The meter bar is an arbitrary measure. You can compare other meter sticks with it, but you can't meaningfully ask the question as to whether the meter bar is the right length."

Says Hart, that's the way it is in legal systems. We can determine whether the individual elements in the system properly fit the system, but we can't ask whether the total legal system is valid or invalid, right or wrong, genuine or not. That kind of a question can't be answered. Thus, H. L. A. Hart is indeed a legal positivist.

In an unpublished but recorded lecture given at the University of California at Los Angeles, Hans Kelsen says this:

> It is of the greatest importance to be aware of the fact that there is not only one moral or political system, but at different times and within different societies several different moral and political systems are considered to be valid by those living under these normative systems. The systems come into existence by custom, or by the commands of outstanding personalities like Moses, Jesus, or Mohammed. If men believe that these personalities are inspired by a transcendental, supernatural, the moral or political system has a religious character. It is, especially in this case, when the moral or political system is supposed to be of divine origin that the values constituted by it are considered to be absolute.
>
> However, if the fact is taken into consideration that there are, there were, and probably always will be several different moral and political systems actually presupposed to be valid within different societies, the values constituted by these systems can be considered to be only relative. Then the judgment that a definite government or a definite legal order is just can be pronounced only with reference to *one* of the several different political and moral systems, and then the same behavior or the same governmental activity or the same legal order made with reference to another moral or political system be considered as morally bad or politically unjust.

What Kelsen is saying is that total legal systems are like trains passing in the night. There is no vantage point on the basis of which we can judge them, except from the standpoint of another system. And if system A makes nasty statements about the immorality of system B, they don't mean anything, because system B can turn around and make nasty statements about system A. The systems stand by themselves. We can tinker with the systems internally, but what we cannot meaningfully do is to criticize the systems per se. Law is the command of the sovereign.

This did not worry nineteenth-century thinkers at all. It particularly didn't worry the English. Why? Because the nineteenth century was the great century of English imperial expansion, and it was a firm conviction, an unquestioned position, of those in England during the Victorian period that the world would eventually become English! And of course under those conditions, different legal systems wouldn't make any significant difference, because ultimately everything would be English.

PROBLEM OF THE POSITIVIST VIEW OF THE NINETEENTH CENTURY

The end result of the expansion of the empire in the nineteenth century was of course the disintegration of that empire early in the twentieth century. And what was the general situation in the twentieth century? Well, we managed to have two perfectly horrendous world wars and several perfectly ghastly totalitarianisms. And at the end of World War II it was discovered that the rumors concerning Nazi activity were underestimated. The Third Reich had attempted systematically to destroy the Jewish population of Europe and all political dissidents. And they had done this by techniques almost too horrible to describe.

So the Nuremberg war crimes trials took place, and at those trials the Nazi leaders of course attempted to defend themselves. How? By virtue of the philosophy of legal positivism!

They said, "Granted, our legal system is not the same as yours. Our fundamental values are not the same as yours—and we simply made our legal system reflect our own cultural values. Our rule involved Aryan supremacy; we did not regard Jews as human beings on the same level as Aryans. From our standpoint, then, Jews certainly did not deserve to benefit from Aryan rights. And the only reason that we find ourselves on trial here is that you won and we lost."

On the basis of legal positivism, of course it's impossible for one legal system to judge another legal system. And the Nazis argued at Nuremberg, among other things, that they therefore did not deserve to be judged by the Allied victors.

Now this put the prosecution at Nuremberg into a very interesting position. In order for the prosecution to justify the criminal prosecution of the Nazi war criminals, it was necessary for them to move beyond legal positivism. They had absolutely no choice. At Nuremberg the American chief prosecutor was Robert H. Jackson, an associate justice of the Supreme Court of the United States, and in his summing up he said: "It is common to think of our own time as standing at the apex of civilization, from which the deficiencies of preceding ages may patronizingly be viewed in the light of what is assumed to be 'progress.' " Note that he put the word *progress* in quotation marks. *No one* put the word *progress* in quotation marks in the nineteenth century. It was simply assumed that civilization was rising to higher and higher levels, and that therefore a cultural millennium was before us and we didn't need to worry about questions such as justifying legal systems. Jackson continues, "The reality is that in the long perspective of history the present century will not hold an admirable position, unless its second half is to redeem its first."[2]

On the basis of legal positivism, of course it's impossible for one legal system to judge another legal system. And the Nazis argued at Nuremberg, among other things, that they therefore did not deserve to be judged by the Allied victors.

Well, we're now looking back on the second half of the twentieth century, and it surely has not done that. We've discovered, for example, that under Stalin there was even more evidence of atrocities than under Hitler! And then there have been Pol Pot and Idi Amin Dada and a whole succession of miserable tyrants who have hurt, maimed and killed their fellow human beings.

> These two score years in this twentieth century will be recorded in the book of years as one of the most bloody in all annals. Two World Wars have left a legacy of dead, which number more than all the armies engaged in any war that made ancient or medieval history. No half-

century ever witnessed slaughter on such a scale, such cruelties and in-humanities, such wholesale deportations of peoples into slavery, such annihilations of minorities. The terror of Torquemada pales before the Nazi inquisition. These deeds are the overshadowing historical facts by which generations to come will remember this decade. If we cannot eliminate the causes and prevent the repetition of these barbaric events, it is not an irresponsible prophesy to say that this twentieth century may yet succeed in bringing the doom of civilization.

Goaded by these facts, we have moved to redress the blight on the record of our era. . . . At this stage of the proceedings, I shall rest upon the law of these crimes as laid down in the Charter [the Charter of the International Military Tribunal, the vehicle by which the war criminals were being judged]. In interpreting this Charter, however, we should not overlook the unique and emergent character of this body. . . . It is no part of the constitutional mechanism of internal justice of any of the signatory nations. . . . As an International Military Tribunal it rises above the provincial and transient, and seeks guidance not only from international law, but also from the basic principles of jurisprudence, which are the assumptions of civilization.[3]

Jackson is saying: Agreed, the law used against the Nazi war crimi-nals is not part of English law, American law, French law, Russian law—not at all. It takes itself from the guidance available in interna-tional law, but also from the basic principles of jurisprudence, which are the assumptions of civilization.

He's saying that we must go to a law that is higher or deeper than national law. We can't simply rest with the law of a nation, because the law of a nation can be damnable, as it was in the case of Nazi jurispru-dence.

A book published in France, *Les lois du Vichy* (The Vichy Laws), ex-poses a rigorously systematic code modeled on the French civil and criminal codes that provided the Pétain regime with the equivalent of the Nazi laws of the time. And as a result of this, Jews in France could not hold any public positions, couldn't be teachers, and were eventually deported to the death camps, just as Jews were throughout Europe.

Human rights violations demand a higher law. Human rights viola-tions, in order to be dealt with, require our being able to find some rights that human beings have that must not be taken away by any government, no matter what the government or legal system. But where can we possibly find that sort of thing?

CONSCIENCE AS A GUIDE

Let's look at the natural law position, which existed for centuries, and which was moved to the wings by legal positivism. Is the answer to go back to natural law? The essence of natural law theory is that we have inherent within us an understanding of human value and an ethic, a morality, an understanding of human rights, which we can use to judge positive law. This approach was first set forth by Aristotle, and then it was baptized, as it were, by Thomas Aquinas and other medieval theologians, and brought within the framework of the medieval West. It continued on by way of the Declaration of the Rights of Man at the time of the French Revolution, and to be sure, the American founding documents. The fundamental idea here is that people really know what's right, and they should use that to judge the positive law.

Why did that viewpoint disappear? Why was it supplanted by legal positivism? In criticizing William Blackstone (an English jurist), Bentham declared that the whole natural law idea was "nonsense on stilts," meaning that human beings maintaining that viewpoint think that their personal consciences can be elevated to the point of criticizing the law of the land. But how can they prove that their conscience represents anything that is capable of doing such?

Bentham had a point. One of the biggest difficulties with natural law theory, and one of the reasons that it disappeared from prominence in the nineteenth century, is the ambiguity and subjectivity of it. In a way, we might say that this is the "Jiminy Cricket" approach to law of human

One of the biggest difficulties with natural law theory, and one of the reasons that it disappeared from prominence in the nineteenth century, is the ambiguity and subjectivity of it. In a way, we might say that this is the "Jiminy Cricket" approach to law of human rights. . . . "Let your conscience be your guide."

rights. Do you remember Jiminy Cricket in Walt Disney? He sings a little song, "Let your conscience be your guide."

What's the trouble with this? The trouble is, of course, that conscience is culturally conditioned, and often culturally determined. When you were a little shaver and you took cookies out of the cookie jar when you shouldn't, Mommy came along and whacked your little hand, and as a result of this you began to feel guilty when you stole cookies. As a result, you stole fewer and fewer cookies.

But that's not the only kind of conditioning of conscience possible. Remember Fagin in *Oliver Twist?* He teaches the street children to steal, to engage in the activity of a cut purse or a pickpocket. Fagin shows them how to do it and makes them feel guilty if they don't bring back valuable watches. So, when the kid gets back at the end of the day and he hasn't stolen a good watch, he's blamed for it and he feels guilty. The next day he's going to work harder to steal something of greater value.

Conscience is culturally conditioned, and therefore it isn't capable of providing the needed objective standard. It's also ambiguous. I'll give you a horrifying example.

Honeste vivere, alterum non laedere, suum cuique tribuere, *which translated means "To live honestly, to harm no one, and to make sure that each one has what he deserves." That's the essence of a natural law.*

One of the greatest statements of natural law theory appears in the Justinian Code, the great sixth-century law code of antiquity. A section of that law code is called the Digest, and at the beginning of the Digest there is a definition of natural law: *Honeste vivere, alterum non laedere, suum cuique tribuere,* which translated means "To live honestly, to harm no one, and to make sure that each one has what he deserves." That's the essence of a natural law.

Surely, no one would disagree with this. But what exactly does it mean? Shortly after World War II, I took friends to the death camp at Buchenwald, just outside of the Enlightenment city of Weimar, Germany. The metal gates leading into Buchenwald have a German inscription on them, *Jedem das Seine.* That means, "Each person gets what he properly deserves." It is the German translation of the third element in the Justinian Code's definition of the natural law.

See what's going on here? The fact of the matter is that the natural law is so vague, so ill-defined, that it can be moved into any context we wish, and it can be employed to create hideous injustice, because it doesn't define what is meant by what each person properly deserves. It doesn't tell what harm actually consists of, and it certainly doesn't define honesty.

Natural law theory may not be as bad as nonsense on stilts, but it certainly isn't going to provide the kind of solid foundation that we need for human rights and for judging inhumanities within legal systems. Where, then, can we go for an answer? Where could we possibly go?

A UNIVERSAL RULE APPROACH

Some attempts have been made in recent years to rehabilitate another kind of natural law approach. It isn't called natural law; it actually goes back to the philosopher Immanuel Kant in the eighteenth century. Kant said, "You can't prove God's existence or anything theological, but you can prove an ethic. You can establish an ethic that stands beyond any and all argument."

This ethic was based on a particular kind of principle, and the principle goes like this: act so that your action can become a universal rule. He termed this *the categorical imperative.* It's an imperative—it tells us what we're supposed to be doing. It's categorical, meaning we can't argue against it. Said Kant, "Everyone must rationally see the value of this kind of principle."

Rawls and a neo-Kantian ethic. Today there are political scientists and legal theorists who have used Kant's fundamental notion in order to try to justify human rights. For example, John Rawls, probably the greatest twentieth-century American political theorist, says that if we can take, hypothetically, human beings in a state of ignorance, so that they don't know anything about any particular advantages that they have over others, then they will necessarily have to form governments that embrace his two principles.

1. Each person is to have an equal right to the most extensive system

of equal basic liberties, compatible with a similar system of liberty for all. In other words, there will need to be civil liberties, and people will logically have to agree to those civil liberties if they are removed from any understanding of the special advantages that they have over others.

2. Social and economic inequalities are to be arranged so that they are both to the greatest benefit of the least advantaged, consistent with what Rawls calls "the just savings principle" (that is, keeping in mind future generations) and attached to offices and positions open to all, under conditions of equality and opportunity.

These two principles are the equivalent of the first and second generations of human rights, as they are termed in contemporary parlance. In a lecture at Oxford, Rawls applied his analysis to the issue of international human rights. He said, in effect, "If you take nations and you can abstract from them their special advantages, nations would also have to agree to these same first- and second-generation human rights." In other words, nations would have to ratify the civil and political covenant of the United Nations, in line with principle number one, and the economic and social covenant of the United Nations in terms of principle number two.

Well, what is the problem with this sort of thing?

First, the problem is simply that there is no way that we can get people to forget their special advantages. We can't put them in that kind of an isolated situation. And there's no point in doing it in theory if in practice people will always operate in terms of their special advantages and privileges.

Second, even if you got individuals and nations to agree that they should always act so that their action could be universalized or generalized, that's no guarantee that they're going to follow it.

Third, the worst of the dictators in human history, those we've had the worst amount of difficulty with, are not going to agree to this at all. They know their personal power and are convinced that they can effectively grind down on other people, and they see no reason why they should stop. For example, let's try to present a neo-Kantian ethic to Genghis Khan.

I say, "Genghis, you've been out raping and pillaging again, haven't you?" And Genghis says, "Yes, I have."

And I say, "Genghis, Genghis, you have got to operate with a principle of universalization. You don't want other people to rape and pillage you, do you? Well, under those circumstances you surely cannot justify raping and pillaging others. So act that your action could become a universal rule."

Genghis grabs me by the throat and says, "Listen, you little pipsqueak. I am Genghis and I am powerful. I can rape and pillage, and the others are not going to be able to do this to me. Moreover, I enjoy raping and pillaging. Some people collect stamps. I rape and pillage."

And he thereupon inverts me and pounds me into the ground, and the discussion ends.

A neo-Kantian ethic is simply incapable of solving fundamental human rights problems. So, where can a solution be found?

NEED FOR A TRANSCENDENTAL SOLUTION: WITTGENSTEIN

We need to do a little bit of epistemology, a little bit of work in the philosophical area of truth claims. And probably the best place to start is with Ludwig Wittgenstein, the great analytical philosopher of the twentieth century. Wittgenstein wrote a work titled the *Tractatus*. It is not good bedtime reading, frankly. It is in numbered propositions and is a very difficult work, but the purpose of this work is to determine how we verify propositions that are not formal in character—factual propositions and ethical propositions.

And when Wittgenstein gets to issues of ethics in proposition 6 and following, he summarizes the situation very simply in a three-word proposition, "Ethics is transcendental."

Ethics is transcendental. What did he mean? Well, he explains it in a lecture he delivered at Oxford, which was posthumously published. He said,

> If a man could write a book on Ethics which really was a book on Ethics, this book would, as with an explosion, destroy all the other books in the world.

Wittgenstein is saying that any ethic arising from the human situation is limited by the human situation. It's culturally conditioned. It can't possibly be absolute because its source isn't absolute. So the only true ethic would be an ethic that doesn't arise from the human situation, that breaks in from the outside. A transcendental, transcendent ethic.

Wittgenstein didn't think there was any such book. One of my professors of philosophy at Cornell University, when I was an undergraduate, was Norman Malcolm. Malcolm was a great friend of Wittgenstein's and wrote a memoir of Wittgenstein. At one point in the memoir he says, "Often Wittgenstein would say, 'Oh my God,' as if imploring a divine intervention." He apparently didn't think there was such an intervention, but he saw perfectly well what the human condition is like without one.[4]

ARCHIMEDES: NEED FOR A FULCRUM

Or we can go to Archimedes. Said Archimedes, "Give me a lever long enough and a fulcrum outside the world, and I can move it." The point being that no matter how great the world is, if he had a lever long enough and a fulcrum properly placed, with his little finger, with his pinky, it would have been possible for Archimedes to move the world.

But the essential condition is that the fulcrum be outside the world. If the fulcrum is in the world, you cannot move it. It would be like trying to pull ourself up by our own bootstraps. One falls on his own derrière! That's painful and accomplishes nothing. The fulcrum's got to be outside the world in order to move it.

Here's a much simpler illustration: water doesn't rise above its own level; that is, we can't get absolute principles from a nonabsolute source. Human beings are finite and self-centered, and the ethics they produce will be limited in precisely those ways. Or to quote Thomas Hobbes, "Human life is nasty, brutish and short," and human rights deriving from the human condition will therefore not reach anything like the needed absolute standards.

The American founding fathers talked about "inalienable" rights. What are they? The rights that cannot be taken away by governments, and which the individual cannot even take away from himself or herself.

Where could we possibly get that sort of thing? If human beings create the rights, of course human beings can take away those rights. Epistemologically, the only way we are ever going to be able to get absolute human rights standards is to go outside the human situation to a non-human source. And incredibly, Jean-Jacques Rousseau, the eighteenth-century political philosopher, understood this. (It is very difficult to find profundity in Rousseau. In this case he actually managed it.) I am not suggesting that Rousseau is a guide in general matters of philosophy, but in the section on law, in the social contract, the *Contrat Social*, Rousseau says:

> In order to discover the rules of society best suited to nations, a superior intelligence beholding all the passions of men without experiencing any of them would be needed. This intelligence would have to be wholly unrelated to our nature, while knowing it through and through. Its happiness would have to be independent of us, and yet ready to occupy itself with ours. And lastly, it would, in the march of time, have to look forward to a distant glory, and working in one century be able to enjoy in the next. It would take gods to give men laws.

The point being: in order to get laws that are going to apply under all conditions, everywhere, we've got to be able to have a perspective that can see into the human condition, past, present and future. And it must be sufficiently independent of the human situation that it will not be locked into a particular viewpoint so as to bias the laws being set forth. Thus, "it would take gods to give men laws."

RELIGION AS BASIS FOR TRANSCENDENT CLAIMS

This inevitably takes us into the realm of religion. It's in the realm of religion that transcendent claims have been made to deity and to revelation. That is to say, religions have claimed that there is a transcendent source, and that the transcendent source has spoken.

The problem here, of course, is that the religious claims of the world through history have been inconsistent with each other in most instances. And the religious positions themselves have sometimes not been at all attractive, for example, the Aztec religion, which I intend to revive when I have particular difficulty with my neighbors. The Aztec solution to the problem of salvation is to sacrifice your neighbor. You simply create a pyre, cut your neighbor open and burn him or her. Instances like this have not encouraged people to look for religious solutions.

And there are not only the obnoxious religious options like that, but there are also religious solutions that are technically meaningless. For example, there is the claim in Hinduism that "Brahman is all." No one can really dispute this. The problem is, what does it mean? Does it mean that everything is God? If everything is God, then I suppose in a sense nothing is God, because our world often displays an appalling absence of human dignity and rights. Or is this an attempted definition? If it is, it doesn't seem to distinguish the transcendent in any way from the immanent. And therefore we find ourselves unable to do very much with it.

If we look at the spread of religions across the centuries, what we really should be looking for is a religion that can demonstrate the truth of its claims, because making claims is easy. Surely those living in California understand this: if people don't like a religion, by next weekend they've started their own. So the number of religions increases. The real issue is not that of making religious claims, but of offering some justification for a given claim.

> *If we look at the spread of religions across the centuries, what we really should be looking for is a religion that can demonstrate the truth of its claims, because making claims is easy. Surely those living in California understand this: if people don't like a religion, by next weekend they've started their own.*

I have a little illustration that may be helpful. This is also a true story. At the time of the French Revolution, an attempt was made to substitute various "rational religions" for historic Christianity, and one of these attempts, a deistic attempt, was created by the French philosopher La Revellière. La Revellière invented a religion he called "Theanthropy," Man Is Godism. He did tracts, booklets and social programs, and worked very hard on this, but it didn't take, and he was very discouraged.

So he went to fellow philosophers for advice. One of them was the French skeptical philosopher Talleyrand. Talleyrand, who had a wonderful sense of humor, said to him, "It seems to me that Jesus Christ, in order to found His religion, first died and rose again on the third day. You could at least do that much."

This suggests that there may be a considerable difference among religious positions, not necessarily in their claims, but in their ability to back them up.

CHRISTIANITY'S CLAIMS AND BASES

I gave a talk previously at this university pointing out how many distinguished lawyers have become Christians on the basis of checking out the evidence for the resurrection of Jesus Christ. Sir Norman Anderson, the head of the School of Advanced Legal Studies at the University of London, for example, the greatest authority on Muslim law outside the Muslim world, became a Christian on the basis of the evidence for the resurrection of Christ, and wrote several books on that subject.

One can engage in historical investigation and discover that the Christian claims are based solidly in empirical, observational fact—and they lead in one direction: Jesus—not as a Jewish boy scout helping little old ladies across the Sea of Galilee, but a person who claimed to be no less than God Almighty come to earth to die for the sins of the world. And he rose again from the dead in order to demonstrate the truth of those affirmations.

Furthermore, Jesus put a stamp of approval on the Bible. As a result of this, the Christian claim is that God was in Christ, reconciling the world unto himself, providing a specific revelation of principles that are inalienable. These principles hold under all circumstances, owing to the fact that they do not derive from a merely human source. They derive from the transcendent. They fulfill Wittgenstein's description of the book, "which with an explosion would destroy all the other books in the world." Now this is a perfectly staggering kind of claim, but it's a claim backed up by solid historical evidence.

In Boston I gave a paper dealing with the specific prophesies in the Old Testament concerning the coming of the Messiah. I used the so-called product rule in statistics. If the Old Testament prophecies are independent of each other (which they are), we can use the product rule to calculate the probabilities against, say, twenty-five of the most specific being fulfilled by pure chance. If the probability of any one of them being valid is taken as only 25 percent, then the likelihood of twenty-five coming to pass by sheer chance would be one in a thousand trillion. *One in a thousand trillion!*

Statistics don't establish cause and effect, obviously. But what are you going to do with a situation like this? The Old Testament was written before the New. So the prophecies can't have been written after their fulfillments. And there is no way that the life of Christ could have been fudged to make it fit the prophesies, because the records of his life were in circulation while hostile religious witnesses were still alive. They would surely have blown the whistle on it. My goodness, the Jewish religious leaders knew their Old Testaments, and if Jesus had not been born in Bethlehem but in Detroit, they would have been the first to raise an objection. We've got a combination of powerful prophetic evidence and solid resurrection evidence that Jesus was the very person he claimed to be.

A CHRISTIAN BASIS FOR HUMAN RIGHTS

Now if this turns out to be the case, notice what we get in the human rights realm.

First, we get that book Wittgenstein talked about. We get the principles, and not in the vague sense of natural law. We get definitive principles, not just the Ten Commandments, but the principles that are running all through Scripture. In my book *Human Rights and Human Dignity*, I've correlated these principles to various human rights conventions today. They are highly specific. And the principles have a solid, transcendent basis for the principles.

But we get more than this. We get something more important than the principles. I began by pointing out that everybody is in favor of human rights. The most greasy dictators are always saying nice things about human rights—meanwhile, they're boiling someone in oil. What does this say? That the real problem with human rights is something beyond the question of the principles—it's the motivation to follow the principle.

Genghis may very well know that it's not nice to rape and pillage, but he enjoys it. The fact of the matter is that the human race is self-centered, and therefore nations are self-centered. It follows that they skew human rights in their own direction to protect themselves, and they don't worry about the next person. *Some are more equal than others.*

In the area of human rights, what is really needed is some device by which human rights can be interiorized, made a part of the human being, so the human being really wants to treat the other person decently. No human rights philosophy, other than the gospel of Jesus Christ, can change people's hearts, and until hearts are changed we can plaster proper human rights principles on every wall everywhere but the results will not be appreciably different from the current ones. Somebody has said, "What we need is not more good advice. What we need is good news."

The Christian message not only makes it possible to know what the principles are and to ground these principles transcendentally, but also opens the avenue—for you and me—to be changed inside. How does this happen? A physician can't force a medicine down someone's gullet if the person doesn't believe he or she has a disease. To do so happens to be a tort against the person in law. We can't do that. People have to recognize they're sick before they're going to take the medicine.

The fact of the matter is that in the area of human rights what is really needed is some device by which human rights can be interiorized, made a part of the human being, so the human being really wants to treat the other person decently. . . . Somebody has said, "What we need is not more good advice. What we need is good news."

So, the first step is to recognize just how radically self-centered we are. And if we see this, then the question is, What's to be done about it? Well, we can't pull ourselves up to heaven by our own bootstraps anymore than it's possible to make the world rise when the fulcrum is on it. We need help from outside. We need a fulcrum outside, and that's exactly why Jesus entered our world as Savior.

Jesus came to earth to die for us on the cross, to take the punishment we deserve and to expiate it, and make it possible for us to enter in to God's presence forever. If we believe this, if we enter into a relationship with him on that basis, then he comes into our heart by way of the Holy Spirit and our life is changed.

"If anyone is in Christ, there is a new creation: everything old has passed away; see, everything has become new!" (2 Corinthians 5:17). Those who have accepted Christ as Lord of their life are the living proof of this. They are not engaged in some kind of subjective religiosity, working themselves up into a mystic state. Not at all. They have accepted God's revelation of himself, based on the historical fact that God was in Christ, reconciling the world to himself.

The objective evidence of the resurrection of Christ and the solidity of the Scriptures offer the basis for entering into that relationship. And when people do that, they really *are* more interested in other people than they are in themselves. They really do go along with Augustine's principle, "Love God and do as you please," because if we love God, what we want to do is what pleases God, and the Scriptures tell us what pleases him. This is precisely the basis we so desperately need for a solid understanding of human rights.

RADICAL MARXIST, RADICAL WOMANIST, RADICAL LOVE

WHAT MOTHER TERESA TAUGHT ME ABOUT SOCIAL JUSTICE

Mary Poplin

The Veritas Forum at Tufts University, 2009

I WANT TO BUILD A CONTEXT so that my talk will make sense. The context is my history. When I went to college, I felt for the first time that I was intellectually awakened. I didn't come from a highly educated family; my dad had not finished high school, and my mother had gone through a couple years in a teacher's college to become a teacher. Even as a teen and young college student, I was deeply drawn to social justice issues.

In high school and college, I was working with handicapped children and adults, and being increasingly drawn to more radical philosophies regarding social justice. Once I became a professor, I fashioned that it was actually my job to bring these radical philosophies into education and to integrate them into my field of education. So in the 1980s I built a teacher education program around social constructivism, which is, for those of you not in the field, the educational equivalent of structuralism and poststructuralism, around radical feminist and womanist theory, and around critical theory (which is basically post-Marxism), and around cultural studies.

In my personal life I also became increasingly adventurous, living on the edge, to the point where, I guess you might say, I was "serially monogamous." I frequented nightclubs, experimented with alcohol and drugs, which were rampant at the University of Texas. In my spiritual life I was experimenting with various spiritual path. I was sort of "surfing the spiritual net," trying transcendental meditation, Buddhist Zen meditation, feminist spirituality and finally, bending spoons—which in California counts as a religious activity.

> *I was sort of "surfing the spiritual net," trying transcendental meditation, Buddhist Zen meditation, feminist spirituality and finally, bending spoons—which in California counts as a religious activity.*

In the late 1980s I met a Native American man, John Rivera, who was a graduate student in the Ph.D. program, slightly older than me. He was the only man to ever take my radical feminism class—and I'm happy to report he's still alive. While we were all discussing how oppressed we were as women, John was silent. In reality, by any measure, he had more experience with oppression than any of us. He had, even as a child, not always attended school because he helped the family by working; he was, among other things, a child farm worker. His whole family of six would sometimes share one potato for dinner.

His peace about all this was very disconcerting to me as a professor who was teaching radical philosophies. I was much more comfortable with people who predictably talked, even complained about their own oppression. He was not naive; he knew and worked against racism and oppression of all kinds in his own way. He had a clear handle on it. He had a clear handle on racism, classism and all forms of what I was calling "oppression," but these things had no handle on *him*. There were no "hooks" in him that this experience had left so he couldn't be trapped or held by it. I was attracted by his peace but confused as to its source.

After he finished his Ph.D., we would work on projects here and there together over the year. Frequently he would offer, "If you ever want help with your spiritual life, I'd like to help," which was very irritating. It seemed to me I *was* doing things with my spiritual life. I didn't know what "spirituality" he believed and lived. He never revealed that.

But in November of 1992, I had an unshakable dream. In this dream, Jesus figured very prominently. When I woke up, I thought—stereotypically—*Native American . . . spiritual life . . . Native Americans can interpret dreams!* So I called him. We met for dinner, and he did offer me some direction still without revealing his own spirituality, which I was to learn quite a bit later is Christian.

Well, because of all of this, I began to hesitantly explore Christianity. After I had begun to open up to Christianity, I went to a monastery in 1994 to a retreat where they said one afternoon, "If you don't have anything else to do, we're going to show a video, a documentary of Mother Teresa, and you are welcome to come and watch." Well, I had not given Mother Teresa any thought before in my life, but when I watched the documentary, I was strangely moved by it. Not only moved by her work, but I was a bit, to be perfectly honest, jolted by it, because here was a woman doing the work that I admired but discussing it in ways that were completely foreign to me.

I admired her, but she kept talking about Jesus. I'd never really heard people talk about justice in that way. But the one thing in the video that really made me want to go to Mother Teresa's mission for two months and work there is that she said, "Our work is not social work, it's religious work." I felt that if I were going to understand that, now that I was seriously exploring Christianity, I would have to actually go to Calcutta and get engaged in the work itself.

So I wrote a letter in the fall of 1995 and asked if I could come in the spring during a sabbatical. So the second jolt to my soul was when I read their letter back to me. I had asked in my letter what I should bring to Calcutta, I was thinking toilet paper, you know, practical things. But their letter said, "All you need to bring to Calcutta is a heart to serve Jesus in the distressing disguise of the poor."

Well, then the questions started really pouring out: Serve Jesus? What does she mean "Serve Jesus"?

Here was a woman who was the head and founder of a worldwide, multiethnic compassion ministry to the poorest of the poor. I professed to support all those things—work with the poor, women in leadership, multiethnic organizations—but she had never made it into my feminist class syllabus, and she had never made it as a model of social justice. So I began to ask myself why this was the case. Was it because she was Christian? Was it because she was Catholic? Was it because she didn't support abortion? Was it because she simply talked too much about Jesus? Why hadn't she made it into my class?

Most people think about Mother Teresa mostly as just a good humanist—actually, maybe an extraordinary humanist. She's more comfortable to us that way.

Most people think about Mother Teresa mostly as just a good humanist—maybe an extraordinary one. She's more comfortable to us that way. It gives us the feeling that if we just tried hard enough, we might be able to be like her. When I came back and wanted to write about the experience, I tried to write it from the secular humanistic position that those of us in colleges and universities understand so well. I thought it would make her less offensive to the world I lived in, fit better with the context of the culture of our times. But she did not think about or live her life this way. So every time I tried to write a chapter that way, I found myself lying about who she was.

Eventually, I stopped trying to exorcise her faith, and as best I could I wrote *Finding Calcutta* from her worldview. So allow me to share a few examples.

MOTHER TERESA'S DEVOTION

We started the day with Mass at the Mother House; I tried to get there early because I knew where she was going to sit. I thought if I could sit close to her, something good might rub off on me—maybe I'd become a nicer person. One day during Mass, a very well-dressed Indian woman came in and started bowing at Mother Teresa's feet.

We're all on the floor (there are no chairs in the chapel at Mother Teresa's) and this woman is kissing her feet and I can see, Mother Teresa is getting pretty disturbed. She speaks to the woman in an Indian language, I don't know what she said, but the woman didn't stop. So Mother takes the woman's hands and she points them toward the crucifix over the altar, and she says to her, in Indian language, and then in English, "It's *him*. Give your thanks to him." Well, the Indian woman kind of pulled back, sat there for a moment and looked at Mother Teresa. Then she looked at the crucifix, and then she just got up and left.

Mother Teresa called herself "a pencil in God's hand." We see the sisters' work with the poor as being their major work, but they do not see that as their primary work. Their first work is prayer and to belong to Jesus. Out of that relationship they have with Jesus, they believe all the work that we see and admire actually emerges. So the stamina, the grace and the strength to work with the poorest of the poor comes from that relationship, according to them.

The work of the Missionaries of Charity is difficult work physically. It's monotonous work, because they're doing the same thing every day. They're cooking, cleaning, feeding, tending people, cleaning up sores and ministering to the poor, the sick and the dying. Something bigger holds them there, and that is their relationship with Christ. As I was watching this, I was thinking to myself of how hard it is to maintain perseverance when doing this kind of service. How easy it is to say, "Well, I'm just not going to go today," or "I'm going to quit." We have had this same problem in many of our "service programs" in colleges and universities.

MOTHER TERESA'S CALLING

Here's a second example. How did Mother Teresa decide to do what she did? Mother Teresa was originally a social studies teacher at Loreto Convent, for middle-school-age girls. Did she just decide that she felt sorry for the poor and wanted to go and help them? Did she do it out of the sheer force of her will and determination? No. Mother Teresa had three mystical visions, beginning on a train ride when she was a thirty-six-year-old nun. In these visions Jesus was speaking to her from the cross. Jesus told her he wanted four things:

> *The work of the Missionaries of Charity is difficult work physically. It's monotonous work, because they're doing the same thing every day. . . . Something bigger holds them there, and that is their relationship with Christ.*

He wanted her to develop an order of Indian nuns who could live like Indians and serve Indian people. Most of the orders in the Catholic Church have European origins and cultural foundations. Mother Teresa told one of her bishops that Jesus did not want her sisters to become *Mems*, which is a word for European women. An Indian girl who joined an order would essentially have to become culturally European. Second, Jesus wanted her to go into the "darkest, deepest holes of the poor" and take him because he loved them. So he asked that she not build an institution like other orders had done in India and elsewhere, but that they live among the poor and go out to them.

Third, they were to *be* poor, live like the poor, inside these poor neighborhoods. Mother Teresa said God called her and Missionaries to live as living sacrifices.

Fourth, they were to serve the poorest of the poor. Mother Teresa served people who had no other options. There are many places in Calcutta that serve the poor, but there is always a fringe of people who are the *poorest of the poor*, the ones living on the streets, in the alleys, suffering and dying there. These are rarely helped and most are ignored, hoping they will go away, or as the man who sold us water said, "They should be left to die. India has too many people."

To these things she was called by Jesus. She did not make this up herself.

A significant aspect of the founding of the order is that Mother Teresa obeyed authority. She thought that obeying the authority of the church, going up through the proper sequence of authority in the church would be a confirmation of her call. The authorities above her would confirm her call if it were real.

MOTHER TERESA'S TRUST IN DIVINE PROVIDENCE

A third example is Mother Teresa's belief in divine providence. Mother Teresa and the Missionaries of Charity *never* ask for money. In fact, their constitution doesn't allow them to ask for money. The reason is that Mother Teresa believed that as long as they are faithful to the calling of Jesus, it is God's responsibility to bring them the provisions they need. So they believe they should never have to ask for money, and they believe no one else should ask for them.

While I was there, Christopher Hitchens came out with his book about Mother Teresa, a nasty little book called *The Missionary Position*. That was before his nasty little book about God, so I guess she is in good company. (He had actually done a BBC film on her called *Hell's Angel* prior to the book.) One of his many complaints about Mother Teresa was that she took money from politically incorrect, maybe even politically corrupt people. Well, Mother Teresa and the Missionaries of Charity don't sit around reading world newspapers all day long to try to figure out where their money's coming from, because they believe the money is sent from the Lord, since they never ask.

I read Hitchens's book while I was there, and soon afterward, I found myself on the bench outside her office talking with her. She was very happy that morning. She told me about how some students from the university had been there and given her some money. She was going to use it for her new ministry to get prostitutes out of jail, put them in homes with some of the sisters, and train them in, well, *other* skills. So she was telling me about this, and I had just read the book. I knew she knew about it because she's quoted in it. I wanted to push her; I just wanted to see what she had to say, so I said to her, "Mother, there are people who write books about you who say you don't need any more money, that you have lots of money."

She looked at me kind of quizzically and then she said, "Oh, the book." She said, "Yes, I haven't read it. It matters not. He's forgiven."

Well, I didn't let that go, because Hitchens knew she said that and was irate about it in the book. So I said to her, "Mother, he knows that you said he was forgiven, and he's kind of angry about that, because he says he didn't need to be forgiven, and he didn't ask you to forgive him."

She said to me, as though I didn't know what I was talking about, "It's not I who forgives. It's God. God has forgiven him."

Then she told me that some of the sisters had read the book, and I should talk to them. So I did. The permanent sisters had passed a copy of the book around and read it; then they fasted for a week and came together at the end of that week. Their prayer, while they were fasting, was that the Lord would show them what the book's message to them was.

I asked them. "Well, what is the message?" The sister who was telling me the story stood there, and smiling gently, she said, "Oh, it's a call for us to become more holy." Well, that was not my response to Christopher Hitchens.

But Mother Teresa believed in radical forgiveness—the decision to let it go, ask God to forgive without anybody asking her to forgive. This, of course, is the kind of forgiveness that Christ gave as he was beaten and crucified on the cross, and the kind he asks us, with his grace, to extend to others. Mother Teresa lived this kind of radical forgiveness. Like John Rivera, all these things were happening to her and being said of her, but she too didn't have any hooks to snare her.

I had many of these kinds of experiences, and they were very foreign to me. I was just beginning to really understand Christianity. India was not as foreign to me as being around the Missionaries of Charity. I knew about cultural difference. It was the Missionaries that confused me—this was not simply a cultural difference but a worldview conflict raging inside of me.

FINDING CALCUTTA

One of the last things Mother Teresa told me—and this is where the book title comes from—she looked at me one day and she said, "You know, God doesn't call everybody to work with the poor like he does us. He calls some people to work with the rich. And he doesn't call everybody to be poor like we are. He calls some people to be rich."

That's why, of course, she could minister to Princess Diana as easily as the poorest people on the streets, which was her ministry. But then she pointed and shook her finger at me (people always say, "Wasn't she sweet?" I always say, "No. She was strong"). Then she said, "But God does call everybody to a Calcutta. You have to find yours."

I came home and began to teach late in August. I would go into my office to prepare, to get things together for class, and I would begin to weep uncontrollably, with no emotion and no knowledge of why I was weeping. This was pretty disconcerting. I'm a thinking type on personality tests, and if you know anyone who's a thinking type, you know that, first, we don't like to cry, and, second, if we are going to cry, we should at least intellectually understand why we're crying.

But I didn't know why I was crying. I would always get myself together in time to go to class, teach the class, and everything would seem fine until I would go back the next time to get ready for class.

This happened throughout September. Then in October I was going to speak at a school administrator's conference on another subject, but the women asked me if I could also speak at their breakfast meeting to tell them a little bit about my time at Mother Teresa's. So I told them little stories, like those in *Finding Calcutta*. At the end of my little talk, they took questions. The last question was from a woman in the back of the room who stood up and asked, "Did you have any trouble coming back from Mother Teresa's?"

> *"God does call everybody to a Calcutta. You have to find yours."*
> —Mother Teresa

At which time, I began to weep just as I was weeping in my office, no emotion, just tears. The women stopped eating and put their coffee cups down. I finally got some semblance of order and at that point, for the first time, I realized why I was weeping. I knew. I had the revelation of *why* I was weeping. And because I was so relieved, I just blurted it out.

I said, "Obviously, I've had some trouble coming back. I've been a Christian now for three years, and I've seen people really *live* this. I'm beginning to understand what the basic principles are, and from all I have seen, I believe it's true. I'm teaching what I've always taught before, but I don't really know how to get from here to there, and I feel like a liar." That's what the whole thing was about—I felt like a liar.

288   A Place for Truth

After Finding Calcutta

I knew then, on the plane back the next day, that I had found my Calcutta. I didn't know what to do with it, but I had found it. So more questions begin to pour out of me. I was such an eager consumer of worldviews; I loved new philosophies and theories. I would try these new ideas, apply them in my work and teaching, and then I would see their limitations and get bored. Then I would try the next philosophy or the next theory. But how had I missed one? Why was there so much resistance to *this one*, even inside my own self? Was Christianity as oppressive as I had been taught? Where was the evidence? Where were women the freest? It is pretty clear if you look around the world, women are freest in countries that have been developed based on Judeo-Christian principles.

Where were the slaves first freed? Where are people still freest? Question after question just jumped out. Was Christianity really that oppressive? If so, why is the largest nongovernment organization in the world, World Vision, Christian? Why were all these little churches everywhere doing what I called social justice? They didn't necessarily call it that, but they were feeding the hungry, helping the homeless, visiting hospitals and nursing homes, sending money to free slaves, adopting new immigrants. Then there was Mother Teresa and the Missionaries of Charity, the fastest-growing order in the Catholic Church. It's wonderful that Oprah Winfrey and Starbucks are digging wells for clean water in Africa, but my student from Ghana tells me that the Catholics were digging wells for clean water in Africa in the 1500s? Where were all those stories when I was going to school?

I think self-proclaimed atheist philosopher Jürgen Habermas, who is probably the reigning continental philosopher, summarizes the situation best. He's German and was part of the early critical theory school. He came to the defense of Pope John Paul II and Benedict XVI when they challenged the European Union's omission of Christianity as part of its history and heritage in its new constitution. Habermas, certainly not a believer, or even defending religion, said:

Christianity and nothing else is the ultimate foundation of liberty, conscience, human rights and democracy, the benchmarks of Western Civilization. To this day, we have no other options. We continue to nourish ourselves from this source and everything else is post-modern chatter.[1]

Now, this is a philosopher who cares very deeply about both justice and truth. His whole life has been given to looking at issues of justice. So I had to ask myself, was Christianity really anti-intellectual? You see intellectuals all over the world—for instance, Francis Collins, Dallas Willard, Carol Swain, Michael Novak, Steven Meyers, George Marsden, Jean Bethke Elshtain, Robert George, Pope Benedict—these are all scholars. There are far too many examples of Christian intellectuals to believe this.

WORLDVIEWS

So I dove headlong into an investigation of the worldviews I had believed before, because from the perspective of any of the worldviews that are currently taught in the university (e.g., naturalism, secular humanism, pantheism) and, clearly, from any of the worldviews *I* had taught in the university, *Mother Teresa is completely incomprehensible.*

Todd Lake, who graduated from Harvard in 1982 when Mother Teresa was the commencement speaker, writes in *Finding God at Harvard:*

> I remember Mother Teresa's speech on the steps of Memorial Church at the Class Day exercise in 1982, where she talked of Jesus incessantly— I mean *incessantly*—and even quoted that verse, John 3:16 (already well known to most of us, thanks to signs in the end-zone bleachers). But in a triumph of brilliant editing, *Harvard Magazine*'s account managed to report almost the entire Mother Teresa speech without once hinting that she might even have mentioned Jesus. We all sensed he could be trouble, and we wanted to make sure he never again became a live issue.

And that is what had happened to me; this spirit had shaped me—the spirit that saw Jesus as so much trouble that the entire worldview had to be excluded from any mention in the university.

From the perspective of naturalism, Mother Teresa was just a unique bundle of brain chemistry with particular psycho-neural processes. From secular humanism, Mother Teresa would've simply been a highly socially evolved woman who took on the responsibility and had the fortitude and determination and will to do good works. Both worldviews would have added the caveat that it was unfortunate that she held to this myth of believing in God. From monism or pantheism, which in the United States is a mix of Eastern religion, New Age belief and postmodernism (things that I was pretty deeply involved in), Mother Teresa would've just been a more highly evolved soul. She would have had a strong spiritual connection to the divine that's in all of us and in the world.

Here is an example of these worldviews clashing in psychology. Let's take the issue of forgiveness. I heard a pastor say that "unforgiveness is like drinking poison and hoping the other person dies." It's a great line. All of us know people with psychological problems. Many of the people who really struggle psychologically are hung up in terms of not being able to forgive someone who has hurt them. The principle of radical forgiveness is that we forgive whether someone asks us or not. When we know something's amiss in our own life and heart, we ask God to forgive us, and he then not only forgives us but also begins a process to change, to heal our spirit and soul. (This is a spiritual transaction.)

From the perspective of naturalism, Mother Teresa was just a unique bundle of brain chemistry with particular psycho-neural processes going on. From secular humanism, Mother Teresa would've simply been a highly socially evolved woman who took on the responsibility and had the fortitude and determination and will to do good works.

On the other hand, in secular psychology, when we have a psychological struggle we may be led to relive our life in a Freudian or psychoanalytic way, or use cognitive behavior modification on ourself by discovering what we are saying to ourself when we get into this particular predicament and learn to tell ourself something different, something more productive. But if forgiveness is actually a true principle, a law by which human beings are designed to operate, the way it's taught in Christianity, then secular psychology will never be that effective. If it is true—then because of the way we're made, unforgiveness will have the same effect that breaking the law of gravity has when we jump off a building. It'll be slower, but things will begin to happen that destroy us—emotionally, intellectually, socially and physically.

So the bottom line is this: Why can't or won't the secular university actually engage these intellectual principles? The rise of the secular Western university was to actually open up options. But through my experience, I came to realize that it had also closed particular options. So my students might hear the options for thinking about justice from Marxism to structuralism to feminism to cultural studies, but not those proposed by Christianity.

The bottom line is this—I teach Ph.D. students almost exclusively. They're getting the top degree in the world. I want them to be well educated. I want them to know the whole range of philosophic and theoretical options that they have when thinking through any problem. I want them to also understand the historic range of considerations. I want them to know enough about the various worldviews that they can look at problems in education through different economic, political, sociological, scientific, religious, psychological frameworks—all of them, in every domain.

I want the same for you. I feel you owe it to yourself to not wait to figure these things out until you are forty-something, like I was. I want you to find the other options, to become fully conscious of all the options and the choices that you've made, and what the consequences of those are. And then, choose the option that best fits reality, because what Mother Teresa taught me is what you believe—and what you disbelieve—makes an enormous difference.

Q&A

Questioner 1. Non-Christians also do social justice. What made Mother Teresa's work special, and could one do her work without following Jesus?

Poplin. That's a great question because it's the first question people really have in their minds. Well, I was only there two months and the thing that Mother Teresa had, I believe, that was different is she had God actually working through her. Through prayer, they stayed very peaceful and very satisfied with what they were doing. I think, for most of us, that work would've been so monotonous; after a while we wouldn't have had the perseverance. We've had a lot of projects at the graduate university and service-learning projects for students, but what we find is after the initial enthusiasm wears off, there's nothing there to keep them going.

For Mother Teresa, it was to fulfill the Scripture around which their ministry was built. The Missionaries of Charity are built on the Scripture where Jesus says to his disciples, "I was hungry and you gave me food, I was thirsty and you gave me something to drink, I was a stranger and you welcomed me, I was naked and you gave me clothing, I was sick and you took care of me, I was in prison and you visited me" (Matthew 25:35-36). Then the disciples say to him, "When did we do that?" And he says, "When you did it for the least of these, you did it for me." So the Missionaries of Charity have a different primary motivation; I believe the power of the Holy Spirit *is* actually working through them to keep them faithful to the project, and to keep them enthusiastic about the project. That was my experience, as well. I could do these projects, but I didn't have the same kind of substance internally in my spirit to continue.

Something C. S. Lewis said is very helpful here. He wrote in *Mere Christianity* that we cannot say that Christians are "better" people than non-Christians, but we can say that everyone who truly comes to Christ will be a better person than he or she would be otherwise. But definitely anyone can work toward social justice. I mean anybody who wants to—we see it all the time.

Questioner 2. Our Calcutta is here at the university. How can we apply your lessons to fit here?

Poplin. Okay, this might not be what you're asking but what came to me when I heard the question was how do you find your purpose while you are here in the university, your Calcutta? I'm going to answer that, and if I didn't answer your question, let me know.

I'm not sure I even knew what my purpose in life was. I felt like I was sort of roaming through life picking up opportunities. I certainly never planned to be a professor; it wasn't really something I planned and followed. But if you want to begin to know, there are several things I think I'd be very attentive to.

One is to begin describe your gifts, what are your special skills, the things that you do really well. There are a lot of people who will tell you that. Your parents have probably informed you. But just begin to ask yourself, What is it that I'm really good at? and I think most of you know some of those things.

Second, and this is maybe the most important thing, what is the desire of your heart? Here is one of the biggest differences between Eastern religions and Judeo-Christian religion. In Judeo-Christianity, God wants a relationship with you and he wants to give you the desire of your heart. So he wants you to *know* what the desire of your heart is, and he wants to help you get that.

Eastern religions tend to advocate giving up desire, because in Eastern religions we're trying to avoid suffering, which Buddha believed came about because of desire. So if we give up desire, we won't suffer because we won't be missing anything. In Judeo-Christianity, we will suffer for our purpose, and suffering can be redemptive and instructive, cause us to grow in the character. We need to attain the desire of our heart—our purpose. Our purposes will also be joyous, but there will be some suffering involved.

Next, I would pay attention to what grieves you in the world. I think a lot of us are drawn to particular issues of social justice. There are many places to serve others, to promote justice. My own research right now is with high-performing teachers in low-performing urban schools in the poorest parts of Los Angeles County. I see these teachers who are really devoting themselves to teaching kids in very difficult situations, really pushing them to learn where they've never been pushed before.

As in my case, sometimes a crisis in your life will actually reveal something about your calling. So it's not always what feels good that reveals your calling. Sometimes, it's what feels bad, like finding Calcutta. I think the reason Mother Teresa called it that is because she loved Calcutta *and* Calcutta was very difficult. Your calling won't be easy, but you will not be happy avoiding it.

Questioner 3. How has your scholarship changed? How has your idea toward radical feminism and how and what you teach changed?

Poplin. My scholarship: that should be the easy one. Basically, I stopped trying to pick my favorite theory and philosophy, and instead sought to see where children who are poor are being best educated, and then I looked at what those teachers are doing. So I stopped trying to do this theoretically, and I began to do it from the ground up. That was one influence that Mother Teresa had on me. For Mother Teresa, everything was one person at a time—"one, one, one, one" she would say. It was very practical, very grounded. So I switched to using grounded theory as a research method, and I began to look at the education of the poor through that lens.

Feminism: I don't know if I've completely worked all this out, but here's where I am now. I began to notice how people who were strongly Christian did not let these "ism's" get to them. I mentioned the case of John Rivera, who had been oppressed (I mean, in terms of critical theory, we call it oppression). I began to be more interested in what I was being called to do and less interested in banging on closed doors. I think about it this way: I'm a woman. Jesus talked to women. The longest dialogue he has in the whole Bible is with a woman, a Samaritan and a big sinner (so I felt comfortable). I began to look so hard at what my purpose was, what I was being called to do and what my opportunities were that the "isms" began to kind of fade away. I think that is also true of Mother Teresa, John Rivera and other people that I began to know.

And then how did my teaching differ? Well, I am just very matter of fact these days about wanting students to know the wide range of options, so I teach them—education from critical theory, liberal humanism, feminism, even the classical Greek traditions. I also teach them the Judeo-Christian tradition and any other mindset or worldview the students or I know. I believe that people should be educated in the widest possible number of options. To me, it makes no sense in the university to have one worldview that is excluded for whatever reason. Every worldview begins with a faith statement; Christianity is no exception.

I began to notice how people who were strongly Christian did not let these "ism's" get to them. . . . I began to be more interested in what I was being called to do and less interested in banging on closed doors.

Questioner 4. Isn't Christianity a means to an end, helping people to get through a tough situation? And therefore, does it have to be Christianity? Couldn't any ideology serve that purpose and end? And what's wrong with seeing Mother Teresa as a secular humanist?

Poplin. The thing that's wrong about seeing her as a secular humanist is that she isn't one. She wasn't one. A secular humanist believes that people, in their own will power, can be good (and we've had a couple centuries of this now), and that we're able, as human beings, without any other values or moral principles from outside, to make right decisions and do the right things. And, yes, people who are secular humanists do serve the poor, and some of them do it brilliantly.

Here's what I found for myself, and this would answer the next question about "wouldn't just any ideology do?" I have tried a lot of ideologies. I found I was really living my life at the moment according to whatever ideology would fit what I wanted to do, to be honest. I had a shifting moral framework based on what I wanted to do with my life at the moment, and that included having relationships with married men, having abortions, doing all kinds of things that I would not do today. But none of those ideologies—even if I had followed them faithfully— had much power in them.

Look—*there is a spiritual reality!* I'm not a naturalist. There *is* a spiritual reality, and there are spiritual transactions happening in the world all the time. There are spiritual transactions going on right now. Things are happening in the spirit realm that obviously affect us. This is what

I believe now: the most powerful force on this earth is the Holy Spirit. Jesus is the most powerful example, and through Jesus, we are filled with the *Holy Spirit* and guided.

So we've been given a guide that I believe embodies a moral framework, and that, as far as I can tell, is superior to the other moral frameworks. Before I came to Christ, I couldn't deal with the junk that was inside me because there wasn't anything to do with it, so I had to pretend it didn't exist. I had to rationalize it.

I'll give you an example, a very personal example for me. When I came to Christ, I had had two abortions. And I began to grieve about this. Every opportunity, no matter where I was, whether I was at a monastery or a church or at home or wherever, I would begin to confess them over and over and over because it says in the Bible, confess your sins and God will forgive you and cleanse you from your iniquity, that is, those attitudes or motivations that caused you to sin.

After I got back from Mother Teresa's, I was at the monastery where I had seen the film about her. We were to write on a card the things we wanted to be forgiven for and people we needed to forgive, and we were going to have a service that night to burn the cards, like an oblation to the Lord, sending the prayers up in the fire. I'd written all these things, including my abortions, on a card. I was walking along the river in the afternoon, and I had the sense of a voice in my spirit—I don't know how to describe this if you haven't heard it. (Now, there could be many voices in your spirit, but I was pretty sure this was a good and true voice, the Lord's voice.) The voice was very firm and stern.

The voice said to me, "Who are you not to forgive someone I forgave?" I thought, okay, I got out my card and I looked for who I haven't written down on the card, and then I walked a little further and I heard exactly the same voice: "Who are you not to forgive someone I forgave?" The third time, I just knelt down on the ground and I said, "I don't know what you're talking about, Lord." Then I heard the following: "I forgave you the first time you asked, and I don't want you to ask me again."

It's very hard not to come at things from a solely human position. What I was trying to do was to work this off, you know, like year after year, moment after moment, I was confessing it to work my way out of it, when God just wanted to take it away and heal me. Well, he couldn't heal me because I hadn't even given it away. I didn't even let him take it away, so there was no way he could fulfill the last part, which was not only to forgive me but also to heal me from it. That's the kind of power that is available to us.

I don't believe any other framework has that kind of power to allow us to be that honest with ourselves, because there's nowhere to take that honesty, except some kind of intellectual rationalization or passing it off as, "Well, I'm just like other people," or "There are people who are worse than me." Those are rationalizations that we build up, and then we become very hard people. Instead of becoming more real, we become less real. I admit, I was much worse than most people. I mean, the kind of things that I did were . . . well, it's a wonder that I'm alive, actually.

I just wanted somewhere I could be real. I wanted to find a real place. And that's what I found in Christ.

Questioner 5. How do we reach the point of understanding radical love and radical forgiveness?

Poplin. The best way to start, in a Christian framework, is by confessing that we don't know how to truly, fully forgive on our own. But we want to. Most of the time, when I'm really praying about something important, I just go to God as a child. I just say, "Here I am, a little baby. I don't know how to do this. Will you help me?"

I think radical love and forgiveness come from the two commandments Christ gave us. We all talk about the second one, which is the one secular humanists would agree with: "Love your neighbor as yourself." But the first one is "Love the Lord your God with all your heart and with all your soul and with all your mind" (Matthew 22:37). I personally believe if we don't do the first one, we can't fully do the second one. The power is actually given to us to live the second one from the first one; there is a reason that they're in that order.

True forgiveness is very hard because you give up your rights to hold a grudge, to retaliate. I'm talking about forgiving other people, things that have happened to you. I think what you have to continue to do is just keep forgiving them (in your head, your emotions and eventually your heart) and asking the Lord to help you. There are lots of great books written about forgiveness. I think R. T. Kendall's book *Total Forgiveness* is probably the best, but you just have to keep giving it up, and knowing for yourself that you don't want to hold onto this. Unforgiveness does poison our lives. To not forgive something that's happened to us leaves hooks in us. So you just keep confessing it. You keep giving it up, and then you begin to try to pray and bless the people that you're forgiving, that they will actually receive some blessing. And eventually you'll find that you have worked it through with God's grace, and then you will finally feel it. You will be free, no hooks to snare you.

Questioner 6. Do you think God will forgive and guide those who do not believe in him?

Poplin. Well, I'm not God, so . . . I believe that God gives people millions of opportunities, probably even to the very moment . . . maybe, even after we die. Hopefully, eventually we get to the end of ourselves and look for something bigger and realize there is something bigger. And I believe, "The last will be first." Even people who confess while they're on their deathbed. I don't know what or how God does what he does, but he says he wants no one to perish.

But I'll tell you what I do know about him. I've finally learned that he loves us. This was really from Mother Teresa—he loves us much more than we can even imagine. There's absolutely no one who can imagine how much God loves us right now, and how much he knows about us; he knows the number of hairs on our head! He knows the good plan for our life, and everything that has happened to us up until now has worked toward that plan, or can be worked toward that plan, for us, including the things that have been really hard, because those things build our character. They build that part of our character that we're going to need to do the purpose to which we're called, which is the desire of our heart. So I would say I don't know the answer to that specific question. All I know is that God loves us more than we can ever even imagine.

Finally, Mother Teresa's "dark night," which some of you may have read about (some have said it was doubt, but she never doubted), is what people for thousands of years have experienced when they have had mystical visions that end. John of the Cross is very articulate here. John of the Cross wrote in the 1500s about the "dark night of the soul," and he said that when we go through this dark night, we experience this deep longing for God. Through this experience, God gives us his divine love. That's what I think happened to her. She didn't have just *agapē* love or *eros* love; she'd gone beyond that. People from all over the world went to Mother Teresa just to touch her, or to have her touch them or their unborn babies, or just be near her. When I was near her, it was amazing. There were days when we would walk out of the chapel—as weird as it sounds—and we would all lower our heads to get her to touch them. And we'd all do it at the same time on the same days! But that kind of divine love, I don't think we can even imagine it. I think she, and other people, have come close to it.

Let me end by reading a line from Mother Teresa. This is the best summation of her ministry. "We, the Missionaries of Charity, carry out an offensive of love, of prayer, of sacrifice on behalf of the poorest of the poor. We want to conquer the world through love and thus bring to everyone's heart the love of God and the proof that God loves the world."

That is radical love. That was Mother Teresa.

15

THE WHOLE GOSPEL FOR THE WHOLE PERSON

Ronald J. Sider
The Veritas Forum at Harvard University, 1995

WHEN I WAS IN UNIVERSITY, I had a lot of questions and doubts about the truth of Christianity. Now, I still wrestle with those questions, but at a different level. I've largely resolved the basic ones except for one. Do you know what continues to bother me as a substantial reason for doubting the truth of Christianity?

It's the church. Precisely the fact that many people who claim to be Christians don't seem to live what they're talking about. If you took church attendance and the claim to be Christian as the criteria, then America is the most Christian nation on the face of the earth. Forty-five to fifty percent of our people are in church every Sunday morning. They tell Gallup that about 80 percent or more are Christians.

But for so many people, attending church doesn't seem to make much difference in whether or not they keep their marriage vows or seek justice for the poor or care for the environment or struggle against racism. How on earth is the most Christian nation on earth among the most violent, has the largest per capita prison population and the highest divorce rate in human history? Half of our kids live in broken homes.

We're doing to our children what no society in human history has ever done to its kids.

That's what tears me apart. That's what brings doubt to my mind. I found solid, intellectual answers to most of my doubts about the existence of God, about whether or not Jesus was alive on the third day. I used to doubt whether an honest thinker in the modern scientific world could really believe that Jesus the carpenter came to life again as Christians have claimed through the centuries.

How on earth is the most Christian nation on earth among the most violent, has the largest per capita prison population and the highest divorce rate in human history?

But I'm an historian; that's where I did my graduate work. And I've examined the historical evidence with great care. Of course, if you start with a bias and assume at the beginning that miracles cannot happen, then of course no amount of evidence would overcome that initial starting prejudice. But if you start with an open mind and examine the historical evidence carefully about Jesus' life, death and alleged resurrection, then the most responsible historical conclusion is that Jesus, in fact, was really alive on the third day.

The historical evidence is so strong that one of the most prominent German theologians today, Professor Wolfhart Pannenberg, has said that nobody would question the claim that Jesus was alive, but for two reasons: The first is that it was a very unusual event—I think we can grant that. Dead people tend to stay dead. Second, if we believe that it happened, we'd have to change the way we live. I believe that Jesus Christ is truly the answer to the toughest problems in our world, not in some silly, superficial way, but the real biblical, historical Christ.

The problem is that many Christians have developed a very one-sided understanding of Christian faith, and so some Christians today think that what we're supposed to be doing is primarily or exclusively leading other people to Christ. And other people in the church think that what we're primarily supposed to be doing is working for social justice. Now the truth is, of course, that most Christians are not doing either. They're simply maintaining the building and the social club.

STORIES OF TRANSFORMATION

Let me tell you two stories: In 1979, I was in South Africa. I spoke to an evangelical university movement that had been divided up into white English-speaking, white Afrikaans-speaking, colored and black. The group that I was speaking to was the white, English-speaking group, although there were a few people from the other races there. I talked about Jesus' resurrection on the third day, about God's concern for the poor, about structural injustice, and I met a guy by the name of James. He was not a Christian; in fact, he was Jewish, but he was intrigued by this circle of deeply committed Christians. We talked for hours; he was deeply involved in the struggle against apartheid. He was trying to be a full-time student and a full-time activist. He gave me a great political education. One night, after a three-hour talk, he said "Ron, I'm burned out." That didn't surprise me, given his two jobs.

He said, "God told me that if I would come to this conference I'd learn something about his Son."

You can imagine I was surprised. I looked at him and I said, "You know, I believe that Jesus died on the cross for your sins, and I believe that he rose on the third day for you."

He said, "I believe all of that, I really do."

But something clearly was in the way, and soon he told me. "I don't want to be like these white Christians here. They sing about heaven, they talk about Jesus, but they don't care about justice in South Africa."

He really thought that coming to Jesus would mean losing his commitment to end apartheid. I said, "Goodness, no, James. Jesus wants to strengthen that, he doesn't want to take it away. It'll have to be on his terms, but I'm sure it'll be more powerful."

Then I said, "I'm not in any hurry, but if you'd like to pray, I'd be glad to do that."

He said, "Let's do." We went to my room. He prayed a beautiful prayer, he confessed his sins, he accepted Jesus Christ as his personal Lord and Savior.

When he was finished and after he left, I looked in the mirror and saw that my face was shining. His face had been shining, believe me, after he prayed. I was so excited that all I could do for the first little while was walk around the room singing praises to the Lord. (Not charismatically, if that would bother anyone.) That illustrates the incredible division between evangelism and social transformation.

Second story: A couple of years later I was asked to be one of the speakers at the thirtieth anniversary of the founding of the National Council of Churches USA, and before I gave my presentation I looked at the seminars being offered. There were about a dozen seminars on ecumenical affairs; that was great. There were about fifteen seminars on peace and justice. I looked for seminars on evangelism, on crosscultural sharing of the gospel. You know how many of those there were? Absolutely zero.

Two snapshots, neither is a full representation of either of those organizations, but they point to the tragic one-sidedness. I want this scandal of one-sided Christianity to end, precisely so that we can show to the world that the real, biblical Christ is the solution to our problems. I have no doubt that if 10 percent of the Christians today would really live the way Jesus called us to, we would transform the world in powerful ways in the next twenty-five years.

I want to tell you about a friend, Wayne Gordon. Wayne grew up in a Christian home in the Midwest. He had perfect Sunday school attendance for about eight years, but he really didn't know Christ personally. One weekend on a camp retreat, he came to know Christ, surrendered his heart to him fully. He was a sophomore in high school. A couple nights later he was back home in bed, praying in the middle of the night, and he looked up and said, "God, I'll do anything you want me to do with my life."

Almost immediately he seemed to hear the words "I want you to be with African Americans—with black people."

He thought, *Africa?*

God said, "No, here."

So he went downstairs and told his parents, "I'm supposed to go to the inner city."

They said, "Just a minute, you can wait a little while. You can finish high school, and you can finish college."

So he did that. And then he worked in the inner city. He got involved in an all-black section of Chicago. He was a football coach, and he also got a teaching job. He was the only teacher in the whole system that lived in the immediate area. He began to form groups for Bible study and for recreational sorts of things, and he began to talk about Jesus Christ with the kids he was coaching on the football team. They began to come to personal faith in Christ, and he walked with them as they struggled with all kinds of things.

One thing led to another, and soon they started a tutoring program, and then they started a medical program, and on it went. Today he runs a multimillion dollar program. They have twenty-one full-time doctors in their medical clinic. They renovated millions of dollars of low-income housing. They start small businesses to provide an economic base in the inner city. And African Americans, strong leaders, joined him to pastor the church that has emerged out of that whole ministry, and now they have a church of about five hundred people, black and white, that are together leading people to Christ and doing all these various ministries.

It hasn't always been easy. When Wayne got married, when he and Ann came back from their honeymoon, their house was broken into. It happened nine more times in the next three years. But Wayne had made a promise, that he would do whatever God wanted him to do in life, and God has used him to develop a fantastic ministry. It's transforming a very significant section of inner-city Chicago. Just think of what God would do with a thousand Wayne Gordons who would say the same thing.

WRONG IDEAS ABOUT CREATION AND GOSPEL

Why are there not more and more ministries like that? It seems to me that it's partly because we have misguided theological ideas. There are two specific areas where I think our theology is messed up: creation and gospel.

I don't think we have a fully biblical understanding of creation in many areas of the church. The Greeks in some important ways have misled us. Plato thought that the material world was rather evil, that the good soul was unfortunately trapped in an evil body, and that the ideal was for that good soul to escape the body. Eastern monism tells us that essentially the material world is an illusion.

Biblical faith is radically different. Biblical faith says that the whole material world around us is finite, limited, but very good, because it comes from the hand of the Creator. In fact, the material world, the body, is so good that the Creator of the galaxies became flesh. It's so good that Jesus, who is true God as well as true man, rose *bodily* from the dead. The material world is so good that, as Romans 8 says, when Christ returns, then even this groaning creation is going to be as restored to wholeness and liberty as the children of God.

That biblical view of creation is a fantastic foundation for caring for the environment. It's also a fantastic foundation for caring for human society. In fact, it's precisely this fully biblical view of creation that provides the foundation we need to go out, knowing that Jesus Christ is Lord of history, and that he is at work, seeking to restore wholeness in the whole created order.

> *Biblical faith says that the whole material world around us is finite, limited, but very good, because it comes from the hand of the Creator. In fact, the material world, the body, is so good that the Creator of the galaxies became flesh. It's so good that Jesus, who is true God as well as true man, rose bodily from the dead.*

We also need a more biblical understanding of the gospel. I suspect if I were to ask you what the gospel is, a number of you would say it's forgiveness of sins. Or, if you're in the divinity school, you'd say justification by faith alone. Thank God, forgiveness of sins is one very important part of the gospel. I never want to stand before our holy God on any basis other than the fact that Jesus died on the cross for my sins. But if the gospel is no more than forgiveness of sins, then you and I can accept Jesus Christ, get our one-way ticket to heaven, and go on being exactly the same racist, environmentally unconcerned, unjust people we've always been.

Jesus tells us that the gospel is more than that. Have you ever gone through the Gospels and noticed how Jesus defines the gospel, the good news? Mark 1:14-15 says, and it's a summary of Jesus' whole preaching:

> After John was arrested, Jesus came to Galilee, proclaiming the good news of God, and saying [in other words, here's the definition of the gospel], "The time is fulfilled, and the kingdom of God has come near; repent, and believe in the good news."

Virtually every time Jesus defines the gospel, he defines it as the good news of the kingdom. What on earth does he mean?

Remember what the prophets had said? They looked ahead to a time in the future, beyond the injustice and disobedience of the people of Israel, and they said, "Some time in the future, the Messiah will come. The messianic order will break in, and God will bring a new right relationship with himself. Our sins will be forgiven and the law will be written on our hearts, and there will be a new right relationship with neighbors. There will be transformation vertically and horizontally, and there will be *shalom*, justice, and wholeness in society."

Then, Jesus comes along and claims to be the Messiah, and says that the messianic kingdom the prophets had predicted was breaking into the present, in his own person and word. He meant the two things the prophets had talked about. He meant a vertical thing. He meant that we get into his kingdom not by good works, not by any kind of works righteousness. We get into his kingdom by sheer grace, because God loves even sinners, and eagerly wants them to change.

But there's more to this good news of the kingdom than that, because Jesus goes on to call a circle of disciples, a new community. He wasn't an isolated, individualistic prophet. He formed a new society, and this new society began to live differently, to live his kingdom ways.

They began to challenge society at all the points that society was wrong, and they cared about the whole person, not just the soul.

Think of the way that Jesus challenged evil in his world. For starters, he obviously challenged the demonic powers and healed people. And think of the way that Jesus challenged the rich. I could go on and on reading texts about God's very special concern for the poor. Matthew

25, for example, says that if we don't feed the hungry and clothe the naked, we depart eternally from the living God. Jesus also said that it's easier for a camel to go through the eye of a needle than it is for a rich person to stop burning fossil fuels, or something like that.

Think of the way that Jesus reached out to the weak and the marginalized. You know how lepers were treated. They had to stay by themselves. The lame and the blind, the disabled, were excluded from the whole religious service of one of the major Jewish groups in Jesus' day, the Qumran community, from whom we have the Dead Sea Scrolls. Their official document says that in the assembly of the righteous, the disabled, the blind and the lame cannot come in. But what does Jesus say when his disciples throw a feast? Invite especially the lame and the blind and the disabled. He's reaching out to the marginalized.

We get into his kingdom by sheer grace, because God loves even sinners, and eagerly wants them to change.

But there's more to this good news of the kingdom than that, because Jesus goes on to call a circle of disciples, a new community. . . . They began to challenge society at all the points that society was wrong, and they cared about the whole person, not just the soul.

We see it probably most powerfully in the way that Jesus treated women. Women in Jesus' day were by no means men's equals. Aristotle had said that women were malformed or misshaped men. They were sort of like slaves and children. First-century contemporaries of Jesus said it was better to burn a copy of the Torah than to give it to a woman. If you taught your daughter Torah, the first five books of the Old Testament, it was like teaching her lechery. It was a disgrace for a man to appear with a woman in public. A woman's word was absolutely useless in court. Women didn't count toward the quorum for a meeting of the synagogue. And there was a regular prayer that men used to say. "I thank God I'm not a Gentile; I thank God I'm not a slave; I thank God I'm not a woman."

Jesus broke through all of that male prejudice. He appeared with women in public; he let Mary Magdalene kiss his feet and wipe them with her hair in public, though she probably was a former prostitute. We have no idea of the outrage that kind of thing caused. He talked theology with women, walked with them in public, and finally, he honored them with the first resurrection appearance. I'm sure it wasn't an accident. Jesus, I think, was a biblical feminist.

Jesus also offended men in another way. In Jesus' day it was very easy for a man to get rid of his wife. He could give her a writ of divorce, and off she went. Women didn't have equal privileges. Our solution, of course, would be to give women equal privileges so everybody could get a divorce real fast. That wasn't Jesus' solution. He called one man and one woman to live together in lifelong covenant.

Jesus challenged the political leadership of his time, saying, "I want servant leaders."

He challenged the violent revolutionaries. The zealots said that the Messiah would come if the whole nation would just rise up in armed rebellion. Jesus said "No, I want you to love even your enemies."

THE GOSPEL AS A NEW COMMUNITY

Jesus was challenging his society at all kinds of points where it was wrong. So when Jesus talked about the gospel as the good news of the kingdom, he meant two things. He certainly meant that his followers were accepted by the holy God. They got into his kingdom by sheer grace because God longs to forgive prodigal sons and daughters.

But he also meant a second very important thing. He meant that a radically new kind of community was actually becoming visible and taking shape as these forgiven sinners began to live what Jesus taught. And this community began to care, as Jesus did, for the whole person. They began to challenge society where it was wrong. In short, they began to imitate Jesus.

One reason the early church was so successful in its evangelism was precisely because it was a new kind of society. People looked at this new community and saw the miraculous power of God at work. They saw men and women, Jews and Gentiles, rich and poor living together, respecting each other, treating each other as equals, and they couldn't understand. They asked, "What on earth is going on?" And in response, people told them about Jesus, because that was the answer. Ephesians 2–3 is very interesting at precisely this point. The text in Ephesians 2 talks about the fact that there's been a great dividing wall between Jew and Gentile, but both get accepted by God on the basis of the cross. So the great hostility, the worst racial hostility in the ancient world, is being overcome in Jesus, and there's one new person.

Ephesians 3 goes on to talk about "the mystery" that Paul preaches. And what is this mystery? Verse 6 tells us. It's a definition of the mystery, which is the gospel, that is, that the Gentiles are fellow heirs and members of the body, and fellow partakers of the promise in Christ Jesus. In other words, it's the new multiethnic body of believers, where Jew and Gentile accept each other and overcome this racial hostility. That's part of the good news.

So what is the gospel then? It's not just forgiveness of sins, although thank God, it includes that. I am still a sinner, and I want to trust in the cross, but it's more than that. It's the fantastic news that the messianic kingdom has broken into history. Now, in the power of the Holy Spirit, you and I can begin to live differently. And in that new community, all of the brokenness, the social, the economic, the ethnic and the emotional brokenness of this old world is being overcome in Jesus' new community. Matthew 9:35 summarizes this: "Jesus went about all the cities and villages, teaching in their synagogues, and proclaiming the good news of the kingdom, and curing every disease and every sickness."

Teaching, preaching, and healing. That's what Jesus was about. That's what I'm pleading for. He cared about the whole person. Jesus never thought that all you needed was a good life here on earth, and then everything would be fine. In fact, he said that it's better to lose the whole world than lose your relationship with God and Christ. But he never drew the conclusion that we Christians sometimes do. Sometimes Christians today say, "Well, that means that we should spend most of our time on evangelism, and if we've got a little bit of time left over we can care about the poor, and so on." Jesus never drew that conclusion.

Look at the Gospels. Look at the space they devote to his preaching and his teaching, and his healing. Vast amounts of time devoted to both. He cared about the whole person, he's our only perfect model, surely we should do the same.

James Dennis is a very dear friend of mine. For eleven years my wife and I attended an inner-city church in an all-black section of Philadelphia. James Dennis and I were elders together in that church. Many years ago, Brother James was a very angry black militant. He told me a little while ago that if he had met me years ago, he might have killed me. (I'm glad he met Jesus first.) But before that happened, his marriage was in trouble, he was abusing alcohol, and he finally went to prison for a major crime. In prison, thank God, he came to know Jesus Christ, and he came out, struggled a bit, got involved in our church discipleship, and God put his life back together.

His family's back together, he's got a decent job, he owns his own home. He wants to be a prison chaplain someday. Fantastic transformation. Anybody who thinks that all he needed was the best government programs of whatever sort, Democratic, Republican or Green, simply doesn't understand. He needed more than that. He needed a living relationship with Jesus Christ that would transform his whole character from the inside out.

At the same time, anybody who thinks that all he needed was to be born again, when the school system wouldn't work and he couldn't get any job or housing, doesn't understand. Surely he needed a decent societal order, and he needed a living relationship with Jesus Christ. How on earth anybody who claims to follow Jesus, the eternal Word become flesh, the perfect combination of word and deed, and then proceeds to separate them in life really puzzles me.

Well, if that's what the gospel is, what does that mean for you and me? How concretely could we begin to live out the implications of what I've been saying?

HOLISTIC APOLOGETICS

I'm going to address what I call holistic apologetics. Holistic apologetics in our universities, right here, perhaps. Let me explain what I mean.

I think we'll all agree that our big universities are among the most secular places on the planet. That's partly because of the Enlightenment; it's partly because of the hypocrisy and tragic failure of Christians. But what do we do about it? How might holistic apologetics begin to make a difference?

I need to tell you another story to illustrate what I mean. Rock Circle is another one of my favorite ministries. (In the book *Cup of Water, Bread of Life,* by the way, I tell a number of these stories at greater length.) Rock Circle is another ministry like the one that Wayne Gordon established, also in Chicago. In this case it's also led by a wonderful, gifted black-white leadership team. It started out, again, with a white kid from a small town who went to Moody Bible Institute, got called to the city, started slowly developing a whole bunch of ministries, the same kind of thing; a medical clinic, a legal clinic and tutoring, and on and on.

Ron Sider talks with law students after his presentation at Harvard.

After about ten years, Glen Kehrein realized that even though he had started out being very committed to integrating evangelism and social transformation, he was doing almost entirely social action. He realized that people weren't being changed very much, and the result was he wasn't producing much long-term change.

Then God sent along Raleigh Washington, a brilliant career Army man who'd been thrown out of the military, because of racism, one day before he would have retired with a twenty-year pension. He had gotten converted a couple of years before that, gone to seminary, met Glen, and they formed a bond that is a wonderful thing to behold, a very strong partnership that they've been developing over the last ten years. Raleigh Washington began to plant a church in the middle of this developing community center. He started to do much more evangelism, and persuaded Glen and the doctors and lawyers and everybody else that they ought to be doing more evangelism—not chucking tracts down people's throats but in fact sensitively, when people had a spiritual need, asking, "Hey, could I talk about that spiritual need?" Or, "Maybe you'd like to talk to the pastoral counselor."

The result is that a wonderful church has emerged in the middle of that community center and all of that ministry. The church at Rock Circle has about 450 members, it's about 70 percent African American and 30 percent white. Rich and poor, black and white, all of them coming together in that congregation.

The story of Cassandra Franklin illustrates what happened. Cassandra came into the community center medical clinic about eight years ago, needing medical help. She got that. The doctor sensed a spiritual need, so he began to talk about that, carefully. And she went to talk to a pastoral counselor. She soon started coming to the church and accepted Christ. She talked to her boyfriend, the father of her child, and he started to come. He soon accepted Christ.

It didn't solve their problems—there was a long struggle and discipleship and growth in the faith, and after several years of real growth on the part of both of them, they decided to get married. It was the first Christian marriage on both sides of the family for a long time. They invited other members of the family as a witness to the goodness of Christian marriage. A number of members of the family on both sides came to Christ. Her husband is now the head of one of the small businesses that this ministry has started in the inner city. Last year, twelve employees working under them cleared a profit of $50,000. Now, that's real transformation.

Take that as the background and imagine that the University Christian Fellowship Group at the University of Chicago was sending a whole bunch of volunteers into Rock Circle, and they were tutoring and working with the folks there, sharing their skills in sensitive ways in whatever they could do. And then imagine that Rock Circle joins the folks at the University of Chicago and says, "Let's do a week-long holistic apologetic campaign, and let's do the usual apologetic stuff, arguments for the existence of God, arguments that Jesus was alive on the third day, and so on. But let's add something else. Let's say to our secular friends, 'Come and see the gospel at work at Rock Circle. Our secular politicians and social scientists simply don't know how to solve the problems of our inner cities. Come to Rock Circle and see what Jesus' new community of rich and poor, black and white, working together in the power of the risen Lord are actually doing. Broken families are being healed, people on welfare are getting jobs. Black and white are becoming trusted partners." I wonder what the secular university would do with that.

Take another example of holistic apologetics—the environment. I know we can argue about some of the science, but I think there's a general agreement today that we face serious environmental problems. More and more of the people in the environment movement realize that they need a spiritual foundation for their environmental concerns. But guess what? They're not going to Christianity for that; they think Christianity's the problem. They're going to Eastern monism, to goddess worship and a whole variety of things. It always puzzles me why somebody who's concerned with the environment thinks that Eastern monism, which says that the whole created order is an illusion, provides any kind of foundation for caring for the created order, but anyway, that's what's happening.

Biblical faith, with the doctrine of creation that I talked about earlier, is a far better foundation for caring for this gorgeous earth, but our words won't do it. We've got to be out there in the middle of the environmental movement, working hard to care for this gorgeous creation. That's cultural apologetics.

If the Gospel is the good news of the kingdom, as I have said, then something very important follows for you and me—something important about how we share the gospel. The only way you and I can faithfully share Jesus' good news of the kingdom is by word and by deed, the way Jesus did it. Remember the Great Commission in John 20:21? "As the Father has sent me, so send I you."

We are sent in the same way Jesus was sent, to do the same kinds of things he was doing. Unless the church today develops thousands and thousands of holistic congregations like Rock Circle and Lawndale in

Chicago, we won't have any credibility. But if we do, think of what will happen. In the world today, fifty thousand people will die of starvation in twenty-four hours. In the same twenty-four hours, fifty thousand will die without ever once having heard about Jesus Christ. And guess what? They're largely the same people.

If you and I go on living in affluence, buying bigger houses, taking fancier vacations, and don't share in costly ways with the poor, we deny the gospel. If we try to evangelize the poor without also helping them overcome their poverty, we also deny the gospel. And if the most visible Christians today in this society are engaged in electing politicians who want to please the white middle class rather than empower the poor, then secular people will rightly walk away in disgust. But when we put it together, when we tell the poor about Jesus Christ, share our best treasure and then walk together with them hand-in-hand to empower them economically, a fantastic transformation takes place.

If evangelical Christians, who have a trillion-dollar annual income, gave 5 percent of their income to this kind of small loan enterprise, we could raise the standard of the poorest 1.3 billion of the world's people by 50 percent in about two and a half years.

David Bussau is one of my special friends. He made his millions as an Australian businessman by the time he was in his thirties. Then God called him to live among the poor. And he learned how to make very small loans to poor people in desperately poor countries like Indonesia, with $50 here, $150 there. In the last thirteen years, he and the organization he works with, Opportunity International, has made seventy-five thousand loans to poor people around the world. Each loan costs about $500 to make, paid back within a year with market rate interest. Every loan on balance improves the standard of living of a whole family of five by 50 percent.

If evangelical Christians, who have a trillion-dollar annual income, gave 5 percent of their income to this kind of small loan enterprise, we could raise the standard of the poorest 1.3 billion of the world's people by 50 percent in about two and a half years.

This holistic approach to evangelism applies of course not just to the poor but to every kind of person. Everybody's hurting in some area, because of alcohol, a hurting marriage, sickness, loneliness. Even the most secular, even the most affluent person needs the whole gospel. They need to know that God loves them; they need to experience God's forgiveness. They need to experience the warm embrace of Jesus' new community, the church, if only the church will walk with them and help them struggle with their deepest problems. Every single person needs that kind of Jesus action. But our word has power and integrity only if you and I are living the gospel as well as speaking it, only if our churches are little pictures of what heaven's going to be like, as Tom Skinner used to say it.

How can we tell our neighbors that Jesus will help them overcome their struggles in their marriage if we Christians don't keep our marriage vows? And how do you suppose that you're going to keep your marriage vows if while you're in university you screw around like everybody else? And how can we tell the world that Jesus is the answer to the racial violence and hatred of our world if the church is not a new community that visibly demonstrates a new kind of love and sharing between rich and poor, between black and white?

If by the power of the Holy Spirit the contemporary church would model faithful marriages in our generation, and generous sharing with the poor, and sacrificial caring for every human need, then our evangelistic words would take on an awesome power. Our secular society is sick of empty words, but our neighbors would stop and listen if they saw that kind of holistic Jesus action. They would come again and again to trust and surrender their lives to the Lord, whom we love and worship.

I end with one final short story. I have a good friend, a graduate student in political science at Harvard, Tim Shaw. He's now on a nine-month leave of absence, working among the poor in a fantastic holistic ministry like the ones I've been describing, run by some very dear friends of mine, Vinay and Colleen Samuel in Bangalore, in one of the big cities in south India. That ministry serves fifty thousand poor people. They're starting churches in the same way as those I mentioned in Chicago. And Tim's there taking some time out of a fast-track career to walk with the poor and share Jesus.

Are the Christians here tonight ready to get that serious about Jesus? There are folk here tonight from ministries in inner-city Boston and Third World Haiti. They'd like to talk with you afterward about the possibility of volunteering with them. You're getting the best education the world offers. Are you going to use it to get rich or to serve Jesus?

Will you join Wayne Gordon and Tim Shaw among the poor, telling them about your best treasure, and helping them overcome injustice? Will you, with Wayne Gordon, look into the eyes of Jesus Christ and say, "My Lord and my God, as you give me the strength, I'll do anything with my life that you want me to do?"

Q&A

Questioner 1. The challenges that are in front of us, particularly as we look at the next century, can be intimidating. The work that we're in sometimes feels exhausting. It feels sometimes like an uphill climb when we look at these problems and challenges. You've been going strong for, if you don't mind me saying, a long time—longer than us, anyway. How can we do the same? How can we keep going, in the words of the prophet, "to run and not grow weary"?

Sider. I'm not committed to a simple lifestyle or to justice, per se. I'm committed to Jesus. And Jesus calls me to live more simply so that I can share with others in evangelism and social justice, and to care for the environment and so on. Jesus calls me to be concerned with the poor. Unless we're grounded there, and in the Scriptures, and grounded in an ongoing, living relationship with him, we simply don't have the staying power.

It's precisely in the power of the risen Lord, and Saint Paul says that it's the same power that raised Jesus from the dead, that now raises you and me to a new life for others. And so it's in that strength that I want to do what I feel called to do.

Finally, we're not even called to success. Sometimes we win, sometimes we lose. We're called to faithfulness. I like to win in anything

I'm doing, including hockey that I used to play, but I want to be faithful to Jesus, and at certain points we may not have a great deal of success and other times, we do. But what we're called to do is to be faithful to Jesus.

I do a course called "Discipleship, Spiritual Formation and Social Change," trying to talk about the relationship between the inward journey of prayer and personal devotions, and outward action in the world. William Wilberforce, that great evangelical British politician who worked for thirty years to end the slave trade and then slavery itself in the British Empire, had a circle of his friends that did that. They used to meet together for three hours a day to pray for that political engagement. So I think it's some of that.

Questioner 2. Given the fact that conservative Christians in the political realm tend to be identified with very conservative kinds of stands, what does that mean for the engagement of others who don't share that concern? Is that a good enough summary?

Sider. The first thing I would say is that I want to approach every political issue not from some kind of ideological commitment to left or right, but because I've gone back to the Scriptures and have looked at the ethical principles that relate to that issue and then have done my social analysis. And when I do that, I find that biblical faith takes me to the left on some issues and to the right on others, and I don't fit into the political parties in their contemporary ideologies. I think that on questions of family, for instance, and on questions of sanctity of human life, I'm pretty conservative. On some other issues, I go a different direction.

So I think we have to first of all start with a biblical analysis. It is a problem with a situation where some of the most visible "Christian" voices don't seem to make justice for the poor one of their primary agendas. I think that's a tragedy. I think it's unbiblical and ultimately heretical. If Jesus and the Scriptures are our guide, then we can't be engaged in politics under any kind of Christian banner and be faithful and not make justice for the poor one of our central agendas. So I think what we have to do is develop an alternative voice that is holistic. That is part of what Evangelicals for Social Action is all about.

NOTES

Chapter 3: Reason for God
[1]Stanley Fish, "One University Under God?" *The Chronicle of Higher Education* 51, no. 18 (2005): C1.
[2]Lesslie Newbigin, *The Gospel in a Pluralist Society* (Grand Rapids: Eerdmans, 1989).

Chapter 5: The New Atheists and the Meaning of Life
[1]Robert Pape, *Dying to Win: The Strategic Logic of Suicide Terrorism* (New York: Random House, 2005).

Chapter 6: A Scientist Who Looked and Was Found
[1]Ed Harrison, *Masks of the Universe* (New York: Macmillan, 1985).

Chapter 7: The Psychology of Atheism
[1]Russell Baker, *Growing Up* (New York: Congdon & Weed, 1982).

Chapter 8 : Nietzsche Versus Jesus Christ
[1]T. H. Green, "Lecture on Liberal Legislation and Freedom of Contract," in *Lectures on the Principles of Political Obligation,* ed. Paul Harris and John Morrow (Cambridge: Cambridge University Press, 1986).

Chapter 13: Why Human Rights Are Impossible Without Religion
[1]H. L. A. Hart, *The Concept of Law* (Oxford: Oxford University Press, 1960).
[2]Hermann Göring, *Trial of the Major War Criminals Before the International Military Tribunal, Nuremberg, 14 November 1945–1 October 1946* (Nuremberg, 1947).
[3]Ibid.
[4]Cf. John Warwick Montgomery, *Tractatus Logico-Theologicus,* 4th ed. (Bonn, Germany: Verlag fuer Kultur and Wissenschaft, 2009).

Chapter 14: Radical Marxist, Radical Womanist, Radical Love
[1]Jürgen Habermas, "In Europe, God Is [Not] Dead," *Wall Street Journal,* July 14, 2007, p. A1. See also Jürgen Habermas, http://sciencestage.com/v/958.

CONTRIBUTORS

Jeremy S. Begbie is the Thomas A. Langford Research Professor of Theology at Duke Divinity School. He teaches systematic theology and specializes in the interface between theology and music. He is an ordained minister of the Church of England and a professionally trained musician. His most recent book is *Resounding Truth: Christian Wisdom in the World of Music*.

Rodney Brooks is director of the MIT Computer Science and Artificial Intelligence Laboratory and is the Panasonic Professor of Robotics. His research is concerned with both the engineering of intelligent robots and with understanding human intelligence through building humanoid robots. His most recent book is *Flesh and Machines: How Robots Will Change Us*.

Francis S. Collins is a physician-geneticist and director of the National Institutes of Health (NIH). As head of the Human Genome Project, Collins led an international collaboration of scientists in sequencing the human genome in 2003. His book, *The Language of God: A Scientist Presents Evidence for Belief*, spent many weeks on the *New York Times* bestseller list.

Os Guinness is an author and a social critic. Born in China to missionary parents and educated at Oxford, England, Guinness has written numerous books, including, *Time for Truth: Living Free in a World of Lies, Hype, and Spin*; *The Call: Finding and Fulfilling the Central Purpose of Your Life*; and his latest, *The Case for Civility: And Why Our Future Depends on It*.

John Hare is a British classicist, ethicist and currently Noah Porter Professor of Philosophical Theology at Yale Divinity School. Educated at Oxford and Princeton, Hare's best-known book, *The Moral Gap*, develops an account of the need for God's assistance in meeting the moral demand of which God is the source.

David J. Helfand is chair of the department of astronomy at Columbia University and the codirector of the Columbia Astrophysics Laboratory. He has also served as part of the university's physics department. His research interests include radio surveys, the origin and evolution of neutron stars and supernova remnants, and active galactic nuclei.

Timothy J. Keller is the senior pastor at Redeemer Presbyterian Church in New York City. He has also served as assistant professor of practical theology at Westminster Theological Seminary. He is author of *The Prodigal God, Counterfeit Gods* and the *New York Times* bestseller *The Reason for God: Belief in an Age of Skepticism*.

Alister McGrath is professor of theology, ministry and education, and head of the Center for Theology, Religion and Culture at King's College London. He is also president of the Oxford Center for Christian Apologetics. He teaches in areas of apologetics, systematic theology, and the interaction of science and religion. He is the author of many studies, including the international bestseller *The Dawkins Delusion?* and *The Passionate Intellect*.

John Warwick Montgomery is emeritus professor of law and humanities, University of Bedfordshire, England; Distinguished Research Professor of Apologetics and Christian Thought, Patrick Henry College; and director of the International Academy of Apologetics, Evangelism and Human Rights in Strasbourg, France. His legal specialty is the international and comparative law of human rights. He is the author of some fifty books in five languages, including *Human Rights and Human Dignity*.

Richard John Neuhaus (d. January 8, 2009) was a prominent American Roman Catholic priest and writer. He was the founder and editor of the monthly journal on religion and society *First Things*. He is author of several books, including the bestseller *The Naked Public Square: Religion and Democracy in America*.

Rosalind W. Picard is founder and director of the Affective Computing Research Group at the MIT Media Laboratory and codirector of the Things That Think Consortium. She has authored numerous peer-reviewed scientific articles in multidimensional signal modeling, computer vision, pattern recognition, machine learning and human-computer interaction. Picard is known internationally for pioneering research in affective computing and in content-based image and video retrieval.

Mary Poplin is a professor of education at Claremont Graduate University in California. She is the author of *Finding Calcutta: What Mother Teresa Taught Me About Meaningful Work and Service*. Poplin's educational research focuses on highly effective people in urban poor schools.

Hugh Ross is a Christian apologist and founder of the science-faith think tank Reasons to Believe (RTB), with degrees in physics from the University of British Columbia, graduate degrees in astronomy from the University of Toronto, and postdoctoral research in quasi-stellar objects, or "quasars," at Caltech. His most recent book is *More Than a Theory: Revealing a Testable Model for Creation*.

Ronald J. Sider is a theologian and activist, professor of theology, holistic ministry and public policy at Palmer Theological Seminary, and president of Evangelicals for Social Action. Sider has spoken and written prolifically on the need for Christians to act for social justice, including in his seminal book *Rich Christians in an Age of Hunger*.

Peter Singer is Ira W. DeCamp Professor of Bioethics at Princeton University and Laureate Professor at the University of Melbourne. His work with ethics has generated intense debate in the academy and beyond. He is founding president of the International Association of Bioethics, and founding coeditor of the journal *Bioethics*. His latest publication is titled *The Life You Can Save: Acting Now to End World Poverty*.

Paul C. Vitz is Professor Emeritus of psychology at New York University and Professor of Psychology and Senior Scholar at the Institute for the Psychological Sciences in Arlington, Virginia. He is also a member of the Fellowship of Catholic Scholars. Among his books on atheism are *Faith of the Fatherless: The Psychology of Atheism* and *Sigmund Freud's Christian Unconscious*.

Dallas Willard is a Christian scholar and author. He has long been a professor of philosophy at the University of Southern California, working in the field of logic and epistemology. His book *The Divine Conspiracy* was selected as *Christianity Today*'s Book of the Year for 1999. Some of his other books include *The Spirit of the Disciplines* and *Knowing Christ Today*.

N. T. Wright is Professor of New Testament and Early Christianity at the University of St. Andrews, and one of today's leading theologians and biblical scholars. He was Bishop of Durham from 2003 to 2010, and has taught New Testament studies at Cambridge, McGill, and Oxford Universities. Among his many published works are *Jesus and the Victory of God*, *The Challenge of Jesus* and *Simply Christian*.

PHOTO CREDITS

Chapter 1
Kay Cole James, Lamin Sanneh, Richard John Neuhaus, N. T. Wright and Nicholas Wolterstorff on a panel at The Veritas Forum at Yale in Levinson Auditorium, 1996: photo by Kelly Monroe Kullberg and used by permission.

Chapter 2
Os Guinness meets with student planners over lunch at The Veritas Forum at Stanford, 2005: photo by Kelly Monroe Kullberg and used by permission.

Chapter 3
Tim Keller presents the reason for God to students at The Veritas Forum at the University of Chicago in Kent Chemical Laboratory, 2008: photo by Sam Park and used by permission.

Chapter 4
Francis Collins head shot: photo by Matt Mendelsohn and used by permission.

Francis Collins answers questions before a packed crowd at The Veritas Forum at Caltech in Beckman Auditorium, 2009: photo by Heather Fuqua and used by permission.

Chapter 5
Alister McGrath, Ron Choong and David Helfand on stage at The Veritas Forum at Columbia in Miller Theater, 2006: photo by unknown.

Chapter 9
Peter Singer head shot: photo by Denise Applewhite, Princeton University and used by permission.

Peter Singer, Eric Gregory and John Hare explore the basis of morality at The Veritas Forum at MIT in Stata Center, 2009: photo by Joel Sage and used by permission.

Chapter 10
Rosalind Picard, James Bruce and Rodney Brooks discuss robots and life at The Veritas Forum at MIT in Kresge Auditorium, 2009: photo by Daniel Nagaj and used by permission.

Chapter 13
John Warwick Montgomery head shot: photo courtesy of the author and used by permission.

Chapter 15
Ron Sider head shot: photo by Obed Arango and used by permission.

Ron Sider talks with law students after his presentation at The Veritas Forum at Harvard in Sever Hall, 1995: photo by David Herwaldt and used by permission.

VERITAS · *Books*
FROM INTERVARSITY PRESS

As a partnership between The Veritas Forum and InterVarsity Press, Veritas Books connect the pursuit of knowledge with the deepest questions of life and truth. Established and emerging Christian thinkers grapple with challenging issues, offering academically rigorous and responsible scholarship that contributes to current and ongoing discussions in the university world. Veritas Books are written in the spirit of genuine dialogue, addressing particular academic disciplines as well as topics of broad interest for the intellectually curious and inquiring. In embodying the values, purposes and mission of The Veritas Forum, Veritas Books provide thoughtful, confessional Christian engagement with world-shaping ideas, making the case for an integrated Christian worldview and moving readers toward a clearer understanding of ultimate truth.

www.veritas.org/books

Finding God at Harvard: *Spiritual Journeys of Thinking Christians*
edited by Kelly Monroe Kullberg

Finding God Beyond Harvard: *The Quest for Veritas*
by Kelly Monroe Kullberg

The Dawkins Delusion?: *Atheist Fundamentalism*
and the Denial of the Divine
by Alister McGrath and Joanna Collicutt McGrath

Finding Calcutta: *What Mother Teresa Taught Me About*
Meaningful Work and Service by Mary Poplin

Did the Resurrection Happen? *A Conversation with*
Gary Habermas and Antony Flew
edited by David Baggett

A Place for Truth: *Leading Thinkers Explore Life's Hardest Questions*
edited by Dallas Willard